Learning how to live faithfully as part of God's good but groaning creation is a defining challenge facing the church and world today. For too long, however, caring for creation has been a blind spot for many Christians. Instead, we have often allowed our cultural and political lenses to dictate how we approach environmental issues. In this rich resource, two highly respected theologians refocus our attention on where it should have always been—the Bible. We have a divine opportunity—and an urgent responsibility—to help the church recover a more faithful role in caring for all God's creation, and this book lays an essential foundation for doing just that. It is an excellent and trustworthy guide for understanding *and* living out the biblical call to creation care. I highly recommend it to Christians, churches, and colleges everywhere.

Rev. Ben Lowe, activist and author, *The Future of Our Faith*
and *Doing Good without Giving Up*

In *Creation Care*, Drs. Moo and Moo do precisely what they promise to—"advance what [they] think is a faithful and balanced vision of the created world as it is presented in the Bible." They do so by engaging historical and systematic theology, cultural analysis, and science, resulting in a balanced understanding of how Christians are to care for creation. I recommend this book to anyone who is looking for a resource on earth keeping that is both faithful to Scripture and incredibly relevant to the pressing environmental concerns of today. A critical contribution and one that will have an impact for years to come.

A. J. Swoboda, pastor, author, professor

This book deserves to become the standard work of its kind. One of its many merits is that it grounds creation care in the whole biblical story from creation to new creation. Another is its well-informed and up-to-date account of the plight of creation today. A third is its thoughtful attention to practical and realistic ways of caring about and caring for creation in our contemporary Western contexts.

RICHARD BAUCKHAM, emeritus professor of New Testament,
University of St Andrews, Scotland

Oh how we need this book! And many more like it. Douglas and Jonathan Moo seamlessly combine their biblical and scientific expertise to achieve two very important objectives. On the one hand, they argue a thorough biblical case for including God's creation within God's redemptive mission—that is, within the full biblical meaning of the gospel itself. The Bible has good news for all creation! The great Bible narrative does not begin in Genesis 3 (sin) and end in Revelation 20 (judgment), but begins with creation and ends in new creation. They expose the sheer unbiblical fallacy of popular "theologies" of obliteration (of the cosmos) and evacuation (of the saints) and make abundantly clear the biblical hope of resurrection (of our bodies) and liberation (of creation), so that our future is not to be saved *out of* the earth (by "going to heaven") but to be saved *with* the earth (by God coming here, as the ending of the Bible graphically portrays). On the other hand, they provide abundant scientific evidence to refute the political and corporate myths that so-called "environmental issues" (like the impacts of climate change) are a "hoax" or still in scientific dispute, while calling us to a range of practical measures that will help us move (as this series intends) from biblical theology to life and its fundamental ethical choices. One of the biggest challenges facing the Christian church (especially in the West) is whether or not those who fervently and evangelically claim to 'love God' and 'love our neighbour' will recognise that you cannot say you love God and trash his property, and you cannot say you love your neighbour and care nothing for neighbours on our planet who are suffering the impact of ecological damage at every level. This book is for those who are willing to be challenged on both counts from the Bible itself.

CHRISTOPHER J. H. WRIGHT, Langham Partnership

At the heart of Christian theology lies the relationship of God and humanity. Yet this relationship—this heart—takes place in the "body" of our natural world, and it is this material world that is the focus of Doug and Jonathan Moo's biblical theology of creation care. Creation, what Calvin calls the "theater" of God's glory, is the stage for the drama of redemption. More than that: the way human creatures engage the natural world, and the way God's Son enters his creation to redeem it, are themselves important parts of the biblical story. Just as Israel honored God by treating the promised land as a gift, so too Christians honor God by treating the earth itself as a good though fragile gift that will eventually realize the purpose for which God originally intended it: to be a place for divine-human fellowship. This is an important book by two biblical scholars that reminds us that the Bible is good news not only for the church but for the whole material creation to which the human creature is inextricably and forever bound.

KEVIN J. VANHOOZER, research professor of systematic theology,
Trinity Evangelical Divinity School

Douglas and Jonathan Moo have written a theologically profound assessment of the critical issue of creation care. Their analysis is scripturally sound and rich, and their understanding of our present predicament is insightful. Rather than browbeating their readers, they present a hopeful vision that will stir the church to action. Every Christian needs to read this important book.

TREMPER LONGMAN III, distinguished scholar and professor emeritus
of biblical studies, Westmont College

It's vital that the evangelical tradition is taking seriously the vast biblical resources pointing toward creation care. No one should be surprised that God would like us to look after the beautiful world we were given—and after reading this book, no one will be.

BILL MCKIBBEN, author of *The Comforting Whirlwind: God, Job, and the Scale of Creation*

Creation Care represents a thorough and thoughtful account of the biblical view of creation and how we should live in light of it. Douglas and Jonathan Moo call us away from the apathy that many, in the church and out, display toward the care of the earth and atmosphere around us. At the same time, they model charity on issues where faithful Christians might disagree on how best to apply these truths. This book will make you think and will help you think as one shaped and formed by Scripture.

RUSSELL MOORE, president, the Ethics and Religious Commission
of the Southern Baptist Convention

Crisply written and clearly organized, comprehensive and yet concise, *Creation Care* is an excellent book. It offers insightful readings of a great many biblical texts while also making judicious use of important early church leaders such as Basil of Caesarea and Athanasius as well as prophetic contemporary writers such as Wendell Berry and Aldo Leopold. A most welcome addition to the literature showing that care for creation is integral to Christian discipleship.

STEVE BOUMA-PREDIGER, Leonard and Marjorie Maas Professor
of Reformed Theology, Hope College

Creation care is an integral part of both our worship of God and of our proclamation of the gospel. This book is rich in clear biblical exegesis of the interrelationships between God the creator, his creation, and us his creatures. It is also rich in practical common sense of how this should play out in the lives and priorities of Christians. Read it, be challenged by it, and do it.

BOB WHITE, FRS, professor of geophysics at Cambridge University and director
of the Faraday Institute for Science and Religion at Cambridge

In 2012 the Jamaica Call to Action, which one of the authors assisted in writing, called for "new and robust theological work," including "an integrated theology of creation care." Douglas and Jonathan Moo's work in *Creation Care* is exactly what we need. Beautifully written, it nonetheless provides a deep understanding of the exegetical, theological, scientific, and even practical issues involved in a Christian examination of this important area. *Creation Care* should become the standard text for any course on environmental theology and required reading for any pastor who wants a solid biblical framework for understanding and teaching about creation care.

REV. ED BROWN, director of Care of Creation

This careful and comprehensive book will be not only a major resource for all those who want to explore the full contours of biblical thinking about the care of creation but should also be understood as a powerful call to action. With deceptive ease, Douglas and Jonathan Moo recapitulate the major areas of debate and discussion from the recent decades of slowly dawning evangelical engagement with our current global, environmental crisis. They argue that our human and Christian calling means that we are to care for God's good earth, and with thoughtful but readable expertise they guide us through a complex landscape of ancient texts and contemporary challenges. As we follow their lead, it becomes increasingly clear that both of these distinguished scholars are writing not just out of their studies but out of a coherent and committed life. So it is a privilege to commend this book and a delight to know that it will now be available to the growing numbers of those who need firm foundations for their Christian worship, work, and witness in a groaning but good creation.

PETER HARRIS, cofounder and president, A Rocha International

CREATION CARE

BIBLICAL THEOLOGY FOR LIFE

CREATION CARE

*A Biblical Theology of
the Natural World*

DOUGLAS J. MOO *and*
JONATHAN A. MOO

general editor JONATHAN LUNDE

ZONDERVAN

Creation Care: A Biblical Theology of the Natural World
Copyright © 2018 by Douglas J. Moo and Jonathan A. Moo

This title is also available as a Zondervan ebook.

Requests for information should be addressed to:
Zondervan, *3900 Sparks Dr. SE, Grand Rapids, Michigan 49546*

Library of Congress Cataloging-in-Publication Data

Names: Moo, Douglas J., author. | Moo, Jonathan A. (Jonathan Andrew), 1975-author.
Title: Creation care : a biblical theology of the natural world / Douglas J. Moo and Jonathan A. Moo.
Other titles: Biblical theology for life.
Description: Grand Rapids, MI : Zondervan, [2018] | Series: Biblical theology for life / general editor, Jonathan Lunde |
    Includes index.
Identifiers: LCCN 2017036847 | ISBN 9780310293743 (softcover)
Subjects: LCSH: Environmentalism--Biblical teaching. | Ecotheology. | Human ecology--Religious aspects--Christianity. |
    Nature--Religious aspects--Christianity.
Classification: LCC BT695.5 .M64 2018 | DDC 261.8/8--dc23 LC record available at https://lccn.loc.gov/2017036847

Cover photograph: Jonathan A. Moo
Interior design: Matthew VanZomeren and Kait Lamphere

Printed in the United States of America

HB 03.26.2019

This book is dedicated to Stacey and Jenny

CONTENTS

QUEUING THE QUESTIONS

ARRIVING AT ANSWERS

REFLECTING ON RELEVANCE

DETAILED TABLE OF CONTENTS

REFLECTING ON RELEVANCE

ABBREVIATIONS

AB	Anchor Bible
BDAG	Danker, Frederick W., Walter Bauer, William F. Arndt, and F. Wilbur Gingrich. *Greek-English Lexicon of the New Testament and Other Early Christian Literature.* 3rd ed. Chicago: University of Chicago Press, 2000.
BECNT	Baker Exegetical Commentary on the New Testament
CEB	Common English Bible
ESV	English Standard Version
HCSB	Holman Christian Standard Bible
JSNT	*Journal for the Study of the New Testament*
JSNTSup	Journal for the Study of the New Testament Supplement Series
KJV	King James Version
LXX	Septuagint (the Greek Old Testament)
NASB	New American Standard Bible
NET	New English Translation
NICOT	New International Commentary on the Old Testament
NIV	New International Version
NJB	New Jerusalem Bible
NKJV	New King James Version
NRSV	New Revised Standard Version
PNTC	The Pillar New Testament Commentary
RSV	Revised Standard Version
SNTSMS	Society for New Testament Studies Monograph Series
TynBul	*Tyndale Bulletin*
WBC	Word Biblical Commentary

SERIES PREFACE

The question "What does the Bible have to say about that?" is, in essence, what the Biblical Theology for Life series is all about. Not unlike other biblical explorations of various topics, the volumes in this series articulate various themes in biblical theology, but they always do so with the "So what?" question rumbling about and demanding to be answered. Too often, books on biblical theology have focused mainly on description—simply discerning the teachings of the biblical literature on a particular topic. But contributors to this series seek to straddle both the world of the text and the world in which we live.

This means that their descriptions of biblical theology will always be understood as the important first step in their task, which will not be completed until they draw out that theology's practical implications for the contemporary context. Contributors therefore engage both in the description of biblical theology and in its contemporary contextualization, accosting the reader's perspective and fostering application, transformation, and growth. It is our hope that these informed insights of evangelical biblical scholarship will increasingly become enfleshed in the sermons and discussions that transpire each week in places of worship, in living rooms where Bible studies gather, and in classrooms around the world. We hope that this series will lead to personal transformation and practical application in real life.

Every volume in this series has the same basic structure. In the first section, entitled "Queuing the Questions," authors introduce the main questions they seek to address in their books. Raising these questions enables you to see clearly from the outset what each book will be pursuing, inviting you to participate in the process of discovery along the way. In the second section, "Arriving at Answers," authors develop the biblical theology of the topic they address, focusing their attention on specific biblical texts and constructing answers to the questions introduced in section one. In the concluding "Reflecting on Relevance" section, authors contextualize their biblical theological insights, discussing specific ways in which the theology presented in their books addresses contemporary situations and issues, giving you opportunities to consider how you might live out that theology in the world today.

Long before you make it to the "Reflecting on Relevance" section, however, we encourage you to wrestle with the implications of the biblical theology being described by considering the "Relevant Questions" that conclude each chapter. Frequent sidebars spice up your experience, supplementing the main discussion with significant quotations, illustrative historical or contemporary data, and fuller explanations of the content.

In sum, the goal of the Biblical Theology for Life series is communicated by its title. On the one hand, its books mine the Bible for theology that addresses a wide range of topics, so that you may know "the only true God, and Jesus Christ, whom [he] sent" (John 17:3). On the other hand, contributing authors contextualize this theology in ways that allow the life-giving Word (John 1:4; 20:31) to speak into and transform contemporary life.

Series Editor
Jonathan Lunde

ACKNOWLEDGMENTS

I (Jonathan) would like to thank my colleagues at Whitworth University, in the theology department and beyond, for their unfailing encouragement and for making Whitworth such a wonderful community in which to work. The joy of teaching at Whitworth has much to do with the remarkable students we are blessed to have, and this book has been deeply informed by the many students who have worked through portions of this material with me, especially those in my January-term "Ecology and the Bible" courses at Tall Timber Ranch in the North Cascades. The passion for Christ and the gospel demonstrated by these students, and their commitment to living out their convictions in how they care well for creation is a profound source of hope and inspiration for me.

I am also thankful to Whitworth for the provision of a sabbatical in which the work for this book was completed. During the sabbatical, I have been grateful to be a visting scholar in St Edmund's College at the University of Cambridge and to be based once again in the Faraday Institute for Science and Religion, which has provided generous support and a stimulating context in which to think, read and write, and discuss ideas. It has also been a gift to have a desk at the Tyndale House library in Cambridge and to get a taste again of the rich and thriving community there. Back in Washington, I am grateful to Bill Mounce who kindly made his cabin available to my wife and me on two occasions for what proved to be wonderfully productive weeks of writing on the banks of the Pend Oreille River. When my wife and I found ourselves unexpectedly without a place to live (besides our tent!) for two months, our dear friends Meredith and Toshi Shimizu invited us to live in their house while they were away, and their front porch proved to be a great place to get a lot of writing done.

Whitworth graduate student Matt Prior served ably as my Welch research assistant for a summer, and I am thankful for his help at the early stage of research. I also wish to express my gratitude to Welch scholar Kylie Guenther for her help at the end of this project. My pastor at Christ Our Peace in Spokane, Billy Gaines, has regularly encouraged me in this work, and I am grateful for his friendship and support. In the final months of this project, my wife and I have also been strengthened and encouraged by our pastor, Jeremy Hobson, and his wife Dawn at our church in London, Trinity Church Islington.

Above all, I dedicate my work in this book to my wife Stacey. She has been my most insightful dialogue partner, reading and commenting on the entire manuscript; she has taught me much about caring well for people and for creation; and her wisdom, creativity, kindness, integrity, strength, and above all her commitment to Christ is a daily example to me. It is an inexpressible joy to be her partner in life and ministry.

I (Doug) began working seriously on the issue of creation care for my "faith and learning" paper, required of all new Wheaton College hires. Writing the paper in the context of a liberal arts environment gave me the opportunity to discuss these issues with colleagues from a wide variety of disciplines: biology, geology, physics, environmental science, as well as, of course, biblical studies and theology. I also had the opportunity to present early versions of the paper I ultimately produced (or portions of it) in a number of venues, and the interactions with varied people (from laypeople to scientists to biblical experts) in these contexts sharpened my thinking significantly.

At the risk of nepotism, I must especially thank my coauthor, my son Jonathan. It was his love for God's creation and deep concern about its parlous state that stimulated my interest in this subject. As most parents will recognize, there are few greater joys than seeing our children mature to the point at which they begin teaching and setting an example for us. The opportunity to write a book like this one with my oldest child is in many respects a fitting capstone to my life as a scholar and father.

My wife, Jenny, is, as always, my greatest source of joy and support; and this book is dedicated to her.

Finally, we both express our thanks to the series editor, Jonathan Lunde, whose wise suggestions improved this book significantly.

PART 1

QUEUING THE QUESTIONS

CHAPTER 1

WHAT DO CHRISTIANS HAVE TO DO WITH CREATION?

My wife, Jenny, and I (Doug) are keen nature photographers. When we travel, we love turning off on back roads, where we find unique perspectives on forests, mountains, and lakes. However, the Chicago area where we live does not exactly have an abundance of spectacular landscape to photograph. We do have a big lake close by, but the nearest forest of any size is five hours away and the nearest mountain ten. But the lack of big-scale scenery has a benefit. During our walks through local parks, our attention is drawn to the details of nature. The well-traveled asphalt path within hearing distance of an interstate is often lined with wildflowers—some of them so small that only a macro lens enables us to photograph them well. As we compose our close-up shot, we are regularly amazed at the intricate beauty God has built into these flowers. And the variety!—all kinds of colors, shapes, sizes. My wife often muses on the decision of God to create such an array of flowers. And, of course, we think of Jesus's well-known words: "Consider how the wild flowers grow. They do not labor or spin. Yet I tell you, not even Solomon in all his splendor was dressed like one of these" (Luke 12:27). But what especially strikes us is the fact that God so "clothes" millions of flowers that no human ever sees: in remote wilderness, in deserts, on steep mountainsides.

God has given us a beautiful world to live in. Our first response to that world should be wonder and praise—wonder at the unbelievable size and splendor of a Mount Denali or the intricate detail of a tiger lily, and praise for the God who made them. This book is about "creation care." The first and vital step in learning to care for creation is to celebrate creation.

From that initial contemplation of creation flows everything else. With appreciation of creation, however, must come understanding of creation. In this book, we hope to help Christians understand the role of the created world in God's plan for the universe. Several key questions will serve as the guideposts that direct our study.

The overarching question is this: What role does the non-human creation play in God's plan? We are convinced that Christians can have the right attitudes and do the right things only if they have the right understanding. The apostle James would of course remind us that right understanding and even acceptance of truth is never enough on its own ("even the demons believe . . . and shudder" [James 2:19]).

But right understanding remains necessary if we are to know how to think and act. It is moreover our conviction that right understanding about ourselves and the world depends on God's revelation of himself to us in his Word. Hence, our focus in this book is on what the Bible teaches us about the non-human creation and our relationship to it. Our basic question about the role of non-human creation in God's plan inevitably leads us to a series of secondary questions. Is there a difference in perspective on creation between the Old and New Testaments? What place do human beings have within the scope of God's creation? How does the non-human creation relate to our call to live out and proclaim the gospel? What is the destiny of the non-human creation? And finally, what role should science play in teaching us about God's creation and our responsibilities within it? This final question requires us also to consider how we translate our biblical understanding about creation into wise and godly attitudes and actions. These are some of the questions to be addressed in this book. But before we can begin to seek answers, we need first to understand a bit more about our topic. In these first two chapters, we will therefore ask and answer three vital questions: *What* is our topic? *Why* write a book addressing this topic? And *how* can we go about seeking answers from the Bible?

WHAT ARE WE TALKING ABOUT?

The phrase "creation care" that we use in the title of this book has become standard language among Christians for referring to our ethical responsibilities for the non-human world. The alliteration is undoubtedly one reason why the phrase is popular, but there are more important reasons why we use this language.

The word "care" nicely captures two sides of the subject. The obvious sense of "creation care" is care "for" creation: specific actions that foster the health of the created world. But the phrase also connotes care "about" creation: a way of looking at creation that grounds our care "for" it. "Creation care" thus refers to two interrelated things at the same time: both our ethical obligation and the fundamental basis for that obligation. We care "for" creation because we care "about" creation. This book will necessarily involve us, then, in asking questions that are relevant for a wider biblical theology of creation, if we are to know why and how we should care "about" the creation. And, as it turns out, we can't unpick one doctrine from the fabric of Christian theology without also having to deal with all the other interwoven threads. John Muir famously said, "When we try to pick out anything by itself, we find it hitched to everything else in the Universe." What is true for living systems is true for Christian doctrine too: in the end, you find that all the great themes of theology are interwoven with each other. So while the focus of this book is on creation—above all, on that bit of creation called earth and on our responsibilities for this place and its life—readers will discover that our inquiries about how to care for creation confront us with central questions about God, the world, and ourselves and cannot be separated from the rest of the Christian gospel.

Our choice of the word "creation" is of central importance for understanding the perspective of this book. Words carry significance—sometimes more significance than we realize. We could, for example, have used "nature" to describe what we are talking about. But the word "nature" is notoriously ambiguous: we use it for all kinds of different meanings, and there are all sorts of possible misunderstandings.[1] For example, two common ways people use the word "nature" carry with them unfortunate baggage. On the one hand, the word is sometimes used to refer to a semi-deified "mother nature," with any idea of a personal God left to the side (though, it should be acknowledged that "mother earth" language on its own has a long pedigree in Jewish and Christian tradition). On the other hand, "nature" is often thought of in a purely mechanistic way, as something separate from God and open to manipulation at human whim. Both of these views depart rather significantly from the biblical view of the world as God's creation.

"Environment" is another way we might have described the focus of our book, and it is certainly the most common way some of the issues addressed here are described in our day. Our schools teach our children to be concerned about it. Hotels encourage us to hang our towels back on the rack so that we will do less damage to it. Large construction projects require "environmental impact" assessments. People especially focused on the "environment" are called "environmentalists" and sometimes form "green" political parties. The word, however, has significant downsides. "Environmentalism" has come to be associated with certain philosophical or even religious (or antireligious) movements. It tends to connote for many Christians the image of tree-hugging druids with antitheistic agendas. But the biggest downside for the word is that it tends to make human beings the focus of attention. According to Merriam-Webster, the word means "the circumstances, objects, or conditions by which one is surrounded."[2] We refer, for instance, to our office as a "good [or bad] work environment." Our city utility departments for things like sewer and waste removal are now sometimes known as "environmental services" departments. Our use of the word "environment" implies that human beings are at the center of things: the created world is important only inasmuch as it is the place *we* inhabit.

Of course, concern about the created world as the environment for humans is appropriate. The Bible makes clear that we humans have a unique place in God's creation, the only creatures made "in the image of God." As we will see, one of the central motivations for creation care is the gospel imperative that we "love our neighbors." To love our neighbors must include doing what we can to enable this

---

1. See Alister E. McGrath, *A Scientific Theology*, vol. 1, *Nature* (Grand Rapids: Eerdmans, 2001), 81–113.

2. To be strictly accurate, this is the first definition of four that they provide.

world to sustain the flourishing of our fellow human beings. The second "great commandment" requires us to assess our lifestyles and priorities in light of the interests of all our "neighbors"—those who live next door and those on the other side of the earth.

However, the command to love our neighbors is preceded by and linked to the greatest commandment of all: to love the Lord our God. The demand to put God above all else is one reason we choose to refer to the world as a "creation." Our cosmos is not merely the accidental by-product of chemical and physical processes. It is something our God called into being, something he created for a purpose, which is nothing less than to bring glory to the One who created it. Speaking of "creation care"—rather than, for example, environmentalism or "nurture of nature"—rightly anchors our topic in a Christian worldview, appropriately privileging *theo*-logy over *anthropo*-logy. As we will see later in this volume, there is good evidence that the rise of humanism and loss of robust belief in a personal, creating God in the last few centuries have fostered a mechanistic way of thinking about the world that has had dramatically unfortunate consequences for the health of God's creation. Christians have not been immune from this fundamentally a-theistic way of thinking. Putting "creation" at the forefront of our discourse can go some way toward rectifying this problem.

> "Both in principle and as a matter of historic fact, alienation sets in when humans lose their awareness of the presence of God and persuade themselves to view the cosmos no longer as a creation, endowed with value in the order of being, a purpose in the order of time and a moral sense in the order of eternity, but as a cosmic accident, meaningless and mechanical."
>
> *Erazim Kohák* [3]

WHY ARE WE TALKING ABOUT IT?

Our world is full of problems and issues. As I write these words, the media is full of stories about a migrant crisis in Europe, global terrorism, conflicts over the implementation of a same-sex marriage decision of the US Supreme Court, and the economic struggles of emerging nations such as China, Brazil, and India. Christians, of course, are deeply involved in these issues and a myriad of others in one way or another. Moreover, we know that all Christians are called in various ways to evangelism, discipleship, mission, and care for the poor and needy. It is therefore natural for Christians to ask, "Why should I add concern for creation to the list of things I am bothering about?" We suggest that there are at least three good reasons why Christians should, indeed, be involved in "creation care": the need to address current challenges facing creation, the need to serve as witnesses to God's kingdom in our time (and to respond to false accusations about Christians and creation), and

---

3. Erazim Kohák, *The Embers and the Stars: A Philosophical Enquiry into the Moral Sense of Nature* (Chicago: University of Chicago Press, 1984), 183.

above all (and the focus of this book), the witness of Scripture to the importance of our vocation as "keepers" of God's creation.

First, then, we'll address the current challenges facing creation. Of course, there have always been "environmental" problems and people concerned with them. We must avoid the error C. S. Lewis dubbed "chronological snobbery," that is, thinking our own era is utterly unique or the only important one.[4] Nevertheless, it is only our own era we can do anything about: God has placed us in this world, at this time. And the evidence that our world faces staggering environmental challenges is overwhelming.

The "environment" as a serious field of scientific study, a political issue, and a topic of everyday conversation is a relatively recent phenomenon. Aldo Leopold's *A Sand County Almanac* (1949), with its focus on the health of the land, foreshadowed some of the most important concerns. Particularly significant also was Rachel Carson's 1962 book *Silent Spring*, which documented the damage that indiscriminate use of chemicals to combat insects was creating (especially on bird populations). "Pollution" became a focus of scientific investigation and public concern, and the issue widened quickly to include all kinds of ways modern technology was exerting harmful effects on the earth. Pressure groups focused on environmental issues sprang up everywhere (e.g., Greenpeace was founded in 1971); political parties focused on the environment took form ("Greens"); and the first Earth Day was celebrated in 1970. Readers of this book will, of course, be familiar with such movements and organizations, which regularly occupy attention in the media. But it should be noted that Christians—and, indeed, evangelical Christians—also quickly became involved. The significant evangelical leader Francis Schaeffer wrote a book on this topic in 1970 (*Pollution and the Death of Man*). Evangelical theologians and scientists, following the lead of pioneering figures such as Loren Wilkinson and Calvin DeWitt, founded organizations such as A Rocha and the Evangelical Environmental Network.

Why was there this sudden outpouring of interest in the environment? There are undoubtedly many reasons, but a combination of two factors is particularly critical. First, scientists developed sophisticated tools and techniques that enabled them to gather data about the environment in a way never before possible (e.g., by satellites that monitor atmospheric conditions around the globe). Second, it was becoming increasingly clear (partly, of course, as a result of these new data) that the unprecedented speed in development of human technologies was having unprecedented effects on the earth.[5] We are well aware that there continues to be debate over the exact extent

---

4. History has witnessed many *local* ecological disasters as great as anything we see today (I [Doug] am indebted to my former Wheaton colleague Joseph Spradley for this point). John Black, writing in 1970, resists the language of "crisis" because it suggests an immediate, one-time problem that ignores the basic long-term changes that ecological healing requires (*The Dominion of Man: The Search for Ecological Responsibility* [Edinburgh: University Press, 1970], 129; cf. also Lawrence Osborn, *Guardians of Creation: Nature in Theology and the Christian Life* [Leicester: Apollos, 1993], 20–22). See also J. R. McNeill, *Something New under the Sun: An Environmental History of the Twentieth-Century World* (New York: W. W. Norton, 2000).

5. See chap. 13 for an overview of these issues.

and nature of these effects—and even more debate about the best public policies to address them. For now, however, we simply note the robust consensus among scientists working in a variety of fields all over the globe that our planet is facing serious challenges. (We will detail some of these problems, and possible responses to them, in the last two chapters.) But one does not need to conduct scientific experiments to see some of the problems. Some of these, as has always been the case, have primarily local causes and effects. When my wife and I (Doug) visited our son and his family in Shanghai some years ago, a brown haze caused by air pollution cast a permanent pall over the city, which led one of our grandchildren to suffer from respiratory problems. Other challenges are global in extent. On another trip, in 2001, we visited Portage Lake in southern Alaska. There, we saw hundreds of chunks of ice—some as large as houses—that had broken off a large glacier visible on the other side of the lake. When we returned in 2008, there remained only a few small pieces of ice. Today, one can no longer even see the glacier from the lakeside. The retreat of the glacier exemplifies a worldwide phenomenon that is linked to the warming of the earth's climate. To be sure, the climate has always changed, and natural warming and cooling phases have characterized the entire history of the earth. But the speed of recent changes, unprecedented in human history, poses serious challenges to agriculture and human health—indeed, even to the very existence of some nations.

Yet here we also face a particular challenge to getting Christians on board with creation care: we often don't really "feel" these issues. Many of us live in suburban or urban contexts in rich countries that make us somewhat immune to the immediate effects of environmental problems; even my own observations above are only those of a tourist. It would be far different if I were a farmer in Peru, for example, for whom erratic weather patterns of a sort not experienced before may already be threatening my family's very livelihood. And many of the environmental issues we face are the product of what seem from our limited vantage points rather gradual changes, however fast they may be in geological time. Jared Diamond has labeled this "creeping normalcy": our personal time line is very short. People living in eastern Virginia, for instance, probably can't remember—or can't remember very well—that it used to be a lot easier to see the mountains in Shenandoah National Park than it is today. We don't notice the loss of species that were common in the time of our great-grandparents, less common for our grandparents, rare for our parents, and never a part of the world we've personally encountered. This is not the place to get into these issues in any detail; some of this is discussed more fully in chapter 13. For now, however, we simply argue that the seriousness of the issues our planet is facing demands a renewed attention to these issues. And, as we will see, Christians are in a unique and special position to address them.

A second reason for Christians to think about and become active in creation care is the need to be faithful witnesses to Christ. That witness is undermined by the sense among many in our culture that Christianity is largely to blame for the environmental challenges we face. The argument of some environmental historians is that the Christian worldview, with its concern for humans and their salvation, has fostered the typical modernist neglect of, or even disdain for, the natural world. In a famous essay, Lynn White, Jr., argued that environmental degradation was the indirect product of Christianity, which he labeled (in its Western form), "the most anthropocentric religion the world has ever seen."[6] The idea that humans are given "dominion" over creation has been, so it is argued, foundational in forming the typically Western "instrumentalist" view of nature: that the natural world exists solely to meet human needs.[7] Wedded to unprecedented scientific and technological advancements, Christian anthropocentrism has brought us pollution, global warming, and widespread species extinction.[8]

White's essay created quite a stir, as historians and theologians debated the degree to which Christian theology, or some streams of Christian theology,[9] might be responsible for the environmental crisis. The pioneering evangelical work on environmentalism, Francis Schaeffer's *Pollution and the Death of Man,* was written to some extent in response to White.[10] Schaeffer and others have faulted White for simplifying a far more complex historical and ideological development and for overstating the role of orthodox Christianity in the formation of the modern Western attitude toward nature.[11] A more nuanced and, we think, more accurate account recognizes that it is not Christianity, as such, or the Bible, as such, that has been responsible for fostering a narrow focus on humans to the detriment of the created world, but certain narrow and superficial readings of the Christian story. William Leiss is right to note that it was precisely when Christianity ceased to be a vital component of the Western worldview

---

6. Lynn White, Jr., "The Historical Roots of Our Ecologic Crisis," in *The Care of Creation: Focusing Concern and Action,* ed. R. J. Berry (Downers Grove, IL: InterVarsity Press, 2000), 38 (a reprint of the article that originally appeared in *Science* 155 [1967]: 1203–7). In basic agreement with White is Roderick Nash, who faults especially Puritan theology for the environmental crisis in North America (Roderick Nash, *Wilderness and the American Mind,* 3rd ed. [New Haven: Yale University Press, 1982]).

7. Often cited as an important source for Christian passivity toward the world of nature is the medieval scholastic "chain of being" perspective, exemplified by Peter Lombard in the *Sentences:* "As man is made for the sake of God, namely, that he may serve him, so is the world made for the sake of man, that it may serve him" (2.1.8). On the theological justification for an instrumentalist view of nature in 17th–18th c. England, see Keith Thomas, *Man and the Natural World: A History of the Modern Sensibility* (New York: Pantheon, 1983), 18–22.

8. To be sure, Thomas Sieger Derr is correct to point out that White's article has frequently been misread as being more hostile to Christianity than it actually is (*Environmental Ethics and Christian Humanism,* Abingdon Press Studies in Christian Ethics and Economic Life 2 [Nashville: Abingdon, 1996], 25–33). As Lawrence

Osborn argues, there is a pervasive ambivalence in Western Christianity toward the natural world (*Guardians of Creation,* 24–40).

9. For instance, Robert J. Faricy claims that it is "the Christianity of the protestant reformation" that created our current problem by introducing an unfortunate split between person and nature ("The Person-Nature Split: Ecology, Women and Human Life," *Irish Theological Quarterly* 53 [1988]: 203–18).

10. Francis Schaeffer, *Pollution and the Death of Man* (Wheaton, IL: Crossway, 1973).

11. For other responses to White's essay, see Alister E. McGrath, *The Reenchantment of Nature: The Denial of Religion and the Ecological Crisis* (New York: Doubleday, 2002); Lewis W. Moncrief, "The Cultural Basis of Our Environmental Crisis," in *Western Man and Environmental Ethics: Attitudes toward Nature and Technology,* ed. Ian G. Barbour (Reading, MA: Addison-Wesley, 1973), 31–42; Max Oelschlager, *The Idea of Wilderness: From Prehistory to the Age of Ecology* (New Haven, CT: Yale University Press, 1991), 33, 43–67; Michael S. Northcott, *The Environment and Christian Ethics,* New Studies in Christian Ethics (Cambridge: Cambridge University Press, 1996), 40–85; Thomas Sieger Derr, *Ecology and Human Need* (Philadelphia: Westminster, 1975), 25–33.

that the dominion mandate, stripped of its theological context, became a basis for environmental neglect.[12] J. R. McNeill puts the matter well: "Few believers knew more than a smattering of the sacred scriptures. And most of those who did, being human, easily allowed expediency and interest more than the scriptures of religious texts to govern their behavior. Every durable body of scripture is ambiguous, self-contradictory, and amenable to different interpretations to suit different circumstances." The upshot of this superficial engagement with Scripture? "In the unusually secular age of the twentieth century, the ecological impact of religions, rarely great, shrank to the vanishing point."[13] We would quarrel with the suggestion that the Bible is, in itself, "self-contradictory," but we must acknowledge that it is susceptible to different interpretations and that we can easily twist and distort its overall teaching because of our own agendas and interests (more on this below). One of our purposes in this book, then, is to advance what we think is a faithful and balanced vision of the created world as it is presented in the Bible. We think such a vision will effectively rebut the kind of charges against Christianity advanced by White and others. Indeed, far from being a hindrance to meeting the "environmental crisis," we argue that Christians have in the biblical story line and worldview unique resources to explain, respond to, and keep in right perspective the "environmental crisis."

Addressing our current environmental crisis and removing misconceptions about the role of Christianity in that crisis are valid reasons to turn our attention to what Scripture says about creation and our role in it. But the most important reason is a more straightforward one: talking about creation care is needed because it is taught in Scripture. As Colin Gunton rightly notes, care for creation does not require a crisis to be justified.[14] Pastors and teachers should be speaking about the issue because it is part of God's revelation to us in Scripture. Believers in general should be concerned for the same reason. Yet concern for creation is a topic infrequently (at best!) mentioned from the pulpit, and it is regularly absent or very low on the agenda of issues that Christians express concern about. In fact, not only do many believers lack any sense of responsibility for creation, but some think that resisting such a focus is a mark of Christian commitment. To be sure, many forms of environmentalism assume or actively propagate ideologies that are anti-Christian. These are often the movements that get the attention of the media, which is always focused on the unusual and sensational. But to turn our backs on creation because of the excesses of some is to turn our backs on an issue that is important to God. What is needed is a positive embrace of the world in which we live as God's creation, aligning our own perspective with the perspective of Scripture. But how can we learn about what Scripture says on the issues? We will address this question in the next chapter.

12. William Leiss, *The Domination of Nature* (Montreal: McGill-Queen's University Press, 1994), 30–35.

13. McNeill, *Something New under the Sun*, 328.

14. Colin E. Gunton, *Christ and Creation* (Grand Rapids: Eerdmans, 1992), 105.

CHAPTER 2

HOW DO WE THINK BIBLICALLY AND THEOLOGICALLY ABOUT CREATION?

In the first chapter, we asked and answered two important questions about this book: *What* are we talking about, and *why* we are talking about it. We explained that our subject is "creation care" and that Christians need to care about creation because we care about the God who brought Creation into being. In this chapter, we turn to a third preliminary question: *How* can we use the Bible to address this matter of creation care?

The environmental crisis has led to interesting developments in the wider religious landscape. Concern about the environment has led many to jettison traditional religions in favor of ones that are perceived to be oriented to the earth and nature.[1] Others argue that we need to introduce significant theological revisions to existing religions in order to provide a solid launching pad for a robust environmental ethic. Several Christian thinkers have gone down this path.[2] Such approaches have stimulated a lively debate about just how we should use the Bible to address many of today's ethical issues. This debate is part of the wider discussion about biblical hermeneutics in general that has occupied theologians and biblical scholars for several decades. We cannot enter this wider debate here. But we do need to say something about how we plan in this book to approach the Bible to discover what it might say about creation care in our day.

---

1. The "deep ecology" movement in particular insists that, along with the jettisoning of Christianity, true environmental healing can only take place when a new ideology is put in its place. See, e.g., Arne Naess, *Ecology, Community and Lifestyle: Outline of an Ecosophy*, trans. David Rothenberg (Cambridge: Cambridge University Press, 1989); George Sessions, ed., *Deep Ecology for the 21st Century: Readings on the Philosophy and Practice of the New Environmentalism* (Boston: Shambhala, 1995). What ideology to put in the place of Christianity as a basis for environmental ethics is, of course, quite contested. See the useful surveys in Oelschlager,

The Idea of Wilderness, 280–353; Northcott, *The Environment and Christian Ethics*, 90–163.

2. See, e.g., Sally McFague, *The Body of God* (Minneapolis: Fortress, 1993); Rosemary Radford Ruether, *Gaia and God: An Ecofeminist Theology of Earth Healing* (New York: HarperOne, 1992); and the discussion in Dieter T. Hessel and Rosemary Radford Ruether, eds. *Christianity and Ecology: Seeking the Well-Being of Earth and Humans* (Cambridge, MA: Harvard University Press, 2002), 97–124.

STRATEGIES OF INTERPRETATION

A useful starting point for our methodological musings is the first part of the 2010 book *Greening Paul* by David Horrell, Cherryl Hunt, and Christopher Southgate.[3] These authors helpfully survey different ways Christians might use Scripture to address concerns about creation. Their focus, as the title indicates, is on the letters of the apostle Paul. Paul's letters seem to be almost entirely concerned with human beings: their original sinful state, God's provision for their salvation in Christ, and the new life in Christian community that God offers them. How does this important part of the Bible help us to think about creation? Horrell, Hunt, and Southgate begin by identifying two main options we have in this matter.[4]

The first option is to "resist" the text, by refusing to allow the allegedly human focus in the letters to shape our approach. This strategy of resistance follows the pattern established by certain liberationist and feminist interpreters, who actively "resist" biblical texts that they perceive to be out of step with their chosen ideology.[5] Critiques of this kind of hermeneutical approach to Scripture are legion, and we don't need to repeat them here. The problem is obvious: this strategy explicitly subordinates the voice of Scripture to another voice—whether of the poor, or women, or the earth. The supreme authority of Scripture in guiding Christian thinking and setting our agenda is lost. As Horrell, Hunt, and Southgate note, "in this approach . . . the Bible is pretty much dispensable."[6] We should note here, however, that the idea of "resistance" might have value, as long as what we are resisting is our own prejudices about what the Bible says rather than the Bible itself. We all read the Bible from a particular perspective, and, too easily, we find in it whatever we want. Sadly, history is littered with examples of people who used the Bible to suppress other people or to exploit the earth. A resolute focus on what the Bible itself is really saying, we believe, will help us to resist these sinful and selfish perspectives.

The second main option in reading the Bible ecologically is what Horrell, Hunt, and Southgate label a "strategy of recovery." As its name suggests, this begins by identifying a core of eco-friendly biblical teaching that is genuinely in the text but has been ignored or muted by cultural assumptions or preoccupation with other issues. A host of books and articles adopting this approach has appeared over the last thirty years, many of them from evangelical writers. Horrell, Hunt, and Southgate are, at best, ambivalent about this strategy. Its basic problem, in their view, is that it is too

3. David Horrell, Cherryl Hunt, and Christopher Southgate, *Greening Paul: Reading the Apostle in a Time of Ecological Crisis* (Waco, TX: Baylor University Press, 2010), 11–32.

4. In identifying these two options, they are explicitly following Francis Watson, "Strategies of Recovery and Resistance: Hermeneutical Reflections on Genesis 1–3 and Its Pauline Reception," *JSNT* 45 (1992): 79–103.

5. Participants in the "Earth Bible" project have been very explicit about their use of this strategy. See, e.g., the opening chapter in *Exploring Ecological Hermeneutics*, ed. Norman C. Habel and Peter Trudinger (Atlanta: Society of Biblical Literature, 2008).

6. *Greening Paul*, 38.

optimistic about the degree to which the Bible supports an ecological agenda. Too often, they argue, interpreters following this strategy engage in facile and simplistic exegesis and find far more in the text than is actually there. The leap from biblical text to contemporary theology and ethics is made too quickly and naively.

Horrell, Hunt, and Southgate therefore opt for a strategy that neither "resists" the text nor simply "recovers" what is there. Following Paul Santmire, they choose yet another "R" word as their label for this strategy: "revisionist."[7] In their own words, this "revisionist" approach means that "We adopt a self-consciously constructive and creative approach, recognizing that we are reading Paul in the light of our context and priorities, *making* new meaning from the texts, but seeking to do so in a way that is in demonstrable continuity with the Pauline material and is thus potentially persuasive as a faithful form of Christian theology."[8]

We may illustrate the process we are talking about with a phrase from the Bible that we talk about later in the book: "new creation" (see chap. 8). As we will see, the meaning of the phrase is debated. Many interpreters think that the phrase refers to Christians, "made new" by their relationship to Christ, and that it therefore has little or nothing to do with the wider non-human "creation." This interpretation is strengthened if the key word, *ktisis,* is taken to mean "creature" rather than "creation." Thus, for instance, 2 Corinthians 5:17 in the NASB reads: "Therefore if anyone is in Christ, he is a new creature; the old things passed away; behold, new things have come." In cases like this, where meaning is debated, the "location" and approach of the interpreter can affect our decision. Some contemporary interpreters insist that we must respond to current ecological challenges by privileging "the earth" in all our interpretations. For these interpreters, then, even if one concluded that "new creation" for New Testament authors referred only to transformed persons, we need to "resist" this tendency in the text and insist that the transformation of the cosmos as a whole must be included in "new creation." Other interpreters, however, think that the problem lies more with the interpreter than with the text. They argue that interpreters in the West have been conditioned by the heritage of Greek dualism to think of religious matters in terms of humans, to the exclusion of "material" issues. What we need to do, then, is to "recover" the broader perspective of the New Testament authors, for whom God's transforming work does indeed embrace the entire cosmos.

We applaud Horrell, Hunt, and Southgate for their desire to map out an interpretive strategy that seeks to "green" Paul (and the rest of the Bible) while remaining faithful to Scripture. However, we fear that they concede too much to the authority of the reader. When we begin talking about making new meaning, we risk dispensing

---

7. Paul Santmire, *The Travail of Nature: The Ambiguous Ecological Promise of Christian Theology* (Philadelphia: Fortress, 1985). The revisionist approach follows the ecological hermeneutic developed in the "Christianity and Ecological Theology" project by Ernst Conradie and his colleagues, who argue that meaning is to be found in the encounter between the text and the reader (see emergingearthcommunity.org).

8. *Greening Paul*, 4.

with the authority of the text itself. To be sure, "meaning" is a tricky word. Anyone who has wrestled with difficult passages in Scripture will have seen how faithful interpreters will come to very different conclusions about what the Bible "means." Nevertheless, while admitting there are difficulties, we are committed to the view that there, indeed, is meaning in the text and that our job, first and foremost, is to discover that meaning. We should be trying to find whatever "green" there really is in Scripture—a color that may, indeed, have been obscured by certain cultural and theological assumptions. What we need to resist is not the text but the assumptions we may inadvertently bring to the text. Our goal is to see whether Scripture itself, not some modern ideological or political agenda, demands such a commitment.

But this brings us back to the problem that bothers Horrell, Hunt, and Southgate: does a "recovery" strategy of interpretation doom us to find in the Bible uncertain and ambiguous support for creation care? We are not convinced this is the case. While some green recovery projects do indeed suffer from the kinds of problems they point out, not all do—as the books and articles of a number of fine interpreters make clear. The way forward is to employ a strategy for biblical interpretation that is broad, integrative, and creative—in the best sense of that word. In what follows, we outline what we think this strategy might look like. Many interpreters are already using this kind of approach, and many others have described elements of it. So we know that we are not saying much—or perhaps anything!—new. But the urgent need to figure out ways to apply genuinely biblical teaching to current issues such as creation care warrants a brief glance at our methods—even if it is by way of reminder.

Our approach fits broadly under the umbrella of biblical theology, as befits a book in a series on topics within biblical theology. But we need to be more specific, because people use the phrase "biblical theology" to refer to a lot of different and even incompatible approaches.[9] The distinction between biblical theology on the one hand and systematic or dogmatic theology on the other hand is no longer clear. Throw into the mix the approach known as "Theological Interpretation of Scripture" and matters become even more complicated. If we were, then, to be more specific, we would characterize the approach taken in this book as biblical theology informed by some of the values of the "Theological Interpretation of Scripture" movement. Two analogies provide a skeleton for fleshing out a bit more what we mean in describing this approach.

---

9. In their recent survey of approaches to biblical theology, Edward W. Klink and Darian R. Lockett comment that "*Biblical theology* has become a catchphrase, a wax nose that can mean anything from the historical-critical method applied to the Bible to a theological interpretation of Scripture that in practice appears to leave history out of the equation altogether" (*Understanding Biblical Theology: A Comparison of Theory and Practice* [Grand Rapids: Zondervan, 2012], 13). Christopher R. Seitz agrees: "'biblical theology' is an elastic and imprecise term" (*The Character of Christian Scripture: The Significance of a Two-Testament Bible*, Studies in Theological Interpretation [Grand Rapids: Baker, 2011], 95).

THE BRIDGE

The metaphor of a bridge is widely used to characterize biblical theology.[10] With one pier sunk in a close reading of the text and the other in systematic theology, the bridge of biblical theology carries us from the world of the text to the world of the contemporary church. Jesus, for instance, talks a lot about the kingdom of God: how it has been introduced into the world at his first coming and how it will have a glorious climax at the end of history. Christians today want to live faithfully as "citizens" of that kingdom. But to spell out what that faithful living should look like requires us to figure out just what the kingdom is. To do this, we use biblical theology, looking carefully at how the language of kingdom is used in the Gospels and trying to synthesize what these various texts say. This, then, becomes the "bridge" from the world of Jesus's day to our day. We need to do the same thing in order to "hear" what Scripture says about creation. Specifically, taking a biblical-theological approach to creation in Scripture requires that we build our bridge out of four materials.

First, to be truly *biblical,* our biblical theology must be *descriptive.* This element of biblical theology is widely recognized and relatively uncontroversial. Biblical theology is what we call a second-level activity. By this we mean that it is one step removed from the text, whose interpretation would be a first-level activity. The purpose of biblical theology is to summarize and synthesize the teaching of the Bible using its own categories and with attention to its redemptive-historical movement.[11] The "recovery" strategy of interpretation we are advocating will obviously require this foundational step. And, to reiterate a point already made, this descriptive task must be done well and with careful regard for the text.

Second, to be truly *theological,* our biblical theology should also be *prescriptive.* Biblical theologians have not always recognized this aspect in their work. Indeed, some have actively resisted it, arguing that biblical theology should focus on "what it meant" in distinction to "what it means."[12] However, we would argue that some element of prescription is inherent in the very word "theology," at least as

---

10. See, e.g., Charles H. H. Scobie, *The Ways of Our God: An Approach to Biblical Theology* (Grand Rapids: Eerdmans, 2003), 46–49, 77.

11. This general description of biblical theology is ubiquitous; see, e.g., Brian Rosner: ". . . *biblical theology may be defined as theological interpretation of Scripture in and for the church. It proceeds with historical and literal sensitivity and seeks to analyse and synthesise the Bible's teaching about God and his relations with the world on its own terms, maintaining sight of the Bible's overarching narrative and Christocentric focus*" ("Biblical Theology," in *New Dictionary of Biblical Theology,* ed. T. D. Alexander and B. S. Rosner [Downers Grove, IL: InterVarsity Press, 2000], 10 [emphasis his]).

12. The distinction between "what it meant" and "what it

means" was stressed by Krister Stendahl in his 1962 article on "Biblical Theology, Contemporary," in *The Interpreter's Dictionary of the Bible,* ed. George A. Buttrick (Nashville: Abingdon, 1962). See also, e.g., James Barr, *The Concept of Biblical Theology: An Old Testament Perspective* (Minneapolis: Augsburg Fortress, 1999); Peter Balla, *Challenges to New Testament Theology* (Peabody, MA: Hendrickson, 1997). Balla says: "A writer of a New Testament theology should not set himself the aim to 'show the relevance of the reconstruction for the present.' If the theology of the New Testament is described, modern readers can make up their minds whether or not they want to accept the content of that theology as authoritative for them" (249).

we understand it.[13] No "theology," whatever adjective we put in front of it, can fully avoid the task of addressing the people of God today. In our biblical theology, our focus will be on the horizon of the text. But that focus must not become tunnel vision that leads us to ignore entirely the horizon of the contemporary reader or listener. We must not put a historical straitjacket around the text, which makes it difficult or impossible to move from that text to its meaning for the contemporary church. The result would be a fatal silencing of the true voice of Scripture in all the work and ministry that God calls us to do. In this book, then, we forthrightly include practical application with our discussion of the biblical text.

Third, to turn back again to the word "biblical," our biblical theology must be *inclusive*. Discussions of biblical theology often focus on whether the adjective in this phrase means that we study the theology found in the Bible or that we develop a theology that does justice to the Bible. We maintain that the adjective implies something more fundamental: it suggests that the theologian operates as a Christian who assumes that, for all their diversity, the books of the Bible are ultimately one book. The special challenge of the sort of biblical theology we pursue here, then, is to do full justice to all the data of Scripture. We don't have the luxury of throwing out inconvenient bits of text or of forcing interpretations on passages in the interest of harmonization. This inclusive principle poses particular challenges for our study of creation care. One of the more obvious is our attempt to formulate a truly biblical view of the destiny of creation. Will God destroy his creation in a fiery conflagration, with a brand new heaven and earth to replace it, as 2 Peter 3 is sometimes thought to teach? Or is it destined to be liberated and transformed, as Romans 8 teaches? In light of our convictions about the authority of all of Scripture, we reject the option of dismissing 2 Peter as a late or semicanonical voice, nor can we be satisfied with exegesis that merely forces the data of one of these texts to fit the shape of the other. An inclusive approach means that we will have to work hard at reading together the very diverse matter of Scripture, letting each text have its own voice and, as the Reformers emphasized, letting Scripture interpret Scripture.

Fourth, and related to this, our biblical theology must be *canonical*. The word *theology* reminds us that we engage in our task as people of the book—the whole book. A canonical perspective is especially critical in addressing the issue of creation care. Teaching about the created world is quite widespread in the Old Testament, but relatively sparse in the New. As Richard Bauckham notes, ". . . the Bible's theology of creation is to a large extent developed in the Old Testament and then presupposed in the New."[14]

---

13. Stephen Motyer's definition of biblical theology is similar: "That creative theological discipline whereby the church seeks to hear the integrated voice of the whole Bible addressing us today" ("Two Testaments, One Biblical Theology," in *Between Two Horizons: Spanning New Testament Studies and Systematic Theology*, ed. Joel B. Green and Max Turner [Grand Rapids: Eerdmans, 2000], 158).

14. Richard Bauckham, *The Bible and Ecology: Rediscovering the Community of Creation* (Waco, TX: Baylor University Press, 2010), 141.

This is a problem for the issue we are addressing because most of the preaching and teaching in our churches is on the New Testament, and most believers spend far more time in the New than the Old in their own reading. This canonical imbalance then breeds an imbalance in the place we give creation within our theology and teaching. By telling the whole story of creation in the chapters that follow, we hope to right this imbalance, even as we do justice to the way in which the New Testament brings this story to its climax.

THE ROUNDABOUT

The bridge metaphor helps us think about the way biblical theology works in our reading of Scripture, but it also has some limitations. Let's think about two kinds of bridges. The first is a one-way bridge, carrying traffic in only one direction. We have used the bridge metaphor in this way above: biblical theology carries traffic from the world of the text to our own world. However, as we will see below, our study of the Bible is often stimulated by and directed toward issues in our own culture. Therefore, it might be more accurate to work with the metaphor of a bridge carrying traffic in two directions. That is, our biblical theology not only moves from text to application, it also moves from our own world back to the text. Perhaps, then, a different metaphor might be used to more accurately describe the "traffic pattern" of biblical theology: the roundabout.[15] The road from the text to our own world is not an uninterrupted superhighway. In reality, our reading of the text is influenced by factors from our own world. Traffic from several secondary roads feeds into the highway leading from text to application. We may identify three general kinds of traffic that will affect our biblical theology of creation care: historical and systematic theology, culture, and science.

Historical and Systematic Theology

First, our biblical theology is affected by historical and systematic theology. When I (Doug) was in seminary, just after the earth cooled, biblical theology had a relatively clear and uncontested meaning: it was the study of the theology taught in the Bible. The movement from text to application was linear. We analyze texts, synthesize those texts into a biblical theology, and then hand this neat package over to the systematic theologian who, armed with philosophical insights and informed by history, provides dogmatic conclusions that instruct the contemporary church. Since those golden days of old, things have become considerably more complicated. As we have already emphasized, we don't want to take anything from the vital descriptive task of biblical

---

15. Another author who uses the roundabout imagery, speaking specifically about the relationship between biblical interpretation and science, is William P. Brown, *The Seven Pillars of Creation: The* *Bible, Science, and the Ecology of Wonder* (Oxford: Oxford University Press, 2010), 15–16.

theology. But we need to be reminded that this deceptively "objective" task is not so simple as we might sometimes think. Because we operate at one level removed from the text itself, biblical theologians must make decisions and adopt categories that are not clearly in the text itself. For instance, if I am trying to develop a biblical theology of the effect that Adam's original sin had on him, his posterity, and the created world, I would have to consider the teaching of several key passages in Scripture. I would have to try to fit them together in a way that makes sense of them. I might even struggle to understand how one passage might relate to another. In doing all this, I have to make decisions. And since I am making these subjective decisions, it would be foolish of me to refuse to make use of insights and even categories developed by systematic and historical theology (such as "the fall," language that does not even appear in Scripture). Of course, we must not allow the categories of historical or systematic theology to dictate how we read the Bible—the Bible must have the last word. Sometimes our study of the Bible will force us to revise historical or systematic categories, but our work is nevertheless influenced by them and would be impoverished and less helpful without them.

Culture

A second road that feeds into our roundabout carries traffic from our culture. Contemporary interpreters, under the influence of postmodernism, are keenly aware of the way all of us are affected by our situation when we read the Bible. None of us comes to it with a blank slate. We all have previously formed ideas about what the Bible says on a variety of topics. While this is true, evangelicals in particular have rightly pushed back against those who use this fact to deny our ability to discover any true meaning in the text of Scripture. However, culture is not just a threat to our work; it can also direct our biblical theology onto a path that enhances its relevance and guards against error.

Our culture can enhance our biblical theology by helping us set priorities in our work. Many discussions of biblical theology focus on "big book" biblical theologies: descriptions of the theology of the entire Old Testament or New Testament, or even of the whole Bible. Such treatments, which seek to reflect accurately and in careful balance the concerns of the text, are vital. But for every such big-book biblical theology, there are a dozen more focused studies, whose very *raison d'etre* often can be traced to influences from outside Scripture.[16] It is no accident that Christian scholars began writing extensively about the biblical teaching on the nature of human personhood and the point at which human life begins in the 1970s or, in recent

---

16. Scobie says in this regard, at the same time giving a nice definition of the "recovery" strategy: "Current theological and ethical concerns (e.g., ecology, feminism, human rights) do not determine or dictate the conclusions of BT [Biblical Theology], but they can prompt biblical scholars to reassess the scriptural evidence that may be obscured or distorted by later nonbiblical prejudices and presuppositions" (*The Ways of Our God*, 48).

times, on the importance of racial reconciliation. A biblical-theological concern with creation and the ethics that arise from that theology should be a persistent focus of the church—simply because Scripture speaks of these matters. But biblical theologians are suddenly spending a lot more time on this theme because of the developments we briefly surveyed above: the realization that the health of our planet is endangered and the rise of the modern environmental movement. Biblical theologians appropriately turn to Scripture to help the church chart a distinctively Christian approach to these developments. As Alister McGrath comments, "Changing situations lead to different articulations, though not to different conceptions, of our vision of the gospel."[17] As we have noted, the comparatively little attention given to the non-human world of creation in the New Testament poses particular challenges for the biblical theologian engaged in this task. But the sparseness of explicit teaching should not deter us from undertaking this important work any more than biblical theologians have been deterred by the lack of explicit teaching in the New Testament about abortion or about the racial injustices we face today. Scripture presents to us a vision of all of reality that has implications for many issues treated only briefly or not at all in its pages.

There is a danger, of course, in coming to Scripture with an agenda, as we may read that agenda into the text. Loren Wilkinson, a leading advocate of a robust Christian commitment to creation care, warns, "We must be careful lest we simply use the gospel as a tool to bring about a program which we have decided on other grounds deserves our attention."[18] The response to this problem, however, is not to pretend to a neutrality that, in fact, can never exist. The proper response, rather, is to make sure that we submit ourselves to the judgment of the text in conversation with the great tradition and with interpreters who come to the task from different cultures.

If culture can help make our biblical theology more relevant, can it also make it more accurate? We think so, though considerable caution is needed here. Let us illustrate with one of the central issues in the current debate about the practicalities of creation care: the place of human beings within creation. Some more radical environmentalists have argued that we must rid ourselves of the focus on human beings ("anthropocentrism") that has dominated Western culture and put in its place a "biocentric" view that gives human beings no special place in the created world. In response, some evangelical theologians simply dismiss this kind of development by reiterating the obvious biblical teaching about the special role that human beings have in God's creation. But this is shortsighted. Shifts in culture can illuminate assumptions that we have unconsciously adopted and that do not, in fact, align with a genuinely biblical worldview. To borrow the language we used earlier, biblical

17. Alister McGrath, "The Doctrine of Creation: Some Theological Reflections," in *As Long as the Earth Endures: The Bible, Creation and the Environment*, ed. Jonathan Moo and Robin Routledge (Nottingham: Inter-Varsity, 2014), 47.

18. Loren Wilkinson, *Earthkeeping in the Nineties: Stewardship of Creation* (Grand Rapids: Eerdmans, 1991), 345.

theologians will sometimes need to resist cultural developments, while at other times those developments may help us to recover a biblical perspective that has been lost or unduly minimized.

In this case, we think there is clear evidence that modern Western culture has tended toward an unbiblical understanding of human dominion over the created world. Admittedly, theologians and biblical scholars are themselves enmeshed in culture, and we think that some scholars and theologians have tended to read our anthropocentric Western culture into their interpretations of Scripture.[19] And, of course, this culture has, in turn, exerted a powerful influence on the way believers view themselves and the created world. As we approach the Bible to see what it says about creation care, then, we may appropriately recognize that our assumptions may be improperly colored by an excessively anthropocentric culture. We then turn to a fresh analysis and teaching of Scripture in an effort to bring the church back to a wider and more accurate view of the role of humans within the world of creation.

Science

A third road feeding into our roundabout carries the traffic of scientific analysis of our world. The data scientists gather about our world affect our biblical theology of creation care in three ways.

First, as we noted above, scientific findings about the state of the earth merge with the traffic from culture to place creation and humanity's role in it high on the agenda of biblical-theological issues. The peer-reviewed research of many scientists working in many different fields has made a compelling case for the severity and extent of the problems we face. Among them are the ongoing catastrophe of biodiversity loss, the destruction of the world's tropical forests, the acidification of the oceans, the degradation and loss of topsoil, the pollution of the atmosphere, the changing of the earth's climate, and the human suffering that these developments are causing.[20] By alerting us to particular issues in the world in which we live, science helps biblical theologians set priorities that will serve the needs of the contemporary church. As William Brown says, "humans remain *homo sapiens*, made in the *imago Dei*, a distinctly wise species uniquely endowed with God-given responsibility. Science provides us the data of danger."[21]

Second, scientific findings provide viewpoints on the natural world that we bring to our reading of the Bible. I (Doug) teach at an institution whose motto for liberal arts education is "All truth is God's truth." Truth discovered by scientists in

---

19. This tendency might be observed in the way some Old Testament scholars so prioritize the history of salvation that the created world is unfairly marginalized. Note, for instance, Emil Brunner's comment: "The cosmic element in the Bible is never anything more than the scenery in which the history of mankind takes place" (*Revelation and Reason* [Philadelphia: Westminster, 1946], 33n).

20. This language is largely borrowed from Jonathan Moo, "The Biblical Basis for Creation Care," in *Creation Care and the Gospel: Reconsidering the Mission of the Church*, ed. Colin Bell and Robert S. White (Peabody, MA: Hendrickson, 2016), 28–42.

21. *The Seven Pillars of Creation*, 243.

the natural world has some bearing on the truth we find in Scripture. Science in this sense is no alien dialogue partner, since the scientist studies the very world that God has made intelligible in the first place. Of course, the matter is complicated by the inevitable uncertainties and sometimes sharp debates about just what "science" is currently telling us. The issue, however, is not scientific theory vs. biblical fact, but, rather, the interaction of the *interpretations* of scientists with the *interpretations* of biblical scholars and theologians. Finding solid ground in this shifting geography of different and sometimes conflicting interpretations will not be easy. Scripture must, certainly, have the last word, and it is important for the integrity of biblical theology that information from outside Scripture not be allowed to dictate what the Bible can or cannot say. Nevertheless, current scientific theory, especially when the theory has stood the test of time and is widely accepted, cannot merely be dismissed. Rather than facilely dismissing a particular scientific finding as incompatible with scriptural teaching, our approach should be to return to the text and open a dialogue between science and Scripture. Theologians have worked like this in the past. The eventual acceptance of Copernicus's heliocentric understanding of the solar system, for example, influenced biblical theologians' interpretation of a number of Old Testament texts. It remains possible that there will be times when Christians find it necessary in the end to hold to what seems to be a clear teaching of Scripture that is in apparent conflict with a contemporary scientific claim. However, even in such cases we ought to acknowledge in humility our limited understanding and not make scientific pronouncements that are beyond our expertise. We can in any case be confident—on the basis of what Scripture itself tells us about God and creation—that there can be no final conflict between science and our Christian faith.

> What we need is ". . . a hermeneutical feedback loop between biblical faith and scientific understanding whereby the former is enriched by the latter. If biblical creation faith is to be intelligible today, then it requires the feedback of science. This does not mean that science would dictate the directions of biblical interpretation and theological reflection. That would turn the dialogue into a hostile takeover. Rather, the process allows science to nudge the work of biblical theology in directions it has not yet ventured and, in so doing, add another layer to Scripture's interpretive 'thickness' (as my colleague Walter Brueggemann would say) or wondrous depth."
>
> *William Brown* [22]

Third, and related to the previous point, our understanding of the natural world has an important bearing on the output of our biblical theology. The traffic from this road affects the direction of the biblical-theological road of creation care. Biblical theology will help establish the values that govern our understanding of, and interaction with, the created world. But our *practice* of those values will be shaped by our understanding of the state of the created world and the particular ways in which its health may be endangered, on the one hand, or enhanced, on the other. If "creation care" is not to remain an empty slogan, we must act on what we know.

22. Ibid., 16.

Theology has an end, a *telos*: the formation of Christian character and the practical living out of biblical values.

The wisdom we need to practice creation care will be informed by scientists, as they illuminate the current state and needs of God's creation. We will therefore conclude this volume with a brief overview of our current environmental challenges and some of the ways that a theology of creation care might address them. But we also need fellow Christians who can reveal to us—through art, poetry, literature, music, and above all lives of faithfulness—the power of the gospel to transform our relationships with each other and all of creation in ways that bring honor and glory to our Creator and Redeemer.

PART 2

ARRIVING
AT ANSWERS

CHAPTER 3

A BEAUTIFUL WORLD

Beginnings and endings reveal a lot about the scope and significance of a story. So it matters that the story of the Bible begins and ends with creation, with a heaven and an earth. The story doesn't begin with *us*—"in the beginning, human beings . . ." It begins with God and the entire universe he made, with earth and sky, with water and land, with birds and fish and animals, with a vast, beautiful world full of creeping and crawling and swimming creatures. Human beings eventually make their appearance on day six, along with the other land animals. But first we learn something about God, the greatness of his creative power, and the goodness of the world that belongs to him.

In this chapter, we will explore what the creation account at the beginning of Genesis reveals about God and creation, especially the non-human creation. Since this is not the only place in Scripture where we find a description of creation, we will also consider other texts, particularly some of the Psalms and Job. There we will discover further reflections on the nature of the world God made, God's ongoing relationship to it, and our place within it. A detailed discussion of our particular role as human beings awaits us in the next chapter, but we will not rightly understand what it means to bear God's image or to rule in his creation if we don't first know something about the God whose image we bear and the creation for which he has given us responsibility.

The spacious and beautiful scene painted for us in the opening chapters of Genesis has sadly become a field of battle in recent decades, as six-day creationists, theistic evolutionists, and everyone in-between have argued with each other about how to relate evolutionary science and biblical faith. These debates are necessary and important: they have significant implications for how Christians with a commitment to the authority of Scripture interact not only with science, but with a host of contemporary issues. Yet it is past time that we step back and look again at Genesis 1 to remind ourselves of our shared commitment to the creator God who is revealed in this text and our shared responsibility for his earth and its creatures. We need to find ways to articulate in our post-Christian society what it means for us to name "nature" and the "environment" as God's good creation, and we must above all ask what it means in our time to faithfully honor God in how we live and love and care for the glorious world that belongs to him. It is time, in short, that we ask again what this text reveals about God, creation, and ourselves and leave aside—for the time being at any rate—questions about precisely how God chose to bring into being the tremendous diversity of life on our planet.

GOD AND CREATION

The Bible begins by centering us on the only one who in his very being is life and love, the uncreated one who is the source of all goodness, the God who made all things: "In the beginning God created the heavens and the earth" (Gen. 1:1). God's act of creation is described using a Hebrew verb, *bara*, that is only ever used for the activity of God. Human beings may also work and make things, but only as subcreators, as those using derivative powers and reshaping what has already been made. God is utterly unique as the Creator who calls into being all that exists. Later reflection on the significance of what this text and others reveal about God's creative activity would lead to the understanding that God creates *ex nihilo*, out of nothing. Paul may allude to such an idea in Romans 4:17, when he describes God as one who "calls into being things that were not." What is in any case clear in Genesis 1:1 is that all that exists is the product of God's creative activity. The expression "heavens and the earth" (or "sky and the land" as we also might translate it)[1] is a merism, two contrasting parts that are used to refer to a whole. Here at the beginning of the creation account, then, is a summary of the rest of the chapter: God is the one who created the whole of the universe, which entails all that exists.

This first sentence of Scripture therefore divides all of reality into God and everything else. There is God, and then there is the world that he made. There is the Creator, and then there is his creation. Wrong thinking about God can usually be traced back to confusion about this basic distinction. When we forget the radical otherness of God, we reduce the Creator to categories that apply only to created things, which leads us, most often, to make God into our own image, so that God becomes merely an inflated, more powerful version of ourselves.

As a result, we cease to have the capacity to hear God's voice when it might challenge us. We impose limits on what God has done and what God might do. We lose the ability to entrust God with our entire lives, the good and the bad. We fail finally to worship God as God. When we forget the otherness of God, the goodness and beauty of creation and the pleasures of life can lead us to live as though these created realities were themselves the sources of life and happiness. These things become gods to us, the center of our lives and the aim of our striving. Genesis 1:1 recenters us on the one from whom and through whom all else derives life and being, and it encourages us to give our entire lives in worship to him, the one true God.

---

1. The Hebrew word *shamayim* is used to refer to what we call the "sky," but English translations often translate it as "heavens" to account for the fact that the word in Hebrew is plural and is also used in the Old Testament to refer to the place of God's throne.

Archaeologists have found other creation stories that were recorded in the ancient Near East, some of which would have undoubtedly been known to the first readers of Genesis. It is fascinating, in this regard, to observe the similarities with the account we have in Genesis: the structure of the universe, the division of the cosmos into heaven and earth, and the subsequent stories of the making of human beings, a garden, and a flood all find parallels in other texts. Yet what is most striking are the differences. What we find in the Genesis account is a startlingly distinct understanding of deity and a radically different assessment of the significance of creation and human life than what is depicted in these other stories. In these texts, there is no fundamental distinction between the one God and all else. Nor is the creation of the world so clearly the result of a decision by the Creator to make a heaven and an earth. Rather, it is the result of bloody conflict between the gods. In the Babylonian *Enūma Eliš*, for example, the god Marduk slays the goddess and chaos monster Tiamat by driving winds into her mouth and piercing her with a spear. He then cuts her in half and uses the two halves of her body to form the heaven and the earth. The contrast with the calm and ordered story of creation's beginnings in Genesis 1 could not be starker:

> The danger of making God in our own image is evident in Ludwig Feuerbach's famous critique of Christianity: "Man—this is the mystery of religion—projects his being into objectivity, and then again makes himself an object to this projected image of himself thus converted into a subject."[2]

Tiāmat and Marduk, the sage of the gods, came together,
Joining in strife, drawing near to battle.
Bēl spread out his net and enmeshed her;
He let loose the Evil Wind, the rear guard, in her face.
Tiāmat opened her mouth to swallow it,
She let the Evil Wind in so that she could not close her lips.
The fierce winds weighed down her belly,
Her inwards were distended and she opened her mouth wide.
He let fly an arrow and pierced her belly,
He tore open her entrails and slit her inwards,
He bound her and extinguished her life,
He threw down her corpse and stood on it. . . .
Bēl rested, surveying the corpse,
In order to divide the lump by a clever scheme.
He split her into two like a dried fish:
One half of her he set up and stretched out as the heavens.
He stretched the skin and appointed a watch
With the instruction not to let her waters escape.

2. Ludwig Feuerbach, *The Essence of Christianity* (New York: Harper, 1957), 29–30.

He crossed over the heavens, surveyed the celestial parts,
And adjusted them to match the Apsû, Nudimmud's abode.
Bēl measured the shape of the Apsû
And set up Ešarra, a replica of Ešgalla.
In Ešgalla, Ešarra which he had built, and the heavens,
He settled in their shrines Anu, Enlil, and Ea.[3]

The second verse of Genesis is sometimes considered to reflect an awareness of such stories: "Now the earth was formless and empty, darkness was over the surface of the deep, and the Spirit of God was hovering over the waters" (Gen. 1:2). The description of the chaotic pre-creation state of things as "formless and void" (*tohu wabohu*), the reference to the shadowy "deep" (*tehom*), associated elsewhere with sea monsters and chaos, and the picture of God's Spirit (or "wind") "hovering over the waters" (or "blowing against the waters," as the Greek translation suggests), all have been characterized as echoes of other ancient Near Eastern versions of creation. Yet the echoes are at best faint. Rather than the result of a divine conflict, the world is called into being by the *word* of God. There is no struggle, no battle, no wresting of the world away from hostile powers. God speaks—"Let there be . . ."—and it is done—"and there was . . ."

In this context, verse 2 functions primarily to prepare readers in dramatic style for the unfolding narrative of creation to follow. We are led to expect that formlessness will be formed, emptiness filled, and darkness made light, as God's life-giving *ruakh*, his "Spirit" or "breath," hovers over the yet lifeless and unbounded waters. The rest of the passage fulfills such expectations and more. In a beautiful, carefully crafted account, we witness the unconstrained power of a God who speaks all things into existence, learn of the order and the goodness of his creation, and discover the delight that God finds in all he has made.

So what kind of world is it, and what difference does this make for us?

GOD'S BEAUTIFUL WORLD
Orderedness and Contingency

The seven-day account is neatly structured to highlight the order and purposefulness of creation. To begin with, we have the structure imposed by the use of a seven-day week. The week itself is divided into two halves of three days each, culminating in God's rest on the seventh day. In the first three days, God creates and separates to form differentiated spaces where otherwise there would be only formlessness

---

3. *Enūma Eliš*, Tablet IV, lines 93–104, 135–146, *Mesopotamian Civilizations: Babylonian Creation Myths,* trans. W. G. Lambert (Winona Lake, IN: Eisenbrauns, 2014), 91–95.

(*tohu*; v. 1); in the second three days, God fills the spaces he has formed, where otherwise there would be only emptiness (*bohu*; v. 1):

The Genesis 1 Seven-Day Creation Account

"formless . . . and empty" (v. 2)	
Day 1	Day 4
Light; day and night	Sun, moon, and stars
Day 2	Day 5
Waters above (sky) and waters below	Birds and sea creatures
Day 3	Day 6
Land separated from sea; vegetation	Land animals
Day 7 God's rest	

This carefully constructed narrative highlights the orderedness and the comprehensiveness of God's creative activity. The entire cosmos is shaped and organized according to God's purposes and filled with abundance—sun, moon, stars, birds, fish, and animals of all kinds.

The distinction between the one God and everything else is hinted at in the curious description in verse 16 of the sun and the moon as the "greater light" and the "lesser light." Hebrew has perfectly good words for the sun (*shemesh*) and moon (*yareakh*), so why not use them? The reason is almost certainly because the sun and moon were considered deities by other cultures in the ancient Near East, and to use their names in the context of a creation account could imply a validation of their divine status. In Deuteronomy 4:19, Moses in fact finds it necessary to warn the Israelites against the worship of sun, moon, and stars (cf. Deut. 17:3; 2 Kings 23:5; Job 31:26–28). Genesis thus describes the sun and moon as they are, merely "lights" that serve to "govern" the day and the night. The sun and moon are not to be worshipped; they are creations of God, like everything else.

In addition, there is no sense in which the world is portrayed in Genesis 1 as *necessary* to God or, as in other ancient Near Eastern accounts, an accident or by-product of something else. It is the result of God's free decision to create. God is under no constraint to make a world at all, nor must any world he makes look like ours. It could have been otherwise. The purpose, the goal, the *telos* of creation is—as later texts will suggest—always and only the glory of God and Christ (Heb. 2:10; Col. 1:16; Rev. 4:11). The creation has its own integrity and role, and it is even called upon to participate in God's creative activity ("let the earth produce . . ."). But the creation exists *contingently*, as the result of God's unconstrained life-giving grace, and is dependent on his sustaining power.

This contingency of creation, the fact that the world is not necessary and could have been otherwise, means that creation can only be known by actually looking at it, exploring it, and studying it. It won't do to sit in a darkened room and puzzle out what sort of a wo[rld] must exist. It is necessary to go out into the world and [ob]serve it if you want to know what it's like, how it works, [w]hat sort of creatures inhabit it, and how they live. Genesis [i]mplies that we need something like empirical science if we [... to] know this world of God's freely given creation. That [the worl]d itself is distinct from God—neither divine in itself, nor[... d]eities—and that it is ordered and sustained in its [regularity by G]od's word suggests moreover that our study of [... a]nd productive. Genuine, reliable knowledge [... poss]ible. The world described by Genesis is [... a world of shifting s]hadows or a world full of capricious [deities that can be invo]ked to explain anything that is as yet [unknown or myst]erious to us. In biblical perspective, the [mystery of crea]tion lies not in its inexplicability but in its [... th]e wonder and beauty.

[... th]e explication and revelation of its wonder and beauty [throu]gh science or art can only enhance its mystery, recalling us [to] humility before the Creator of it all and inviting us into his worship. The command given to human beings to "rule" over other creatures (Gen. 1:26, 28), the charge to "work . . . and take care of" the garden (Gen. 2:15), and Adam's naming of the animals (Gen. 2:19–20) all serve to challenge us to undertake study of the world and to come to know it as well as we can so that we might appropriately rule in it and serve our Creator well. In this light, science, art, and many forms of work we sometimes label "secular" ought instead to be recognized as high and holy callings. If we are to care well for the earth, we need scientists to help us understand the thing for which we are called to care, and we need artists to help us see this world anew.

Goodness

It may be surprising that the consistent emphasis on the uniqueness of God in Genesis 1 and the rejection of the notion that created things are divine in themselves do not lead in any sense to a denigration of the created world. In fact, it is quite the other way around. The value and goodness of the entire world of God's creation is one of the

"The lived quality of Genesis 1 [...] my efforts in trying to raise th[...] in the living quarters of so [...] I know and have kno[...] blinds and get th[...] between Sun[...] vast, rhyth[...] and h[...] smell[...] creating [...] plants and [...] fish and birds, [...] hounds, and the [...] and woman—look [...] of wonders, male and [...]

. . . Everything we se[...] and taste carries within it the [...] 'And God said . . . and it w[...] and it was good . . . .' W[e ...]more deeply in and at home in the creation than ever."

Eugene Peterson[4]

4. Eugene H. Peterson, *Christ Plays in Ten Thousand Places: A Conversation in Spiritual Theology* (Grand Rapids: Eerdmans, 2008), 71.

central themes of this first chapter of Genesis. No fewer than seven times (a number appropriately symbolic of completeness), God looks at what he has made and sees that it is "good" (vv. 4, 10, 12, 18, 21, 25, 31). The seventh time, God's assessment includes "all that he had made" (v. 31). In de-divinizing the world, Genesis does not demote it. Rather, creation is seen for what it is so as to be rightly appreciated, valued, and even loved.

We have all known someone who falls hopelessly in what they think is love for someone whom they idolize and treat as though they were a god or goddess. Such a projection onto the beloved cannot, we know, sustain a relationship, nor can it enable the sort of intimate knowledge of the other that is necessary for genuine love and care. Rather, seeing someone for who they really are, being free to be oneself with them, and being willing to risk knowing them deeply and truly in a relationship of mutuality, trust, and give-and-take are the sorts of things we hope for in human relationships. So when Scripture dethrones the created world from its idolized status as divine and calls readers away from nature religions and pantheism, this is not—as is sometimes claimed—a reason to conclude that biblical religion leads to the devaluation of creation or serves as a license for its exploitation. It serves instead as an invitation to know creation as it is in itself and, as we will see, to learn to live in it well. We are invited, in fact, to care for creation in ways that are in keeping with its true nature.

The emphasis on the goodness of the world throughout Genesis 1 challenges readers to adopt God's own perspective on the world he has made. This "goodness" of the world does not mean that it is necessarily perfect, or that there is no possibility of change or development. As we will see, Scripture suggests that God intends a direction for his good creation, a purpose for it that is finally fulfilled in the new creation. The Hebrew word for "good" used in Genesis 1 (*tov*) is as broad in its meaning as the English word. Yet this recognition of the goodness of every part of God's creation is perhaps the most important thing that Genesis 1 contributes to a biblical theology of care for the earth.

> "And they do wrong unto the Deity,
>   Who Nature and her goodness do despise,
>   And God blaspheme and in their hearts deny."
>
> *Dante*[5]

God discerns the truth of things, so when Genesis says that God looks at what he has made and finds it to be "good," we are being told unequivocally that what God has created is of *value*. It has a goodness that belongs to itself—what we might call *intrinsic* value—by virtue of having been created by God and assessed by him as good. The value of the rest of creation is not dependent on what we think about it or merely on its apparent usefulness to human beings. Our aim must be to come

---

5. Dante, *Inferno: Canto XI*, lines 46–48, *Dante's Divina Commedia: Inferno*, trans. C. H. Ramsay (London: Tinsley Brothers, 1862), 73.

to see the world as God sees it, to learn to love and value it as he does. Notice, by the way, that God sees goodness in every part of his creation, even before humanity enters the scene (vv. 4, 10, 12, 18, 21, 25). It is, then, the *fullness* of creation, with human beings finding their appropriate place alongside all else, that evokes God's final summative assessment that "all" that he made is "very good" (v. 31). In an age when many secular environmentalists have found it necessary to abandon any attempt to argue for the value of the earth and its creatures beyond narrowly utilitarian arguments about their service to us, Christians ought to reclaim a distinctively biblical perspective on the intrinsic worth of all of God's creation.

Diversity and Abundance

In the next chapter, we will consider what makes human beings unique within the vast array of created life, but it is important at this stage to observe that our species is portrayed in Genesis 1 and 2 as having kinship with the rest of God's creatures and as sharing membership within the community of creation. In chapter 1, we don't even get a special day to ourselves but are created alongside the other land animals on day six. In chapter 2, humanity is described as having been formed from the "dust of the ground" (v. 7). We are humble, earthy creatures; *adam* from the *adamah*, or "human" from the "humus," as some have suggested we translate the wordplay here. We learn a few verses later that, just as we are formed out of the ground, so too "the LORD God had formed out of the ground all the wild animals and all the birds in the sky" (v. 19). We share our earthly origins as human creatures with all of life.

"God's original plan was to hang out in a garden with some naked vegetarians." This quote from a bumper sticker (courtesy of Restoring Eden) reminds us that Genesis 1:29–30 (and 2:16) assigns a vegetarian diet to human beings and, indeed, to all animals. There is a suggestion here of God's intentions for a peaceable creation, which finds an echo in depictions of the messianic kingdom in Isaiah 11:6–9 and 65:25. The vegetarian diet is broadened after the flood, when God tells Noah and his family that now "Everything that lives and moves about will be food for you. Just as I gave you the green plants, I now give you everything." (Gen. 9:3)

When God breathes into the man whom he has formed, the man is said to become a "living being," a *nephesh khayah*, translated by the King James Version as a "living soul" (v. 7). Yet it is not a "soul" in this sense that distinguishes humanity from other creatures. In chapter 1, the sea creatures (vv. 20–21), "all the beasts of the earth," "all the birds in the sky," and "all the creatures that move along the ground" are also described as being (or having) *nephesh khayah* (v. 30). All creatures are animated and sustained by the life-giving breath of God. So too do all creatures share in their dependence on the produce of the earth for their food. To human beings, God gives "every seed-bearing plant on the face of the whole earth and every tree that has fruit with seed in it" (v. 29); to the other creatures, God gives "every green plant for food" (v. 30). We, and all other creatures with us, derive our sustenance from the earth and its abundance.

And what a diverse world of living creatures God made, in both the sea and on land!

> God created the great creatures of the sea and every living thing with which the water teems and that moves about in it, according to their kinds, and every winged bird according to its kind. (Gen. 1:21)

> And God said, "Let the land produce living creatures according to their kinds: the livestock, the creatures that move along the ground, and the wild animals, each according to its kind." And it was so. (Gen. 1:24)

The British biologist J. B. S. Haldane, commenting on the extraordinary number of beetle species that inhabit our planet, is reputed to have remarked that the Creator, if there is one, must have "an inordinate fondness for beetles." Haldane intended his comment as a joke, but Genesis 1 does indeed portray a God who seems to delight in the richness of species he creates "according to their kinds"—including, presumably, all 350,000 (and counting) beetle species!

Genesis 1 reveals that the staggering diversity of life on our planet is not an accident; it was God's intention that the world be *filled* with a rich variety of species, and God considers it all to be good. God also apparently delights in the sheer abundance of life. Human beings are famously told to "be fruitful and increase in number" (v. 28). But we should not miss the fact that the birds and sea creatures too are given precisely the same blessing in verse 22, to fill the seas and to increase upon the earth. The picture of the whole chapter is of a richly diverse, abundant, and good world, teeming with life and blessing.

How then should we respond to God's creative work?

> "For you love all things that exist, and detest none of the things that you have made, for you would not have made anything if you had hated it."
>
> *Wisdom of Solomon 11:24 (NRSV)*

RESPONDING TO GOD'S BEAUTIFUL WORLD
Celebrating God's Expansive Care

If Genesis 1 were the only time the Bible gave such attention to creation, perhaps we could be excused for thinking it was merely a minor theme in the drama of Scripture. Yet God's concern for his creation is woven into the fabric of the entire biblical narrative, culminating with the renewal and restoration of all things, the new creation. Above all, it is in the psalms that the celebration of God's creation reaches its crescendo, and of all the psalms, Psalm 104 rings out the loudest and clearest in its praise of God for the richness and diversity of his world. The importance of this psalm for a biblical theology of creation and care for the earth justifies quoting it in full—and we urge readers not to skip reading the psalm before turning to our discussion below!

[1] Praise the LORD, my soul.

LORD my God, you are very great;
>> you are clothed with splendor and majesty.

[2] The LORD wraps himself in light as with a garment;
>> he stretches out the heavens like a tent
>>> [3] and lays the beams of his upper chambers on their waters.

He makes the clouds his chariot
>> and rides on the wings of the wind.

[4] He makes winds his messengers,
>> flames of fire his servants.

[5] He set the earth on its foundations;
>> it can never be moved.

[6] You covered it with the watery depths as with a garment;
>> the waters stood above the mountains.

[7] But at your rebuke the waters fled,
>> at the sound of your thunder they took to flight;

[8] they flowed over the mountains,
>> they went down into the valleys,
>> to the place you assigned for them.

[9] You set a boundary they cannot cross;
>> never again will they cover the earth.

[10] He makes springs pour water into the ravines;
>> it flows between the mountains.

[11] They give water to all the beasts of the field;
>> the wild donkeys quench their thirst.

[12] The birds of the sky nest by the waters;
>> they sing among the branches.

[13] He waters the mountains from his upper chambers;
>> the land is satisfied by the fruit of his work.

[14] He makes grass grow for the cattle,
>> and plants for people to cultivate—
>> bringing forth food from the earth:

[15] wine that gladdens human hearts,
>> oil to make their faces shine,
>> and bread that sustains their hearts.

[16] The trees of the LORD are well watered,
>> the cedars of Lebanon that he planted.

[17] There the birds make their nests;
>> the stork has its home in the junipers.

[18] The high mountains belong to the wild goats;

the crags are a refuge for the hyrax.
¹⁹ He made the moon to mark the seasons,
and the sun knows when to go down.
²⁰ You bring darkness, it becomes night,
and all the beasts of the forest prowl.
²¹ The lions roar for their prey
and seek their food from God.
²² The sun rises, and they steal away;
they return and lie down in their dens.
²³ Then people go out to their work,
to their labor until evening.
²⁴ How many are your works, Lord!
In wisdom you made them all;
the earth is full of your creatures.
²⁵ There is the sea, vast and spacious,
teeming with creatures beyond number—
living things both large and small.
²⁶ There the ships go to and fro,
and Leviathan, which you formed to frolic there.
²⁷ All creatures look to you
to give them their food at the proper time.
²⁸ When you give it to them,
they gather it up;
when you open your hand,
they are satisfied with good things.
²⁹ When you hide your face,
they are terrified;
when you take away their breath,
they die and return to the dust.
³⁰ When you send your Spirit,
they are created,
and you renew the face of the ground.
³¹ May the glory of the Lord endure forever;
may the Lord rejoice in his works—
³² he who looks at the earth, and it trembles,
who touches the mountains, and they smoke.
³³ I will sing to the Lord all my life;
I will sing praise to my God as long as I live.
³⁴ May my meditation be pleasing to him,
as I rejoice in the Lord.

[35] But may sinners vanish from the earth
    and the wicked be no more.
Praise the LORD, my soul.
Praise the LORD.

The psalm begins and ends with a call to praise God, reminding us that the purpose of creation is, from first to last, to bring glory and praise to the Creator. The bulk of the psalm describes in extravagant detail some of the richness of this wild and beautiful world. Much of the first half, in particular, echoes the order of the creation account in Genesis 1. In the psalm, however, God does not merely speak the world into existence, but he is also active in both creating and sustaining it. He "makes springs pour water into the ravines" (v. 10), he "waters the mountains" (v. 13), he makes grass and other plants grow (v. 14), he brings darkness at night (v. 20), he gives food to all creatures (vv. 21, 27–28), he causes earthquakes and volcanoes (v. 32). When God removes the breath of life, creatures die and return to the dust (v. 29), and when he pours out his life-giving Spirit, "they are created" and he renews "the face of the ground" (v. 30). The God of the Bible is not the god of the Deists who makes a world and then leaves it to its own devices; this is a God who remains at work in the world. The very regularity of the creation that we observe and depend upon and that scientists study is the result of the sustaining, creative work of the same God who called it into being.

What is most striking in Psalm 104 is the breadth of God's concern with and delight in creation, which extends beyond the neat boundaries of settled human life and civilization. God does indeed provide richly for human beings, making grass grow for cattle, "plants for people to cultivate—bringing forth food from the earth: wine that gladdens human hearts, oil to make their faces shine, and bread that sustains their hearts" (vv. 14–15). Yet this evocative picture of the goodness of God's provision for abundant agricultural life is but a part of God's provision for *all* creatures. So too does he water the mountains and make springs that flow down ravines and "give water to all the beasts of the field," including the "wild donkeys," or onager (v. 11). Onager are known in Scripture for their undomesticated freedom from human restraint; they are creatures of the desert wilderness (Job 39:5; Jer. 2:24; cf. Gen. 16:12). Here, they remind us of God's concern even for those parts of creation that do not serve humanity.

It is sobering to note that the "wild donkeys" (also known as onager) described in Psalm 104 are threatened across much of their traditional range and were entirely extirpated from Israel until reintroduction efforts brought back a small number. Many of the wildlife species described in the Bible are in fact no longer present in Palestine due to overhunting and the loss of habitat.

The cedars of Lebanon, which elsewhere serve as building materials for the palaces of David and Solomon (2 Sam. 5:11; 7:2; 1 Kings 7) and for the Jerusalem temple (1 Kings 5–6), are here celebrated solely for their provision of nesting sites for birds (Ps. 104:16–17). So too are the junipers, where the stork (probably the carnivorous white stork) "has its home" (v. 17). The high mountains, meanwhile, belong to the "wild goats," or ibex, while the rocks provide refuge for the hyrax (v. 18). These are places and creatures that do not directly serve or provide for the people of ancient Israel, yet they are singled out as among those creatures for which God cares and provides. Even more dramatic is the description of the beasts of the forest that prowl by night (v. 20) and the lions that "roar for their prey and seek their food from God" (v. 21). These are creatures that not only fail to serve or provide for ancient Israelites in any obvious way but also pose a threat to their livelihoods by regularly preying on their livestock. They can also, of course, kill human beings, and regularly did so. When, in Judges 14:5–6, a roaring young lion comes at Samson, the Spirit of the Lord comes upon him and enables him to kill the lion, presumably saving Samson from being killed himself.

No ancient Israelite, including the writer of Psalm 104, could be naive about the realities of death and predation. "Nature red in tooth and claw" was a part of daily life. Yet, in Psalm 104 (and, as we will see, also in Job 38:39–40), roaring lions find their appropriate place in the community of God's creation. God is even portrayed as providing prey for them (v. 21). The psalmist has an expansive view of the goodness of God's world, recognizing God's care and provision even for the wildest parts of creation. It is a vision that challenges any exclusively human-centered narrative of God's purposes in and for the world he made.

Verse 24 (along with the beginning and ending calls to praise) provides the interpretive key to the entire psalm: "How many are your works, Lord! In wisdom you made them all; the earth is full of your creatures." We are encouraged to celebrate the diversity of life God made, seeing *all* of it as testifying to his wisdom and glory and recognizing that other creatures belong not to us but to God himself. In case we missed the point, the next two verses expand the scope of the celebration of God's creation to the vastness of the sea, teeming with life, including even the mythical Leviathan. This is a creature that more than any other represented for ancient Israelites the threatening power of unconstrained chaos, the terror of the wild. How shocking then to learn that Leviathan itself is but one of God's creatures, created for the sheer delight of allowing it to "frolic" in the ocean. This is a God who is bigger and more powerful than can be imagined, a God whose

It is not because of their potentially important roles in fully functioning ecosystems (as an ecologist might tell us today) that the author of Psalm 104 celebrates onager, ibex, lions, and all living creatures, nor is it because of a recognition that the fruitfulness of the earth ultimately depends on such things as volcanoes and earthquakes (as an earth scientist might tell us today) that the psalmist sees such so-called "natural disasters" as coming from God's hands. It is rather because the psalmist has a vision of the creator and sustainer God that is expansive enough to encompass the whole of reality, a vision that is rooted in Scripture, engaged with the world, and centered in praise. Science can help us appreciate more fully the wisdom and beauty of God's creative design, but Psalm 104 reminds us that, first and foremost, a stance of humility and awe before God and his creation will foster discernment and wisdom and enable us to embrace even that which we do not understand.

purposes are beyond our understanding. In verse 32, we learn that this is a God whose very glance can cause an earthquake, a God at whose touch volcanoes erupt. The "glory" of the Lord, the weight of his presence and the power of his reign, ought to be discerned in *all* of his works, just as he too rejoices in them (v. 31).

Recognizing Creation's Testimony

The revelation of God's glory through his creation is a theme that is evident elsewhere in Scripture. It may, for example, lie behind the well-known praise of God's glory in Isaiah's vision of God on the throne in Isaiah 6:3. This verse is usually translated, "Holy, holy, holy is the LORD Almighty; the whole earth is full of his glory" (NIV). But, as Hilary Marlow has suggested, the use of the noun *melo* ("fullness") here rather than the verbal form suggests the possible translation, "the fullness of all the earth is his glory."[6] In other words, as in Psalm 104, it is precisely in the diversity and abundance of his creation that God's glory is made visible. In Psalm 19:1, we learn that "the heavens declare the glory of God, the skies proclaim the work of his hands." They do not use human words (v. 3), and yet their voice is heard throughout the earth, accessible to all (v. 4). So too in Psalm 97: "The heavens proclaim his righteousness, and all peoples see his glory" (v. 6). The apostle Paul develops this theme in Romans, where he likewise assumes that something about the nature of God can be discerned by looking at the created world: "For since the creation of the world God's invisible qualities—his eternal power and divine nature—have been clearly seen, being understood from what has been made" (Rom. 1:20).

Theologians debate the extent to which it is possible to learn true things about God through natural theology, without having recourse to Scripture or special revelation. That there are profound limitations is clear. For example, consider the supreme revelation of God in the person of Jesus Christ. There is obviously no way we could intuit the story of Jesus's life, death, and resurrection or discover it through mere study of nature. Moreover, experience teaches us that it is perfectly possible to understand much about the world of God's creation without actually knowing God himself. Paul himself seems to assume that, although God's power and divine nature are "clearly seen" in creation, in practice people suppress what can be known about God and turn aside to worshipping creation rather than the Creator (Rom. 1:21–25). The fullness of who God is and the particularity of his revelation of himself in his Word (both Christ and the Scripture that bears witness to him) cannot be learned through natural theology. Moreover, our creaturely limitations, and above all our inclination to sin, mean that even what we really ought to be able to learn about God through creation is often obscure to us.

---

6. See Hilary Marlow, *Biblical Prophets and Contemporary Environmental Ethics* (Oxford: Oxford University Press, 2009), 237.

Yet the texts we have examined make it unmistakably clear that this world that God made continues to testify to its Creator and to reveal the glory of God. Whatever we think about the limitations and possibilities of natural theology (and it is beyond the scope of this book to pursue the question further here), we should not miss the fact that, in the light of Scripture and in the light of Christ, we ought to be enabled all the more to discern the beauty and power and glory of God as it is revealed in the things he has made. To become a follower of Christ is to have the world opened up to us as it really is, shot through with the grandeur of God. Christianity is *not*, in this sense, a world-denying religion. Moreover, since this creation is the "real world" that God made (and not a phantasm or merely a projection of our own subjectivity)—an ordered world that can be studied and known, and which in its very existence bears testimony to the Creator—natural theology retains an important place in our apologetics. We can describe for others how we perceive the world in light of our Christian faith, and we have reason to expect that this vision will resonate with what they observe too. For if the God of the Bible is the Creator and Sustainer of all things, then the world as it exists in itself will be consonant with what Scripture teaches us about God and creation.

> Conversion is about stepping "into the real world God made; and then begins the delicious process of exploring it limitlessly."
>
> Evelyn Waugh[7]

In the whole of the New Testament recorded for us, there are only two times that any preaching is directed toward people who apparently have no knowledge of the Old Testament. It is intriguing that, in both cases, proclamation of the gospel begins with creation and what we might call natural theology. Thus, in his well-known Areopagus speech in Athens, Paul, after observing the Athenians' worship of an unknown god, begins with a description of God's action in creation. This is the God who "made the world and everything in it" and who reigns over it as Lord (Acts 17:24), who is not far from anyone and desires that they reach out and find him (v. 27). Paul moves on to call the Athenians to repentance, to turn from their worship of idols to the true God, the Creator and judge of all, who has now definitively revealed himself in the resurrection of Jesus Christ (v. 31). For Paul, the good news about Jesus needs to be understood as the revelation of the one God who is Creator, Sustainer, and Lord of all, and since this is the creator God, and we are all his offspring (v. 28), Paul assumes that there are things about the God he proclaims that "pagans" will have already glimpsed.

An even more compelling example of natural theology at work occurs earlier in Acts, when Paul and Barnabas are in Lystra. The residents of Lystra are amazed at the healing of a lame man and begin to hail Paul and Barnabas as gods themselves.

7. Evelyn Waugh, *Letter to Edward Sackville-West*, cited in Michael de-la-Noy, *Eddy: The Life of Edward Sackville-West* (London: Bodley Head, 1988), 237; quoted in McGrath, "The Doctrine of Creation," 33.

Horrified at this, the two evangelists tear their clothes and rush into the crowd. Emphasizing that they too are only human, Barnabas and Paul proclaim, "We are bringing you good news, telling you to turn from these worthless things to the living God, who made the heavens and the earth and the sea and everything in them" (Acts 14:15). What is striking in the proclamation here of the "good news," the gospel, is not only that it begins with an emphasis on God as Creator, but also that Barnabas and Paul then go on to assume that those in Lystra have actually already received some testimony about the living God. For God "has not left himself without testimony: He has shown kindness by giving you rain from heaven and crops in their seasons; he provides you with plenty of food and fills your hearts with joy" (v. 17). What is sometimes called God's "common grace," the blessings of his provision in creation and even the experience of "joy" that finds its source only in him, is here considered to be part of the way in which God reveals himself even to those who have not yet had the fullness of the gospel proclaimed to them.

Above all, then, we must supplement our care for the poor and our proclamation of the gospel with an attitude toward this world as God's creation, broadening our praise of him as the Creator and Redeemer. Perhaps then we can more confidently hope that others will be drawn into the vision of reality held out to us in Scripture and come by God's grace to know and worship him as well. As we will explore in later chapters, it is therefore sobering to consider how our cavalier treatment of God's good creation, our carelessness in how we live on the earth, and our diminishment of the abundance and diversity of life have not only made us unfaithful stewards, but have also profoundly hindered our witness to the glory of God in Christ. In what ways do we prevent others from perceiving creation's testimony to God when we fail to care well for creation, to enact justice, and to ensure that the abundance of the earth is shared with all?

Perceiving Creation's Enduring Goodness

This returns us again to Psalm 104, which ends, just before its final call to praise, on a rather sobering note. Following line after line of praise and celebration, we are brought up short by verse 35: "But may sinners vanish from the earth and the wicked be no more." The psalmist recognizes that not all is right in the community of creation. To borrow from the picture painted for us in Psalm 148, there are some members of the cosmic choir who have introduced a discordant harmony, who fail to praise God alongside his other creatures, who in fact threaten God's good purposes for his earth. Thus, while the psalmist prays that God may be pleased with the praise and meditations that he offers (Ps 104:33–34), he finds it necessary to pray too for the banishment of evildoers, the end of sin and evil (v. 35). It is instructive for our attempt to develop a biblical view of creation that the same psalmist who celebrates such things as lions and Leviathan—seeing even in the violence of predation and the wildness of the great sea creature God's sustaining providence and care—perceives in the sinfulness of human beings the real threat that needs to be dealt with.

Psalm 104 describes and addresses a world this side of the fall. It is a world—this world—where there are sinners and wicked people. The significance of this is that it confirms for us, if we needed the confirmation, that the goodness of the world, as described in Genesis 1 and elaborated in Psalm 104, endures even in a world of human sin and brokenness. The psalmist does not—as many later interpreters of Genesis 3 do—use the story of the "fall" as an excuse to denigrate those parts of creation that might make us uncomfortable or cause us pain or seem inexplicable to us. The psalmist prefers instead to celebrate the wonder and goodness of a world that yet bears testimony to the Creator, even in its wildest and most frightening aspects. We will consider in chapter 6 what it means to claim that the creation is indeed subject to frustration and enslaved to ruin (as Paul says in Rom. 8:20–21). There is clearly a tension between celebrating the goodness of a wild world that has things like lions and earthquakes in it and feeling sorrow for the suffering and loss of life that is the inevitable result of such things. We are caught up in mystery here, and there are no easy answers. Yet the psalmist would teach us humility and reverence before God and invites us into awe and wonder at the world he made and all its creatures.

Psalm 104 is recited every evening in the Eastern Orthodox tradition, where it is a part of the Daily Vespers, and it is also sung in the All-Night Vigil. Whatever our church tradition, it is important to find ways to include creation in our regular readings and hymns if we are to reflect its prominence in Scripture itself.

Acknowledging Humanity's Limits

The vision of Psalm 104 is one of the most beautiful in all of Scripture, with its inclusion of a place within God's good creation both for settled human life and agriculture, as well as wilderness and wild creatures of all kinds. In the book of Job, especially in the speeches of God at the end of the book, we discover a similar celebration of God's power and providence in creation. But here we begin to wonder if there is any place for humanity at all. When God addresses Job out of the storm, he launches into a series of rhetorical questions that reveal the incomparable power of a God whose purposes are beyond human imagining and who exceeds all our attempts to know him. This is a God who cannot be reduced to merely human categories or constructs, a God whose creation—in all its beauty and mystery—exists for his own good pleasure and not simply to satisfy human needs. The theme of these chapters is in fact summarized earlier in Job, when Job himself describes the power of God in creation and concludes by acknowledging, "And these are but the outer fringe of his works; how faint the whisper we hear of him! Who then can understand the thunder of his power?" (Job 26:14).

Job is not, to be clear, rejecting all possibility of knowing God. He has just elucidated in some detail God's acts of power and wisdom in creation, making positive statements about the character and acts of God. Yet he recognizes the folly of thinking that he has fully comprehended God, of thinking that God can be reduced to what we know of him. In fact, Job's friends provide a devastating example of the risk of a narrow theological perspective that assumes God and the world must operate in a particular way—in this case, that suffering must be the result of an individual's sin. We, the readers, know Job's friends are wrong; we know more of the story than they do. And so we are prepared to see the truth of Job's acknowledgement of God's exceeding greatness and the limitations of human knowledge. Yet even we as readers can hardly be prepared for the shattering power of God's speeches at the end of the book.

The rhetorical questions in God's first speech (Job 38–39) highlight above all God's power in creation. In language that sometimes echoes Genesis 1 and Psalm 104, God makes it unmistakably clear that neither Job nor any other creature can hope to exercise the power God has, nor to know and understand the world in the way God alone can. How all of this serves as an answer to Job's suffering and complaints in the rest of the book is disputed. But for our purposes, it is important to observe the scope of God's care for creation as it is described in these chapters. The vision is all-encompassing. In fact, a particular focus emerges on those parts of creation that are most distant from civilization and settled human life.

> "There are no unsacred places; there are only sacred places and desecrated places."
>
> *Wendell Berry*[8]

Thus, Job is asked if he waters (as God does) "a land where no one lives, an uninhabited desert, to satisfy a desolate wasteland, and make it sprout with grass" (38:26–27). God asks Job if "you hunt the prey for the lioness, and satisfy the hunger of the lions when they crouch in their dens or lie in wait in a thicket" (vv. 39–40). In what can sound like an invitation to become an ecologist, God asks Job, "Do you know when the mountain goats give birth? . . . Do you count the months till they bear? Do you know the time they give birth?" (39:1–2). The point is that, even if Job were to learn something of the ways of mountain goats or lions or ravens (38:41), these creatures have a life of their own, lived largely apart from humankind and remaining mysterious to us. Their young "grow strong in the wilds" (39:4). God gives to the wild donkey the "wasteland" as "home" and "salt flats" as "habitat" (v. 6). It "ranges the hills" (v. 8) and "laughs at the commotion in the town" (v. 7). The same laughter is heard from the ostrich (v. 18), whose ways may be inexplicable to Job and even suggest that God failed to give this creature wisdom and good sense (v. 17), and yet whose ability to outrun a horse and rider ought to remind Job that here too human standards of assessment are inadequate for determining God's purposes. Even the

---

8. Wendell Berry, "How to Be a Poet," in *Given: Poems* (Berkeley, CA: Counterpoint, 2006), 18.

warhorse, apparently domesticated and of use to human beings, reveals by its sheer power and fearlessness something that is beyond our ability to create or even fully control (vv. 19–25). The chapter ends with hawks and eagles, those dwellers on cliffs and rocky crags that can see their food from afar and whose "young ones feast on blood," including the blood of the slain (v. 30). Perhaps even more than in Psalm 104, we encounter here a wild and irreducibly mysterious creation that does not conform easily to human standards or categories.

Job unsurprisingly has nothing to say to all of this (40:4–5). But God is not finished. Challenging Job's ability to question God's justice (v. 8), he calls on Job to demonstrate that he stands on the same level as God. Can Job exercise the same sort of power and justice and bring about salvation on his own (vv. 9–14)? Job is confronted with Behemoth, which, God says, "I made along with you" (v. 15)—in other words, as merely another creature in the community of creation. And yet this creature (which, like a land-based version of the Leviathan, seems to be a mythical embodiment of wild and untamable creation, modeled perhaps on the hippopotamus) possesses a power that is beyond human power to control or manage. Only "its Maker," God himself, can approach it, this creature that "ranks first among the works of God" (v. 19). God then turns to the terrifying Leviathan for his final example, raising the absurd spectacle of Job trying to keep "a pet of it like a bird" or putting it on a leash (41:5). Yet, though no one is able to subdue the Leviathan (vv. 9–10) and "nothing on earth is its equal" (v. 33), God reminds Job that "everything under heaven belongs to me" (v. 11). Even Leviathan, then, remains a part of God's creation and fulfills the purposes for which God intended it. As Job says of God at the end of the book, "I know that you can do all things; no purpose of yours can be thwarted" (42:2), and Job acknowledges that he has spoken "of things I did not understand, things too wonderful for me to know" (v. 3).

Job and readers of the book that bears his name are confronted with the limits of human understanding and power. Yet these limits are not cause for sorrow or despair; on the contrary, they are a cause for celebration. They mean that Job can neither save himself (40:14), nor need he. For the same God whose power is seen so dramatically in creation is also powerful enough to save and redeem. Job's cause, if left with God, will find resolution (as indeed it does in a way, in the epilogue of the book . . . and, for Christian readers, in the person of Christ, the redeemer whom we discern in Job's claim: "I know that my redeemer lives, and that in the end he will stand on the earth" [19:25]). If God cares for this vast creation in the ways that have been described, does he not care too for Job in his suffering? In fact, the shock of the book is that the God of the universe should have put his reputation on the line by investing the person of Job and his response to his suffering with such significance.

In accepting who we are as mere creatures, we are enabled to find the freedom to be ourselves as we are created to be. We are not gods striding about the earth.

When we act like it, we make a mockery of God and fools of ourselves. Such hubris is usually rooted in a temptation to reduce the world and God to categories that we think we know and understand. Once having reduced creation, for example, to a machine that we consider to exist for our sole benefit and whose operations we think we fully understand, we are tempted to treat it like a machine. We never suspect that there may be things we have not understood as well as we think, that perhaps the purpose of creation is greater than just the service of our wants and needs, that perhaps reverence and awe are required of us first and last. Moreover, once we reduce God to convenient categories that we think we fully understand, we begin to find it easier to imagine that we might take his place. What a shock, then, when we rouse Leviathan!

> "Praise ignorance, for what man has not encountered he has not destroyed."
> Wendell Berry[9]

Acknowledging God's Ownership

The next chapter will consider more positively just what role Scripture does envision for human beings in creation. For the time being, however, it is necessary to reiterate that Job, like Psalm 104, portrays for us a wild and stunningly diverse creation. We discover a God who cares and provides even for those places and creatures that serve no human purpose and in fact can threaten our well-being and our lives, a God who apparently delights in *all* of his creation. Indeed, what unites the texts we have examined in this chapter are the twin convictions that all of creation belongs to God and that its purpose is to bring him glory.

These convictions are often stated explicitly elsewhere in Scripture. Consider the following examples:

- "The whole earth is mine." (Ex. 19:5)
- "The earth is the LORD's, and everything in it, the world, and all who live in it." (Ps. 24:1; quoted by Paul in 1 Cor. 10:26)
- "Every animal of the forest is mine, and the cattle on a thousand hills. I know every bird in the mountains, and the insects in the fields are mine. If I were hungry I would not tell you, for the world is mine, and all that is in it." (Ps. 50:10–12)
- "The heavens are yours, and yours also the earth; you founded the world and all that is in it." (Ps. 89:11)

Again and again, we are reminded that God is the owner of the earth and all that inhabits it. Moreover, as Psalm 50 suggests, he knows every one of his creatures, as only their Creator and Lord can. On the other hand, Psalm 115:16 suggests that

---

9. Wendell Berry, "Manifesto: The Mad Farmer Liberation Front," in *The Country of Marriage* (Berkeley, CA: Counterpoint, 1973), 14.

in some sense God has given the earth to us: "The highest heavens belong to the Lord, but the earth he has given to mankind." As we saw in Psalm 104, God clearly intends the earth to provide for humankind, as well as the rest of life, and we will see in the next chapter the unique responsibility that human beings are given in and for creation.

But this is not the same as *ownership*. If we consider the context of Psalm 115:16, we see that the purpose of the psalm is to highlight the incomparability of Israel's God, who "is in heaven; he does whatever pleases him" (v. 3). This suggests that the contrast in verse 16 between the "highest heavens" that "belong to the Lord" and the earth that is "given to mankind" is not about ownership, then, but rather about where we live. The psalmist is emphasizing the transcendence of God, who is not limited to the earthly realm as are his human creatures. God dwells in the highest heavens, while he grants the earth to us as our home. There is therefore no disparity between the giving of the earth to mankind in Psalm 115 and the clear assertions elsewhere that the earth—all of creation—belongs entirely to God.

Christians sometimes assume that the creation was made for human beings, and a few non-canonical Jewish texts and later Christian ones do indeed make this claim (e.g., *4 Ezra* 6:55; 7:11). But Scripture tells us otherwise. As we might have gleaned from the picture painted for us in Job and Psalm 104, it is God "for whom . . . everything exists" (Heb. 2:10). In Revelation, the praise of God on the throne ends with a focus on his role as Creator: "You are worthy, our Lord and God, to receive glory and honor and power, for you created all things, and by your will they were created and have their being" (4:11). The NIV quoted here, along with many other recent translations, renders this last phrase as if it indicates the *means* by which God created ("by your will"), but it may in fact be better translated as the *purpose* for which God made all things, as in the KJV: "for thy pleasure they are and were created" (cf. NASB). The theme of creation finding its purpose in the glory of God is given a Christological focus by Paul in Colossians 1:16, where we learn that Christ, as the image of the invisible God, is the one through whom all things have been created and *for whom* all things exist. Creation does not belong to us, and neither does it exist for us. It exists for God and his glory.

Joining the Cosmic Choir

This chapter has considered the beautiful world of God's creation primarily as an object to be studied and analyzed. We would be remiss if we did not conclude by acknowledging that the community of creation is also a *subject*, an actor in its own right in the drama of Scripture. The earth and its non-human creatures are not portrayed in Scripture as machines nor merely as an "environment" or backdrop for human action and history. They have their own value and integrity and, if we continue with the metaphor of a drama, they have their own roles, their own parts in the play. We will later explore how all of creation cries out against evil and injustice, groaning under the weight of human sin, and the ways in which God enlists creation to accomplish his purposes in bringing about his kingdom. But, in keeping with the focus of this chapter, we should first consider how the role of creation as portrayed in Scripture is first and foremost about praising and glorifying God simply by being what it was created to be.

Isaiah, after describing the efficacious word of God, which, like rain that waters the earth and causes it to bud and flourish, does not return to God empty, envisions a time when "You will go out in joy and be led forth in peace; the mountains and hills will burst into song before you, and all the trees of the field will clap their hands" (Isa. 55:12). And the psalms in particular are full of depictions of creation's celebration and praise of God (e.g., Ps. 65:13; 69:34; 89:12; 96:11–13; 97:6; 103:22; 145:10; 150:6),[10] a theme that reaches its culmination in Psalm 148. Here, in an expansion of a theme we see elsewhere (e.g., Ps. 103:19–22), all parts of the created realm are called upon to praise their Creator: the sun and moon, mountains and hills, sea creatures and all ocean depths, fruit trees and cedars, wild animals and all cattle, small creatures and flying birds. Only at the end of the psalm are human beings also invited to join in the praise that all of creation is already offering to God. We are asked to become a part of the cosmic chorus of praise that the rest of God's world offers him just by being what it was created to be. The *Benedicite* has preserved a similar canticle (derived from the Greek text of Daniel) in the church's liturgy, calling Christians through the centuries to add their voices to the cosmic praise offered to the Creator, to become who we were created to be.

"When man accepts his destiny in Jesus Christ . . . he is only like a late-comer slipping shame-facedly into creation's choir in heaven and earth, which has never ceased its praise."

Karl Barth[11]

The New Testament does not contain a book of prayers and songs like the Psalms, no doubt in part because early Christians went on using the Psalter as their songbook. But the theme of creation's praise of God emerges even here. Most dramatically, Jesus observes that if his (human) disciples did not rejoice and praise God for the miracles that they had seen, the stones themselves would cry out (Luke 19:40). As in the psalms, creation cannot help but respond to the coming of its king. The book of Revelation paints a particularly magnificent picture of creation's praise of God. In John's vision of the heavenly throne room in chapters 4 and 5, all of creation gives God and Christ the glory for what has been accomplished in the creation and redemption of all things. John makes it clear that no creature is left out: "Then I heard every creature in heaven and on earth and under the earth and on

10. See Bauckham, *The Bible and Ecology*, 76–82.

11. Karl Barth, *Church Dogmatics II.1: The Doctrine of God* (Edinburgh: T & T Clark, 1957), 648; quoted in David G. Horrell, *The Bible and the Environment: Towards a Critical Ecological Biblical Theology* (London: Equinox, 2010), 133.

the sea, and all that is in them, saying: 'To him who sits on the throne and to the Lamb be praise and honor and glory and power, for ever and ever!'" (Rev. 5:13).

SUMMARY

In this chapter, we have been invited into a way of seeing the world of which we are a part as God's good, abundantly diverse, and beautiful creation. God is the Creator, sustainer, and owner of all things. The world belongs to him, not to us, and it exists for his glory. The entire creation testifies to this reality, serving as a witness to God's creative power and goodness. Our aim must be to begin to see the rest of creation as God sees it, and to join in with all of nature in its praise of our God.

In the next chapter, we consider in detail what our role within creation is intended to be, what it means to bear God's image, to rule over other creatures, and to work and keep the earth. But there is perhaps no more compelling vision of our place within the community of God's creatures than as members of a choir as vast as the cosmos and as diverse as God's creation, all gathered around the throne of our Creator and Redeemer, worshipping him in endless praise.

RELEVANT QUESTIONS

1. Which of the major themes of the Genesis story of creation is most important for the church and our society to hear today? How can this theme best be communicated in our time?
2. In what ways does the biblical emphasis on the value of all of creation to God challenge contemporary approaches to environmental and economic issues?
3. Does the biblical perspective on the limits of human, creaturely life have any implications for how we understand our role on earth and for our appropriate use of technology? If so, what are these implications?
4. How can non-human creation praise and worship God? How can we as human beings join in the rest of creation's praise of God?

CHAPTER 4

MEMBERS, RULERS, AND KEEPERS OF CREATION

As I begin writing this chapter, I (Jonathan) am sitting near the shore of the Pend Oreille River in the far northeastern corner of Washington State on an unusually cool and cloudy August morning. The breeze is rustling the aspen leaves above me and causing the mixed forest of aspen, western redcedar, hemlock, Engelmann spruce, Douglas fir, larch, white pine, grand fir, and lodgepole pine on the hills across the river to sway gently back and forth. Three large white-tailed deer bucks are slowly picking their way along the opposite shore, and a red squirrel is chattering loudly behind me. An osprey has just flown into a Douglas fir nearby. A few minutes ago, a flock of geese flew up the river, honking as they went. The quiet is occasionally broken by the cry of two hawks high overhead, which elicits excited responses from the squirrel and a host of birds feeding up the hill behind me. Every once in a while, I hear a splash when a fish—probably smallmouth bass—jumps in pursuit of an insect or smaller fish, and it takes great willpower for me to leave the fishing to the osprey for the moment, to keep writing and not pick up the fly rod instead.

All of these creatures—along with the wolves I heard howling last night and the impertinent raccoon that kept me awake with its noisy attack on a bird feeder outside my window—and even the inanimate rocks and soil and water and clouds are, I know, bringing God praise and glory simply by being what they were created to be. Yet what, then, I wonder, of me and my kind? There are plenty of human sounds here too: the deep hum of a passenger plane far overhead, the occasional rumble of a car or motorcycle or logging truck on the road across the way, the roar of a boat or Jet Ski motoring up the river, and earlier this morning, the buzz of a chainsaw and, strangely (for it is not hunting season), two gunshots rather close by. Are we too praising God in all of this? What does it look like for us to join the chorus of praise that all the rest of creation offers God?

As we will see in this chapter, the answer lies in becoming who we are created to be. We are called to fulfill the purpose for which God made us, as other creatures do merely by being themselves. Our true worship of God involves, as Paul tells us in Romans 12:1, the giving of our whole selves to God, offering our bodies as living sacrifices to him. In Christ, God's image is renewed in us, and we are enabled to become who we most truly are in offering ourselves to his service. The challenge of fulfilling our responsibilities as God's image bearers in creation, which we will confront in this chapter and later in the book, ought therefore to be seen not as a burden that weighs us down, limits our potential, or hinders our progress; rather, when we enter into our true identity and purpose, we are liberated from our slavery to ways of living that are finally destructive both of ourselves and others and represent a denial of who God has made us to be.

To live the life God calls us to, to join in the worship of the rest of creation, to offer ourselves in sacrificial service to him, and to rule rightly as his image bearers is to discover the sort of freedom and joy that can be experienced only when our lives align with God's purpose. "It is hard for you to kick against the goads," the risen Jesus tells Paul on the Damascus Road (Acts 26:14). We cannot find true joy and rest if we live our lives in opposition to God and against the grain of who he has created us to be, no matter how convenient it may seem for a time, nor how difficult the path of righteousness. "Come to me, all you who are weary and burdened, and I will give you rest," Jesus tells his disciples, "Take my yoke upon you and learn from me, for I am gentle and humble in heart, and you will find rest for your souls. For my yoke is easy and my burden is light" (Matt. 11:28–30).

> The joy of discovering who we are made to be in Christ is memorably portrayed in the film Chariots of Fire. Eric Liddell, the sprinter and soon-to-be Christian missionary to China, explains to his sister why he considers competing in the Olympics a part of his service to God: "When I run, I feel his pleasure."

In this chapter, we explore the place of humanity within creation by considering the meaning and significance of the image of God and the commands God gives human beings in the opening chapters of the Bible. We also look briefly at how this plays out in in the rest of the creation story, especially in the subsequent chapters of Genesis. We will consider in the next chapter how Israel's relationship to the land further elucidates something of what our human vocation on earth might look like, and later, in chapter 7, we will look to Jesus, who reveals definitively for us what it is to bear the image of God. Before we spend time focusing on our particular *significance* as human beings, however, it is necessary to be reminded again, as we were in the previous chapter, of just how *insignificant* human beings sometimes appear in the pages of Scripture.

MEMBERS OF THE COMMUNITY OF CREATION

We observed in the last chapter that human beings are created alongside the other land animals on the sixth day of creation and that the blessing of fruitfulness, of multiplying on the earth, is one we share with other life. We, like all other living things, are earthy creatures, formed from the dust of the earth, *adam* from the *adamah*. Our possession of the life-giving breath of God, making each of us a *nephesh* or *psychē* or "soul," does not distinguish us from other living things, all of whom are also animated by God's same life-giving Spirit. The prophets and the psalmists regularly remind us of our place within this wider community of creation and of our relative insignificance:

> All people are like grass, and all their faithfulness is like the flowers of the field. The grass withers and the flowers fall, because the breath of the LORD blows on them. Surely the people are grass. The grass withers and the flowers fall, but the word of our God endures forever. (Isa. 40:6–8)

> [The Lord] knows how we are formed, he remembers that we are dust. The life of mortals is like grass, they flourish like a flower of the field; the wind blows over it and it is gone, and its place remembers it no more. (Ps. 103:14–16)

In the New Testament, Peter quotes and reaffirms Isaiah's contrast between the brevity of human life and the enduring word of God: "'All people are like grass, and all their glory is like the flowers of the field; the grass withers and the flowers fall, but the word of the Lord endures forever'" (1 Peter 1:24–25; cf. Isa. 40:6–8). Though he employs a different metaphor, James picks up on the same theme in his challenge to our self-importance and temptation to make plans without considering God: "What is your life? You are a mist that appears for a little while and then vanishes" (James 4:14; cf. Hos. 13:3). Both the Old and New Testaments recall us to a humility that we too easily forget. Our modern world has inherited an optimism about human beings and their accomplishments that goes back at least to the Enlightenment of the late seventeenth and eighteenth centuries. Scripture challenges that optimism, reminding us that we are fallible and transient creatures. Scripture wakes us from the comforting delusions of technology (and the human-centered world that technology enables us to construct around ourselves), and it recalls us to our true place within the wider community of creation. We also glimpse in the pages of Scripture something of the joy we can have when we recognize who we are and embrace the role that God intends for us within this community.

The discovery that we share 96% of our DNA with chimpanzees, that in every physical respect we are no different than other animals, and that in fact our lives are so dependent upon and entwined with the rest of creation that even our bodies would not function without the other organisms that make them their home (e.g., our

"In short, a land ethic changes the role of Homo sapiens from conqueror of the land-community to plain member and citizen of it. It implies respect for his fellow-members, and also respect for the community as such. In human history, we have learned (I hope) that the conqueror role is eventually self-defeating. Why? Because it is implicit in such a role that the conqueror knows, ex cathedra, just what makes the community clock tick; and just what and who is valuable, and what and who is worthless, in community life. It always turns out that he knows neither, and this is why his conquests eventually defeat themselves."

Aldo Leopold[1]

---

1. Aldo Leopold, *A Sand County Almanac* (New York: Oxford University Press and Ballantine Books, 1966), 240.

humble gut bacteria) should hardly cause consternation for those committed to a biblical worldview. Scripture has always taught that we stand firmly on the "creature" side of the Creator/creation divide and that we share a close kinship with the rest of life.

It is only from such a realistic assessment of our humble natural state that we can hope to appreciate the sheer grace of a God who cares for us and gives us the unique role and responsibilities he does. This is in fact the point of Psalm 103, quoted above (and which, not incidentally, is twinned in the Psalter with Psalm 104). God knows that "we are dust," that we are but mortal creatures formed from the earth. Yet, "As a father has compassion on his children, so the LORD has compassion on those who fear him" (Ps. 103:13). Though our lives are fragile, short, and apparently insignificant, nonetheless "from everlasting to everlasting the LORD's love is with those who fear him, and his righteousness with their children's children" (v. 17).

In Psalm 8, we find an expression of this wonder that the God of the universe should care for his humble human creatures:

> When I consider your heavens, the work of your fingers, the moon and the stars, which you have set in place, what is mankind that you are mindful of them, human beings ["the son of man"] that you care for them? (Ps. 8:3–4)

As the psalmist (identified in v. 1 as David) looks up at the brilliance of the night sky and recognizes that all he sees is but the work of God's "fingers," he cannot help but question how human beings can possibly matter to God or the universe that he made. We are sometimes tempted to think that our own age's questioning of humanity's place within the cosmos, prompted by science's newfound ability to quantify the unimaginable vastness of space, is something new or historically novel. Yet the questions we ask are not so very different than the ones an ancient shepherd might have asked, tending to his vulnerable flock of sheep in a world wilder and less explored than our own and looking up into a black sky sparkling with more stars than most of us ever will see. What is humanity in the face of such awesome splendor?

The answer the psalmist gives would have been, on the face of things, an even more improbable claim in his time than in ours:

". . . only by our completely not wanting to be God can the divine life take root in us. Discipleship in the body of Christ is in one sense simply a matter of constantly battling to be a creature, battling against all those instincts in us which make us want to be God or make us want to be what we think God is. There, of course, is the catch. And that's why discipleship challenges at every level those unrealities which distort humanity, which distort creatureliness. That's why discipleship challenges those enterprises in our world and our culture which feed the illusion that actually we could be God if we tried hard enough."

Rowan Williams[2]

2. Rowan Williams, "Creation, Creativity and Creatureliness: The Wisdom of Finite Existence" (lecture, St Theosevia Centre for Christian Spirituality, Oxford, April 23, 2005). Available at: http:// rowanwilliams.archbishopofcanterbury.org/articles.php/2106/ creation-creativity-and-creatureliness-the-wisdom-of-finite -existence#sthash.MaZFUc5k.wOtczjYe.dpuf.

You have made them a little lower than the angels and crowned them with glory and honor. You made them rulers over the works of your hands; you put everything under their feet: all flocks and herds, and the animals of the wild, the birds in the sky, and the fish in the sea, all that swim the paths of the seas. (Ps. 8:5–8)

The basis for such a startling assertion of the place of human beings within creation is, of course, Genesis 1:26–28. The psalmist puts particular emphasis on the breadth of humankind's dominion: "everything" is put under their feet, including even those creatures, like the fish of the sea, over which it would have been unlikely for ancient Israelites to have had any reason to think they had power. (In fact, the reference to "all that swim in the paths of the seas" could hint to later readers that even the untamable Leviathan is included here in the scope of humankind's dominion [cf. Job 41:1; Isa. 27:1]—and hence lead them to think that the "son of man" in view here might be none other than the Messiah.)

> "Equally incapable of seeing the noth-ingness from which he emerges and the infinity in which he is engulfed."
> *Blaise Pascal,* Pensées [3]

The picture painted in this text may seem more plausible to us today, when the outsized role of human beings on earth has become so evident that some scientists have dubbed our age the "Anthropocene," or age of humanity. But for the psalmist (and for us too, if we are honest about the limits of our power and our understanding), there is an inevitable gap between lived reality and the assertion of faith in a God who intends human beings for such an exalted role. The gap, as we will see, is finally bridged, according to the author of Hebrews, only by Jesus, the true human being and "son of man" (Heb. 2:5–9). As Christians, we will finally only understand what humanity's rule ought to look like by focusing on Christ.

In the immediate context of Psalm 8, it is in any case instructive to note what frames the entire psalm, the praise with which it begins and ends: "Lord, our Lord, how majestic is your name in all the earth!" (vv. 1, 9). The "Lord" is the personal name of God (YHWH), and "Lord" identifies his role as *adon*, the "Sovereign" (NRSV) or ruler of all. As we consider what it means to have dominion over other creatures, we must always keep in view both our place as members of the community of creation and God's place as the ultimate ruler over all things, the one to whom the earth belongs and to whom we will finally answer for how we have exercised our rule in his kingdom.

IMAGE OF GOD

Psalm 8, we have seen, develops what God says in Genesis about the place of human beings within creation:

---

3. Blaise Pascal, *Pensées*, trans. A. J. Krailsheimer (London: Penguin, 1995), 61.

Then God said, "Let us make mankind in our image, in our likeness, so that they may rule over the fish in the sea and the birds in the sky, over the livestock and all the wild animals, and over all the creatures that move along the ground." So God created mankind in his own image, in the image of God he created them; male and female he created them. God blessed them and said to them, "Be fruitful and increase in number; fill the earth and subdue it. Rule over the fish in the sea and the birds in the sky and over every living creature that moves on the ground." (Gen. 1:26–28)

It should be evident by now that there are plenty of other texts besides Genesis that help us understand who we are as human creatures. Yet Genesis 1:28 has understandably played a central role in Christian reflection on our place within creation. Much of this reflection has taken the form of wide-ranging theological and philosophical speculation about what it means for us to bear the image of God, sometimes taking us far from the actual text of Genesis. Part of the reason for this is that there are in fact very few further references to the "image of God" in the rest of Scripture that might help us interpret the phrase.

In the Old Testament, we find only one more explicit reference to humans being created in God's image, in Genesis 9:6. We do learn earlier, in Genesis 5:3, that Adam's son Seth is "in his own likeness, in his own image," and the parallelism with Genesis 1:26 suggests that readers are meant to perceive the connection: even after the tragedy of the "fall," the image of God that Adam bears will continue in Adam's offspring. But the only explicit reference to the "image of God" is found immediately after the flood: "Whoever sheds human blood, by humans shall their blood be shed; for in the image of God has God made mankind" (Gen. 9:6). We will return to Genesis 9 soon, but for the time being, we can observe two things about the function of the image of God in this text. First, the image of God serves to distinguish human beings from other creatures. Other animals may be killed and eaten (v. 3), but human blood may not be shed. A certain respect for the life of other creatures is still engendered by the proscription against eating "meat that has its lifeblood still in it" (v. 4), and there will be other sorts of moral considerations that apply to our treatment of animals. But human beings are unique and distinct in bearing God's image, and so murder is strictly forbidden. The distinctive value of human life is such that an accounting will be demanded even from animals that kill human beings (v. 5).

Second, Genesis 9:6 implies, as does Genesis 1, that all human beings without exception are created in the image of God and are to be treated as such. As Paul will tell the Athenians in Acts 17, all people and nations share the same humanity, all are creations of God, and hence all are his offspring (Acts 17:26–29). This "democratization," as it is sometimes called, of the image of God is a distinctive biblical belief. In other nations of the ancient Near East, it is the king alone who bears the image of the god. But according to Genesis, the image of God is shared by all of humanity, including male and female alike (1:27).

Returning to Genesis 1, then, in what does the image of God consist? Our argument, in keeping with that of many other contemporary interpreters, is that the image of God means being placed into a particular set of relationships with God, each other, and the rest of creation, for the purpose of ruling as his royal representatives. This meaning comports with what we find in the text of Genesis itself and makes best sense within its original ancient Near Eastern context.

We have observed that all creatures and all parts of the cosmos exist necessarily in relationship with God, bringing him praise and glory simply by being what they are created to be. Yet human beings are distinctively given the responsibility of subduing the earth and ruling over other creatures. This seems in fact to be the stated purpose of human beings being created in God's image: ". . . so that they may rule" (v. 26).[4] In the ancient world, "images" were erected by a king to remind people of his unique role as sovereign. In a similar way, God establishes his human creatures, made in his likeness, to reflect his sovereignty throughout the earth. This responsibility to reflect God's rule entails a particular relationship with God, with each other, and with the earth. If we are to rule as God would have us rule, it is to God that we must look if we are to reflect him and his purposes in how we live and reign. This requires our active response and obedience to God if we are to take our appropriate place in the choir of creation and fulfill our divinely ordained role. Our relationship with the rest of creation will be not only as one creature among others (though it is this too), but also as ones who have a responsibility that is uniquely ours. We relate to God and to other creatures in ways that are different than aspen trees and white-tailed deer and osprey and smallmouth bass and wolves and raccoons. We are set into a network of relationships that might be said to reflect in a limited way the relationality that exists within God himself.

Christians have usually read the plural that suddenly occurs in the creation narrative in verse 26 ("Let *us* make mankind in *our* image, in *our* likenesss . . .") as a signal of Trinitarianism, a hint of God's existence in three persons as Father, Son, and Holy Spirit. This reading has some resonance with the common ancient Near Eastern conception of a deity with his divine council, whom God may be considered to be addressing here. At the same time, the portrayal of a God whose life-giving Spirit is at work and who creates by his Word hints at the later biblical theme of the Spirit, who gives life to God's people, and Christ, the Word through whom the universe came into being. In any case, singular pronouns return again in the very

---

4. The NIV here, correctly in our view, takes the *waw* connective as indicating purpose.

next verse ("in *his* image . . ."), suggesting that whomever God is addressing in verse 26 is not outside of God (*elohim*) himself.[5]

It is intriguing that the plural pronoun should appear just here, and only here, at the creation of human beings. The description of our creation is also unique in the narrative in that it emphasizes the creation of male and female together, and that God is said to have created *them* (the plural pronoun is used in the Hebrew at the end of v. 27) in his image. There is a sense of the irreducible relationality of human beings made in God's image, created for community and intended to reflect in our relationships the unifying love that is at the center of the being of the triune God. To be human is to be known and loved by God as his image bearers, and we are intended to reflect that love as we reflect his image and rule in the community of his creation.

We bear God's image not by virtue of our wisdom, our reason, our stature, our strength, or even our capacity for moral judgment. A baby bears God's image just as you or I do, and as do the physically and mentally infirm. The stress in Scripture on the universality of the image of God demands that we recognize the image of God in all human beings. In fact, it is often especially through children and the apparently weak that God reveals his purposes. Consider Psalm 8 again, where God is said "through the praise of children and infants" to "have established a stronghold against your enemies, to silence the foe and the avenger" (v. 2), a text later cited by Jesus (Matt. 21:16; cf. Mark 9:35–37; 10:13–16; Matt. 18:1–6; Luke 9:46–48; 18:15–17). In Isaiah's vision of the peaceable kingdom brought in by the Spirit-anointed one, we find a picture that highlights, above all, the security of this newly harmonious world but which also hints at the restoration of humankind's role within creation, invested in a little child: "The wolf will live with the lamb, the leopard will lie down with the goat, the calf and the lion and the yearling together; and a little child will lead them" (Isa. 11:6). The point is that to be human is to bear God's image and to deserve to be treated as such; and it is also to recognize that sometimes it is from the apparently weakest members of our human family that we have the most to learn about what it is to relate to God in trust and faith and dependence.

This is not to ignore the significant ways in which characteristics that may be considered either unique to human beings or possessed at a higher level than other creatures enable humankind collectively to represent God's rule in creation in ways that other creatures could not. Nor is our emphasis on the democratization of the image of God intended to rule out the possibility that there are better and worse ways of ruling in creation as God's image bearers. Quite the opposite. Paul's emphasis on the need for us to be renewed in the image of our Creator (Col. 3:10) reminds

---

5. It is hence unlikely that God is addressing the earth or the rest of creation in v. 26, an interpretation that otherwise would be consistent with the way God involves the earth in the process of creation elsewhere in the narrative.

us that something has gone wrong in how we live and rule as God's image bearers. When—as Genesis 3 describes—we look to ourselves or to any source that is not God to determine who we are and how we are to live, when we seek to define apart from God what is right and wrong, good and evil, we deny and deface God's image. Like shattered mirrors, our reflection of his image becomes fragmented and distorted. The catastrophe that this represents for ourselves and the rest of creation, the way in which it causes our rule on earth to become tyrannical and self-serving and our dominion to become domination, is explored in the next chapter. It is important first, however, to consider more positively what God might intend for our rule as his image bearers to look like.

DOMINION

The purpose of God's creation of humanity in his image is "so that they may rule" over other creatures (Gen. 1:26). When God then blesses the human beings he has just created, he both entrusts them with this rule and also instructs them to "fill the earth and subdue it" (v. 28). Other creatures are also given the mandate to "fill" space: the sea creatures are to "fill the waters in the seas" (v. 22). Fish, birds, land animals—all need their appropriate space to experience the shared blessing of fruitfulness that God intends. But the commission to subdue the earth and to rule over other creatures is given uniquely to humankind.

The Hebrew word for "subdue" (*kabash*) has the strong, sometimes even violent connotation of bringing something or someone under the subjection of another. It is not a gentle word; in fact, the Greek word used in the Septuagint translation of Genesis 1:28 (*katakyrieuo*) is used in the New Testament to describe precisely how followers of Christ are *not* meant to exercise leadership over others (Mark 10:42–45; Matt. 20:25–28; 1 Peter 5:3). The most relevant parallels in the Hebrew Bible, where "land" or "earth" is the object of the subduing, are in the context of the conquest of the land of Canaan, "when the land is subdued before the LORD" (Num. 32:22, 29; cf. Josh. 18:1; 1 Chron. 22:18). This connection is indicative of a deeper link between the creation and exodus/conquest stories in the Old Testament, which, among other things, suggests that Israel's place on the land can be seen as a microcosm of humanity's place on earth. What is particularly important here, however, is that Israel "subdued" the land by fighting against the enemies of God so that God's people could inhabit it as God intended.

In the context of Genesis 1, then, the charge to "subdue" the earth suggests at a minimum the active work of bringing the earth under the appropriate rule of those who bear God's image. Whether this work involves battle against hostile forces is less clear, however. Genesis 1, with its ordered picture of a good world that fulfills God's purposes for it, does not include any mention of such forces (though of course a clever and deceitful serpent will turn up in the garden). The military metaphor may prove more relevant in a post-Genesis 3 world where the world lies under threat of corruption and ruin, where there are more obviously destructive forces at work. In any case, the commission given to humankind in Genesis 1:28 indicates that hard work will be required if human beings are to rule in the earth as God intends.

In his popular poem "The Glory of the Garden," Rudyard Kipling compares England to a garden and observes that "such gardens are not made / By singing: — 'Oh, how beautiful!' and sitting in the shade." There is a "needful" job for everyone to do; it takes hard work and all kinds of work. And, as the last stanza of his poem suggests, "half a proper gardener's work is done upon his knees."

If we ask what such subduing and ruling looks like, we could do no better than to begin with the way humanity's role is explained in the very next chapter of Genesis. In Genesis 2, we find a way of expressing God's purpose for humankind that moves from what is potentially abstract and general to the rooted and the local: "The LORD God took the man and put him in the Garden of Eden to work it and take care of it" (v. 15). The "man" is of course the *adam*. Even when later in the narrative his name becomes personalized and appropriately translated (or, rather, transliterated) as "Adam" (the article drops off in 4:25), the "man" here is clearly intended as a representative figure for all of humanity, much as Jacob will come to represent and stand in for the nation of Israel (e.g., Gen. 32:28; Deut. 32:9). The man is set in a garden, a temple-like space where God dwells intimately with his creatures. Or, to put it the other way around, the garden described here becomes the template for Israel's tabernacle and temple where God's presence with his people will be especially represented.

Eden's location is enigmatic (Gen. 2:8–14), deliberately so, for what the garden of Eden represents—the intimate dwelling of God with humanity; right relationships between God, humanity, and the rest of creation; and the hope held out in the tree of life of eternal life with God—cannot now be found through mere geographical exploration. The garden in Genesis 2–3 may represent the whole of creation, but the way the story is told suggests rather that it represents a marked-out space within creation. In fact, when read within the context of the whole of Scripture, which ends with a city-garden-paradise in which God's presence fills the entire cosmos, we see that what pertains to Eden is intended finally to encompass the whole of the earth. Taken together, the commands to subdue the earth in Genesis 1:28 and to work and take care of the garden in Genesis 2:15 suggest the potential—the need even—for change in God's creation, for movement toward a *telos*, an "end" or "goal." God's good world is not a static place in which nothing new can come about. It is a world in which God himself remains at work (John 5:17), and he intends, by his grace, to include his human image bearers in his work.

That work is described in Genesis 2:15 as to *abad* and *shamar* the garden. The NIV translation is particularly helpful here: "to work and take care of it." A very common word in the Hebrew Bible, *abad* can connote a wide range of different ways of working or serving. In the context of a garden, to "till" (NRSV) or "cultivate" (NASB) makes good sense (cf. Gen. 2:5; 3:23; 4:2, 12), but it probably is best in 2:15 to maintain the breadth of possible meanings in the NIV "work" (or else we risk excluding, e.g., no-till agriculture!). If we take seriously the context of work that is done for God as his servants, in a garden that is described like a temple (as interpreters both ancient and modern have recognized), we might even consider translating *abad* here as "to serve," that is, to serve God in the service of the earth. The same two verbs, *abad* and *shamar*, are used together in the book of Numbers, for example, to describe the service of the Levitical priests in the tabernacle (3:7; 8:26; 18:7).

The second verb, *shamar*, usually refers to "keeping" God's commandments, or, as here, "keeping watch over," "guarding," "preserving," and "protecting" people, animals, or places. As the "keeper" of a castle, stationed in the "keep," is charged with guarding and protecting the place,[6] so is humankind given the vocation of watching over and protecting the garden. In the great priestly blessing, "keeping" is what God does for us: "The LORD bless you and keep (*shamar*) you; the LORD make his face shine on you and be gracious to you; the LORD turn his face toward you and give you peace" (Num. 6:24–26; cf. Ps. 12:7). As the image bearers of God, our care and protection of the earth is thus a reflection of the care and protection that God shows to us.

Our human vocation is to work and take care of the place where God has planted us, to serve him in our rule in creation as priests in his temple. Caring for the earth is not, in this light, a peripheral biblical theme; it is central to our identity as God's image bearers. The purpose of the dominion that we are given over other creatures is the peace and blessing that God intends for us and all his creation. As the queen of Sheba observes of Solomon's reign over Israel, God appoints kings "to maintain justice and righteousness" (1 Kings 10:9). Indeed, if we look to the description of God's ideal king in the Old Testament as our guide, we find that the king is meant to rule as a first among equals, and as one whose rule is first and foremost for the benefit of those under his care. He is not to use his position selfishly to accumulate things for himself, and he is to rule under God's law as one subject to God, just as his fellow Israelites are:

> When he takes the throne of his kingdom, he is to write for himself on a scroll a copy of this law, taken from that of the Levitical priests. It is to be with him, and he is to read it all the days of his life so that he may learn to revere the LORD his God and follow carefully all the words of this law and these decrees and not consider himself better than his fellow Israelites and turn from the law to the right or to the left. (Deut. 17:18–20)

---

6. Daniel L. Brunner, Jennifer L. Butler, and A. J. Swoboda, *Introducing Evangelical Ecotheology: Foundations in Scripture, Theology, History, and Praxis* (Grand Rapids: Baker Academic, 2014), 26.

Endow the king with your justice, O God, the royal son with your righteousness. May he judge your people in righteousness, your afflicted ones with justice. May the mountains bring prosperity to the people, the hills the fruit of righteousness. May he defend the afflicted among the people and save the children of the needy; may he crush the oppressor. May he endure as long as the sun, as long as the moon, through all generations. May he be like rain falling on a mown field, like showers watering the earth. (Ps. 72:1–6)

Such a biblical understanding of kingship makes impossible any interpretation of *dominion* in Genesis 1:26–28 as *domination*, and it rules out any notion that God's entrusting of other creatures into our care means that we may use them or the rest of creation however we like.

This is all the more evident when we consider again that our rule is not absolute. Not only does God remain the owner of his creation, but—as we saw in Psalm 8—he is also its true Lord and master under whose reign we and all other creatures live. "Dominion belongs to the LORD" (Ps. 22:28; cf. Job 25:2); he is the "great king over all the earth" (Ps. 47:2, 7); he "has established his throne in heaven, and his kingdom rules over all" (Ps. 103:19).

> "The hands of the king are the hands of a healer, and so shall the rightful king be known."
>
> J. R. R. Tolkien,
> The Return of the King[7]

As Psalm 97:1 exclaims, God's rule is something for all creation to celebrate: "The LORD reigns, let the earth be glad; let the distant shores rejoice." The same God who "gives life to everything" is, according to 1 Timothy, "the blessed and only Ruler, the King of kings and Lord of lords" (1 Tim. 6:13–15).

The character of God's rule is captured most beautifully perhaps in Psalm 145. God is described as the "King" (v. 1), the Lord who "is gracious and compassionate, slow to anger and rich in love" (v. 8). He "is good to all; he has compassion on all he has made" (v. 9); faithful and trustworthy, he "upholds all who fall and lifts up all who are bowed down" (v. 14). In an echo of one of the key themes of Psalm 104, we learn that God the king is also the great provider: "The eyes of all look to you, and you give them their food at the proper time. You open your hand, and satisfy the desires of every living thing" (vv. 15–16). "The LORD watches over (*shamar*) all who love him" (v. 20); and "every creature" is called upon to praise him forever (v. 21).

Our reign in God's creation is subsumed under the reign of God, and it is his rule that defines for us the priorities and purposes of the derivative powers he has granted us. How, then, can we rule as God's image bearers and not also seek to be "good to all" as he is, to provide as we are able for the thriving of all his creation, and to be rulers whose governance is life-giving and a cause for celebration? Like the "kings and rulers of the earth" described in Psalm 2, we are called to be "wise"

---

7. J. R. R. Tolkien, *The Return of the King* (New York: Del Ray, 2012), 138.

(v. 10) and "serve the LORD with fear and celebrate his rule with trembling" (v. 11). It is only in the awe of God and under his rule that we can find the wisdom to reign as he intends. David, at the end of his life, paints an evocative picture of what such God-honoring rule looks like: "When one rules over people in righteousness, when he rules in the fear of God, he is like the light of morning at sunrise on a cloudless morning, like the brightness after rain that brings grass from the earth" (2 Sam. 23:3–4). Does the rest of creation experience our rule like this? This should be our aim as bearers of God's image.

Near the start of his reign as king over Israel, Solomon recognizes that wisdom is what a king needs the most. He asks God to "give your servant a discerning heart to govern your people and to distinguish between right and wrong" (1 Kings 3:9). To rule well requires wisdom and the ability to discern what is best, "to distinguish between right and wrong." Such wisdom is not the same as knowledge, yet it requires knowledge. It is unsurprising that the very first thing Adam does in Genesis 2:19–20 is to name the animals. To name is to begin to know; if Adam is to serve and protect the garden and rule over other creatures, he needs first to be able to name them. Solomon too provides us with an example of one whose wisdom includes intimate knowledge of the natural world: "He spoke about plant life, from the cedar of Lebanon to the hyssop that grows out of walls. He also spoke about animals and birds, reptiles and fish" (1 Kings 4:33). Solomon is not a perfect model of kingship; he ends up contravening the principles laid down in the law for the king, using his power to accumulate wealth and wives for himself, and as a result he goes astray from the exclusive worship of the God of Israel. Yet 1 Kings 4 praises Solomon for his wisdom and, in this at least, offers a biblical model of a king. He is a poet and a naturalist (vv. 32–33). Under his rule, his subjects prosper and live in peace and safety (vv. 20, 25). His reputation for wisdom draws people from all nations (v. 34).

If we are to rule wisely and well in creation, we need to learn all we can about the earth and other creatures for whose care we bear some responsibility; we must aim for the prospering of all of life; and, above all, we must fear and honor God. And to fear and honor God necessarily entails, as we have seen, recognition of our limits and of the fact that our rule is always derivative of and subservient to the rule of God.

NOAH AND THE PRESERVATION OF LIFE

We have thus far considered how humanity's role is described in Genesis 1–2, in conversation with other biblical texts that help illuminate what it means to be created in God's image, to subdue the earth, to rule over other creatures, and to work and take care of the garden. In the next chapter, we will consider how Israel's call to honor God in the ways the nation lived on the land of Canaan provides some examples and principles for how human beings live on earth. In chapter 6, we will then wrestle with the reality of humankind's and Israel's rebellion against God and the catastrophic results that ensue for the land and for all of creation. Chapter 7 will focus on Jesus, who both saves us from the catastrophe described in chapter 6 and definitively reveals for us what it is to bear God's image and to rule as God's anointed king. It should be stressed that the present chapter on human beings as bearers of the image of God cannot possibly stand alone for Christian readers of Scripture: it is only in Christ that we discover finally who we are created to be.

Before moving on, however, we should consider the paradigmatic example that Genesis provides us of a person whom God uses to keep and preserve his creation. The story of Noah is well-known, though it presents many unresolved riddles and questions that could be wrestled with at length. We narrow our focus here to just two themes of particular importance for our understanding of the relationship between humanity, God, and creation: (1) God's use of the righteous Noah to save other creatures and (2) the covenant God establishes at the end of the narrative with all of creation.

Before we focus on these themes, however, there is one particularly troublesome question we must at least acknowledge: How are we to understand God's decision to judge human evil by "destroying" the earth? Consider the sad echo of the creation account with which the story begins:

> The LORD saw how great the wickedness of the human race had become on the earth, and that every inclination of the thoughts of the human heart was only evil all the time. The LORD regretted that he had made human beings on the earth, and his heart was deeply troubled. So the LORD said, "I will wipe from the face of the earth [*adamah*] the human race [*adam*] I have created—and with them the animals, the birds and the creatures that move along the ground—for I regret that I have made them." (Gen. 6:5–7)

Why should other creatures—"the animals, the birds and the creatures that move along the ground"—be wiped out because of the wickedness of humanity and God's regret at having made them? This is a question that will continue to confront us in the next chapter, as we look at the effects that human sin and God's judgment have on the earth, and it is admittedly a question for which we are not likely to find a satisfactory answer. There are, however, two considerations that should be kept in view.

First, such texts remind us of the picture that has emerged in the opening chapters of Genesis of an interdependent relationship between human beings and the rest of creation. We are on the one hand merely a part of the community of creation and inseparable from it, but on the other hand, we have also been given a particular responsibility for the rest of creation, which means it experiences both the blessing and the curse of having its fate linked to ours.

Second, we should observe that God's judgment is often described in Scripture as essentially confirming or rubber-stamping the results of the actions of sinful humanity, representing, in a sense, his abandonment of us to our fate. It is as if God withdraws his life-giving Spirit and hands us over to the forces of evil and destruction that our wickedness has unleashed. Thus, even in the flood story, where God is obviously active in sending the rain and the flood—"destroying" the earth in this sense (e.g., Gen. 6:17)—his action is also represented as enacting what has in fact already become the case:

> God saw how corrupt the earth had become, for all the people on earth had corrupted their ways. So God said to Noah, "I am going to put an end to all people, for the earth is filled with violence because of them. I am surely going to destroy both them and the earth." (Gen. 6:12–13)

The word for "destroy" in verse 13 is a different form of the same Hebrew root (*shkht*) that is used for "corrupt" and "corrupted" in verse 12. So, to suggest another possible translation of *shkht*, human beings have "ruined" their ways, which has meant the "ruin" of the earth, and so God is going to ruin "both them and the earth." Our ruin means the ruin of the earth and its creatures too.

But if one of the things we learn from the story of Noah is that sin has consequences, the focus of the story is on God's use of Noah to preserve life through the waters of the flood. It is important to recall that God can act however he chooses in this story; after all, he is about to open the floodgates of heaven and the springs of the abyss and send unimaginable rain on the earth. At the end of the flood, he will send a wind so that the floodwater recedes, and he will set a rainbow in the sky. God clearly could save Noah and his family and the other creatures in any way he chose. Yet he elects to use Noah to accomplish his purposes, to call him to be the instrument through which life is preserved. This means that Noah has work to do. Incidentally, Noah is *not* given the task of implementing God's punishment; his sole job in the story is to preserve life, even through the waters of God's judgment.

The work of preserving life that Noah undertakes is done under the direction of God; it requires planning and preparation; and it involves skillful labor, the use of human ingenuity and technology. The construction of the ark is perhaps the preeminent biblical symbol of conservation efforts and the preservation of biodiversity ("the animals going in were male and female of every living thing" [Gen. 7:16]). The ark, then, reminds us that our role of working and taking care of the earth includes the good use and application of technology. A biblical approach to creation care may well necessitate, as we have begun to see, a re-envisioning of what it means to be limited human creatures, and it may require of us a willingness to let go of our endless pursuit of "progress" (at least as our societies have defined it) in order that we might embrace richer and simpler ways of life that give space for and promote the flourishing of all of life. But, however reconfigured it all may need to be, such an approach will not involve a retreat from technology, science, art, innovation, and exploration. We need instead to reconsider the purpose of all these human endeavors, to redefine what progress would look like, and to clarify what constitutes good work.

The good work that Noah undertakes at God's command is to "keep alive" (6:19, 20; 7:3) all the diversity of life on earth. The text emphasizes that Noah is to take "every kind" (NIV; or "according to their kind," NRSV) of bird and animal and creature that moves along the ground (6:19–20; 7:2–3; cf. 8:17). At the key turning point of the narrative, after the destruction of the flood is complete, we learn that then "God remembered Noah and all the wild animals and all the livestock that were with him in the ark" (8:1). We see yet again that God's care and concern extends to nonhuman life; he knows and "remembers" them all. When the flood waters have receded, we again have the same emphasis on the diversity of life that is now ready to repopulate the world:

> "Bring out every kind of living creature that is with you—the birds, the animals, and all the creatures that move along the ground—so they can multiply on the earth and be fruitful and increase in number on it." So Noah came out, together with his sons and his wife and his sons' wives. All the animals and all the creatures that move along the ground and all the birds—everything that moves on land—came out of the ark, one kind after another. (Gen. 8:17–19)

The emphasis here on the diversity of life is of course the same as that in Genesis 1, where God creates everything "according to their kind." God is concerned in both cases with the wide variety of species on earth, and we also find here again the blessing of abundance applied to all living creatures.

God's valuing of all of life is seen finally in the first covenant explicitly described in Scripture. This covenant is sometimes referred to as the Noahic covenant (since it does indeed involve Noah and his family), but it is perhaps more accurately called the cosmic covenant or the covenant with all creation. For, in an extension of the commitment God has made to Noah in Genesis 6:18, we discover in chapter 9 a covenant relationship that encompasses all of life: "I now establish my covenant with you and with your descendants after you and with every living creature that was with you—the birds, the livestock and all the wild animals, all those that came out of the ark with you—every living creature on earth" (Gen. 9:9–10). God's commitment in this covenant is to preserve his creation, to never again send the waters of the flood to destroy all of life (v. 11).

For the early readers of Genesis, this assurance would have been particularly important. They would have known other versions of the story of an ancient catastrophic flood, and such accounts could lead them to question the reliability of God and his commitment to his creation. For example, in another ancient Near Eastern version of the story, the Atrahasis Epic, the cause of the flood is not the violence and evil of humankind but merely that the gods are annoyed by the noisiness of the growing population of human beings. The character of the gods seems capricious; there is no underlying commitment to justice and goodness. Moreover, there is no reason to think that the gods might not act similarly in the future. The Genesis account, by contrast, serves to underline the Creator God's faithfulness and commitment to all his creation. Just as God "remembered" Noah and his family and all the animals and so ended the flood (8:1), so whenever he looks at the rainbow set in the sky will he "remember" (9:14–15) his commitment to preserve the earth and its creatures.

As in the Abrahamic covenant to come, God is the one who puts himself on the line to fulfill the terms of the covenant he makes with all of creation. It is an unconditional commitment. God knows that, despite having sent the cleansing waters of the flood across the earth to judge human sin and violence, his human creatures have not changed in their basic inclination to evil (8:21). Yet he binds himself to his creation nonetheless, promising never again to "curse the ground because of humans" (8:21) nor to destroy all living things. The earth and its rhythm of life will be preserved: "As long as the earth endures, seedtime and harvest, cold and heat, summer and winter, day and night will never cease" (8:22); "Never again will all life be destroyed by the waters of a flood; never again will there be a flood to destroy the earth" (9:11). But if God's commitment is unconditional, that does not mean there is nothing for human beings to do. The vocation given to humanity in Genesis 1 and 2 has not changed. We even have a repetition of the blessing of fruitfulness and multiplication given both to human beings and all the other creatures (8:17; 9:1). Yet there is also a darker note now:

> The fear and dread of you will fall on all the beasts of the earth, and on all the birds in the sky, on every creature that moves along the ground, and on all the fish in the sea; they are given into your hands. Everything that lives and moves about will be food for you. Just as I gave you the green plants, I now give you everything. (9:2–3)

This serves primarily to expand the diet of human beings from the vegetarian diet of Genesis 1 and 2 to a diet that includes meat (cf. Deut. 12:15–16, 20), and it describes perhaps the natural fear prey have for those who have now become predators. The eating of meat and animal sacrifice will become a part of the life of Israel (although it is already there in Gen. 4:4), and the provision of meat along with grain and vegetables becomes something to celebrate and a particular feature of Israel's festivals. Yet "fear and dread" hints at a deeper brokenness in the relationship between animals and the human beings who are meant to be the rulers and keepers of the earth and its life. This broken relationship is one we will examine at greater length in chapter 6.

What is important to note here is that, even in this new context in which the taking of animals for food is explicitly permitted, the prohibition of eating blood (9:4; cf. Lev. 17:10–14; Deut. 12:16, 23–25; 15:23) indicates that a certain respect is still due to the life of other creatures. And as we explore in the next chapter, God's people Israel will still have duties and responsibilities toward other creatures and the land itself, duties and responsibilities that may reflect something of the role that God intends human beings to have within creation.

DOMINION AS STEWARDSHIP?

Before looking more closely in the next chapter at how Israel's vocation is reflected in the nation's relationship with the land, it is worth taking a step back to consider what words we use to describe the role of human beings within creation. Many Christians use the language of "stewardship" as the default or only way of describing our responsibilities in and for creation. "Stewardship" is admittedly a useful term, and so we ourselves use it at times in this book: among other things, it is broad enough to encompass a wide range of views for how we care for creation, both within and beyond Christian contexts (see also our remarks on this in chap. 11). Yet this very looseness in definition can also be a liability. Its common use to describe exclusively the "stewardship" of money and financial resources can be confusing and can lead to the erroneous notion that the rest of creation is nothing more than a larder of resources to be distributed and used. The popularity of the term also means it has been hijacked by groups whose interpretation of "stewardship" would seem in the view of the authors of this book to contravene nearly everything Scripture says about who we are called to be as God's people in our relationship to the rest of creation.

The term "stewardship" is not in fact used in Scripture to describe our role in creation, though I (Jonathan) have elsewhere explored the potential of Jesus's parable of the wise steward (*oikonomos*) to illuminate something of the nature of our responsibilities within creation. Although it is not a perfect parallel, Jesus's parable, where the "steward" or "manager" is the one who oversees and manages a household, does provide us with some biblical principles about how "stewardship" needs to be defined.[8] Among the key principles that emerge from Jesus's parable are the following: (1) stewards, whatever unique responsibilities they may have, remain members of the household within which they serve and are not themselves the owners or masters; (2) stewards care for those people and things entrusted to them on behalf of the true owner and master; and therefore, (3) stewards do not serve themselves or take

---

8. See Jonathan A. Moo and Robert S. White, *Let Creation Rejoice: Biblical Hope and Ecological Crisis* (Downers Grove, IL: IVP Academic, 2014), 142–45. The parable is found in Luke 12:42–48.

advantage of their position to exploit what has been given into their care. As should be evident, the role of steward resembles in certain respects the biblical role of the ideal king who rules on behalf of those ruled and only under the authority of God as the true lord and king, but here the model of servanthood perhaps comes even more to the fore. What is strikingly different in a biblical model of stewardship compared to a secular one is that, whatever benefits may or may not accrue to the one doing the stewarding or to the future offspring of the steward, the purpose of stewardship is always first and foremost for the sake of the master and secondarily for the sake of fellow members of the household.

It is important to consider the connotations of the words we choose and what they might evoke for others, but we should not become pedantic about it. What is crucial is to define what we mean by the words we use. In my own university, for example, I (Jonathan) teach within what is called the "environmental studies" program. It should already be evident that "environment" is not a word that adequately captures what Scripture says about creation and our place within it; in fact, it can be downright misleading in its connotation that there is this thing out there called the "environment" from which we can separate ourselves. Yet "environmental studies" is a widely used descriptor of the sorts of things we do in this program, and so it seems better to use the recognized term and, where necessary, to clarify and redefine what we mean by it in our teaching and our research. So too with "stewardship." Inasmuch as we use the term, let us seek to define it carefully in ways that are consistent with the biblical witness concerning how we relate to creation as those bearing the image of God.

SUMMARY

Regardless of what we call our work on behalf of creation, this chapter reveals the importance of caring for the earth as an inescapable part of who God has created us to be. Indeed, the risk inherent in the use of any specialized term is that it can imply that creation care involves a particular set of tasks reserved for experts or the particularly keen, something we can safely leave in the hands of others. There are of course some who are called especially to devote themselves full-time to what we might call creation care, just as there are those who are full-time missionaries, or pastors, or aid and development workers. But creation care is first and last simply about being human. It's about becoming who we have been created to be as God's image bearers in the community of creation, living as God calls us to in all of life—in our eating and sleeping, our working and playing, our planting and harvesting, our buying and selling, our loving and dying. The biblical vision is a holistic, all-encompassing one, and it includes us all.

RELEVANT QUESTIONS

1. In what ways do we stray from the biblical perspective on humanity by either thinking too highly or too lowly of ourselves? What are some practical ways we can avoid both errors and remain rooted in a fully biblical view of what it is to be human?

2. What difference does it make to how we understand and care for creation if we believe God created it for a purpose, a goal or *telos*?

3. What do biblical examples like Noah, David, and Solomon reveal about how we ought to rule and care for creation today? How are we collectively failing or succeeding in our vocation today?

4. How does God's unconditional commitment to creation, made after the flood, affect our understanding of our own responsibilities to work and care for the earth?

HUMANITY AND THE EARTH, ISRAEL AND THE LAND

If we are going to care well for God's creation, we have to take into consideration the entirety of the earth and all its life. This is especially true in our globalized age, when our decisions and actions can have an outsized impact even on distant parts of the world. Yet what has always been required of us, no less today than at any other time, is responsible care for and attention to our own local place. We might imitate the popular saying that "all politics is local" by reminding ourselves that "all creation care is local." Our care for creation must first and last be connected to ordinary, everyday life and be rooted in the particular places where we live and love and play and worship and eat and raise our food and make our homes. The practice of creation care is necessarily shaped and informed by the particularities and idiosyncrasies of our various and diverse communities, with their own unique mixtures of people and landscapes and soils and climates and assemblages of creatures. There are certainly principles of ecology and what we might call Christian ecological virtues that apply in all times and places, but their practical outworking often looks different in my backyard in Spokane, Washington, than it does in yours or in our neighbors' on the other side of the globe.

> "There can be no such thing as a 'global village.' No matter how much one may love the world as a whole, one can live fully in it only by living responsibly in some small part of it. Where we live and who we live there with define the terms of our relationship to the world and to humanity. We thus come again to the paradox that one can become whole only by the responsible acceptance of one's partiality."
>
> *Wendell Berry*[1]

LIFE IN A LAND OF ABUNDANCE

In the life of biblical Israel in the land of Canaan, we get a glimpse of how the general responsibilities given to human beings to rule over other creatures and care for the earth are worked out in the life of God's people in one particular place at one particular time. Israel's life on the land is shaped by all the idiosyncrasies of its particular vocation as God's chosen nation, by its geography and climate, and by the technological, agricultural, political, and social realities of the day. Yet, in the

---

1. Wendell Berry, "The Body and the Earth," in *The Art of the Commonplace: The Agrarian Essays of Wendell Berry* (Berkeley, CA: Counterpoint, 2002), 117–18.

law given to Israel, it is possible to identify the outworking of certain principles that are relevant for the people of God in other times and places too.

What first should be observed is the simple and obvious fact (though it is often overlooked) that the earth itself is necessarily caught up in the network of relationships established between God, Israel, and the land. When God calls Israel out of all the other peoples of the earth to be a nation set apart from others, a "kingdom of priests and a holy nation" (Ex. 19:6), he leads them to a place and gives them this particular land as their home (even if we acknowledge, of course, that the land of Canaan itself consists of a variety of landscapes and ecosystems). That this land is distinct from others and will require practices particularly suited to its conditions is hinted at in Deuteronomy, where the land of Canaan is compared to Egypt:

> The land you are entering to take over is not like the land of Egypt, from which you have come, where you planted your seed and irrigated it by foot as in a vegetable garden. But the land you are crossing the Jordan to take possession of is a land of mountains and valleys that drinks rain from heaven. (Deut. 11:10–11)

Yet what is most distinctive about the land is that "it is a land the LORD your God cares for; the eyes of the LORD your God are continually on it from the beginning of the year to its end" (v. 12). Of course, this could be said to be true for the whole of the earth. But just as God's love for and desire to bless all peoples is now mediated through his covenant with Israel, so too is God's attention now focused in a particular way upon the land in which they dwell. Indeed, the state of the land itself will become a visible sign to the wider world of the status of Israel's relationship with her God.

The entirety of God's creation, the "heavens and the earth," is called upon to witness the covenant between God and his people whom he is establishing on the land (4:26). Israel's God is not a local God who belongs only to the land of Israel but is the true Lord and owner of all of heaven and earth (10:14). And just as the whole of creation is "good" and ought to elicit worship and obedience to the creator, so the land that Israel inherits is a particularly "good land" (4:21; 9:6). And the only appropriate response to what God has done and to his gift of good land is worship and obedience:

> Observe the commands of the LORD your God, walking in obedience to him and revering him. For the LORD your God is bringing you into a good land—a land with brooks, streams, and deep springs gushing out into the valleys and hills; a land with wheat and barley, vines and fig trees, pomegranates, olive oil and honey; a land where bread will not be scarce and you will lack nothing; a land where the rocks are iron and you can dig copper out of the hills. When you have eaten and are satisfied, praise the LORD your God for the good land he has given you. (Deut. 8:6–10)

"We are connected by work even to the places where we don't work, for all places are connected; it is clear by now that we cannot exempt one place from our ruin of another. The name of our proper connection to the earth is "good work," for good work involves much giving of honor. It honors the source of its materials; it honors the place where it is done; it honors the art by which it is done; it honors the thing that it makes and the user of the made thing. Good work is always modestly scaled, for it cannot ignore either the nature of individual places or the differences between places, and it always involves a sort of religious humility, for not everything is known. Good work can be defined only in particularity, for it must be defined a little differently for every one of the places and every one of the workers on the earth."

Wendell Berry[2]

"Examine each question in terms of what is ethically and aesthetically right, as well as what is economically expedient. A thing is right when it tends to preserve the integrity, stability, and beauty of the biotic community. It is wrong when it tends otherwise."

Aldo Leopold[3]

The land is celebrated here especially for its bounty, its ability to provide food of all kinds and even copper and iron for the people. Incidentally, we are reminded again that Scripture holds together the intrinsic value of non-human creation and the instrumental value of creation for human use. A biblical ecological vision will necessarily include a vision of how agriculture, mining, and industry can be pursued in ways that are just, respectful of other life, and consistent with the recognition that all of creation exists first and last for God's glory. In other words, a biblical ecological vision includes an understanding of what "good work" looks like. As we have seen, the earth serves human needs only as part of its wider service in bringing God glory and praise.

In light of God's provision, then, the people are charged to "acknowledge and take to heart . . . that the LORD is God in heaven above and on the earth below. There is no other" (4:39). It is only in fidelity to the one true God that Israel—and the land itself—will be sustained and find life and blessing:

> He will love you and bless you and increase your numbers. He will bless the fruit of your womb, the crops of your land—your grain, new wine and olive oil—the calves of your herds and the lambs of your flocks in the land he swore to your ancestors to give you. You will be blessed more than any other people; none of your men or women will be childless, nor will any of your livestock be without young. (Deut. 7:13–14)

> So if you faithfully obey the commands I am giving you today—to love the LORD your God and to serve him with all your heart and with all your soul—then I will send rain on your land in its season, both autumn and spring rains, so that you may gather in your grain, new wine and olive oil. I will provide grass in the fields for your cattle, and you will eat and be satisfied. (Deut. 11:13–15; cf. Lev. 26:3–5[4])

---

2. Wendell Berry, *Sex, Economy, Freedom and Community: Eight Essays* (New York: Random House, 1993), 35–36.

3. *A Sand County Almanac,* 262.

4. Lev. 26:6 goes on to describe, as a part of this promised reward for faithfulness, the removal of "wild beasts" as part of the "peace in the land" when no one will make the Israelites afraid.

Later, in a description of the curses that will befall Israel in the event of her disobedience, "wild beasts" are sent against the people to rob them of their children and cattle, until the land is desolate (v. 22; cf. Deut. 32:24). The contrast between this negative portrayal of "wild beasts" and the joyful celebration of wild animals—even threatening ones like lions—that we saw in Genesis, Job, and some

The LORD will establish you as his holy people, as he promised you on oath, if you keep the commands of the LORD your God and walk in obedience to him. Then all the peoples on earth will see that you are called by the name of the LORD, and they will fear you. The LORD will grant you abundant prosperity—in the fruit of your womb, the young of your livestock and the crops of your ground—in the land he swore to your ancestors to give you. The LORD will open the heavens, the storehouse of his bounty, to send rain on your land in season and to bless all the work of your hands. You will lend to many nations but will borrow from none. (Deut. 28:9–12)

The abundance and fruitfulness of the land is not to be taken for granted but is always to be a source of thanksgiving to God. It is a gift, not a given. The health of the land and its ability to sustain human life are moreover dependent at least in part on how God's people choose to live on the land. The risk is that the people become proud and forget the true source of their life and blessing. They are warned against the temptation to say, "My power and the strength of my hands have produced this wealth for me" (8:17), when in fact it is God alone "who gives you the ability to produce wealth" (v. 18). The result of forgetting or rejecting God will be disaster for the land and the people together:

Be careful, or you will be enticed to turn away and worship other gods and bow down to them. Then the LORD's anger will burn against you, and he will shut up the heavens so that it will not rain and the ground will yield no produce, and you will soon perish from the good land the LORD is giving you. (Deut. 11:16–17)

The LORD will send on you curses, confusion and rebuke in everything you put your hand to, until you are destroyed and come to sudden ruin because of the evil you have done in forsaking him. The LORD will plague you with diseases until he has destroyed you from the land you are entering to possess. The LORD will strike you with wasting disease, with fever and inflammation, with scorching heat and drought, with blight and mildew, which will plague you until you perish. The sky over your head will be bronze, the ground beneath

---

of the Psalms, is perhaps understandable when we observe that the focus here in Leviticus is entirely on the mortal danger that some wild animals can pose to people and their livestock. However much we recognize that predators have been created by God to be predators and ought to be celebrated as such, the death of human beings (and their dependent domesticated animals) at the hands of other wild animals is still considered a sign of brokenness in the relationship between humanity, God, and the rest of creation. Gen. 9:5 even suggests that animals are held responsible when they cause human death: "And for your lifeblood I will surely demand an accounting. I will demand an accounting from every animal" (cf. Ex. 21:28–32). Leviticus labels the animals in view here not simply as "wild" (as in the NIV) but actually as "evil," or, perhaps most accurately, "harmful" (Hebrew *ra'ah*). In Isaiah's portrayal of the messianic peace, we find an analogous portrayal of the removal of the threat of death at the hands of wild beasts described in Lev. 26, but here such predators are not removed. Instead, wolves, leopards, lions, bears, and venomous snakes all exist in peaceable harmony with settled human life (Isa. 11:6–9).

you iron. The LORD will turn the rain of your country into dust and powder; it will come down from the skies until you are destroyed. (Deut. 28:20–24)

You will sow much seed in the field but you will harvest little, because locusts will devour it. You will plant vineyards and cultivate them but you will not drink the wine or gather the grapes, because worms will eat them. You will have olive trees throughout your country but you will not use the oil, because the olives will drop off. You will have sons and daughters but you will not keep them, because they will go into captivity. Swarms of locusts will take over all your trees and the crops of your land. (Deut. 28:38–42)

We will see in the next chapter that the Hebrew prophets will turn again and again to this covenant language from Deuteronomy to challenge God's people in subsequent generations and to interpret their experiences of drought and ruin and conquest. Ultimately, rejecting God would lead even to dispossession from the land. According to Deuteronomy, it was the sin of the nations who lived in Canaan before Israel that led to them being driven out of the land (9:1–6); and the Israelites would be treated no differently if they too failed to honor God (e.g., 28:63). To avoid these curses, the challenge is for God's people to live in daily dependence on God, to give him thanks and praise for all he provides, to keep his commands, to walk in his ways, to serve him alone, to fear and to love him. Israel's relationship to the land then will become a sign and example to other nations of the sort of life on earth that God intends, and the health of Israel's relationship with God will be reflected in the health of the land itself.

THE LIVES OF OTHER CREATURES AND THE SACRIFICIAL SYSTEM

Not only is Israel's relationship with God reflected in the health of the land itself, but Israel's law reveals that the land and its creatures are considered morally significant. At first glance, this may seem a surprising claim, given how much of the law provides stipulations for Israel's sacrificial system—in which, of course, Israel is instructed to take the lives of many animals. And Israel's law clearly assumes a profound difference between the moral weight assigned to human versus animal life: consider, for example, the difference in penalties assigned to the taking of a human life versus the life of a domestic animal. Yet the entire sacrificial system is predicated on the assumption that animal life has distinctive value in itself and that there is in fact a certain kinship between human beings and other creatures.

The animal sacrifices offered to atone for sin would remind Israelites of the weightiness of sin and its potential to separate them from God and to result finally in death. Yet the fact that other animals can stand in their place and suffer the penalty of death that they otherwise would face is above all a sign of the grace of God, who provides this means for his people to have ongoing life with himself, even in the context of their inevitable sin and impurity. New Testament writers will observe that, in an ultimate sense, "It is impossible for the blood of bulls and goats to take away sins" (Heb. 10:4; cf. Rom. 3:25), and hence there remains the need for the perfect sacrifice of Christ. Yet the shedding of the blood of animals for the people's sins that the Old Testament requires and which New Testament writers consider a foreshadowing of the final, once-for-all sacrifice of Christ, implies an intimate connection between human life and the life of other creatures.

This connection perhaps is seen most clearly in the stipulations for how the blood of animals is to be handled. The blood is never to be consumed, and the blood of slain animals is to be poured out and covered with earth, because it represents the life of the animal (Lev. 17:10–14; Deut. 12:23–25; cf. Gen. 9:4). So significant was this stipulation in the self-understanding of the people of God that it remained in force for the early church, even when the practice of circumcision was considered no longer to be necessary for Gentiles who became followers of Christ (Acts 15:19–20, 29).[5] But our point here is simply that the respect that Israelites were to afford to the life of the animals they killed for food and sacrifice served in part to remind them of their kinship with other creatures and of the gift of life and breath that they shared with them. The God who breathed life into humanity and created them to be "living being[s]" (Gen. 2:7) bestowed that same breath of life into other creatures too (Gen. 1:30; cf. Job 12:10).

In other contexts, we see that, although animals may be killed for food and sacrifice, they still deserve to be treated with respect appropriate to their kind. An ox is not to be muzzled when treading out grain (Deut. 25:4), and animals, along with everyone else, are to be given rest on the Sabbath (Ex. 20:10; Deut. 5:14). As Proverbs says, "The righteous care for the needs of their animals" (Prov. 12:10).

SUSTAINABILITY AND RESTRAINT IN THE LAW OF ISRAEL

"Sustainability" has become a contemporary buzzword. It is overused to the point of meaninglessness, especially in advertising and in corporate and educational contexts. Nevertheless, it remains a useful word, encapsulating the important idea that people should use resources in a way that is healthy for both people and the land. And it is there already in the law of Israel. If a practice is sustainable, it can hypothetically be carried on indefinitely into the future, so sustainable living means adopting

---

5. The ability of blood to represent life takes on a fresh significance in the Eucharist: "Very truly I tell you, unless you eat the flesh of the Son of Man and drink his blood, you have no life in you. Whoever eats my flesh and drinks my blood has eternal life, and I will raise them up at the last day" (John 6:53–54).

practices that preserve or enhance the ability of people and all of life to thrive now and into the future.

Such a principle lies behind the prohibition against taking the mother along with her young when raiding a bird's nest for food (Deut. 22:6–7). This restriction and the restraint it requires is, at minimum and most obviously, simply a wise practice if there is to be any hope of the bird producing more offspring in the future. To take all that could be taken, the mother along with the young (trusting, perhaps, that there are plenty of other breeding pairs or that God will always provide), would be an abrogation of the significant responsibility with which God has invested his people. The God who provides abundantly and establishes his people in a land overflowing with the good things they need is the same God who calls his people to exercise wisdom and care and restraint in their use of all that he provides.

A similar restraint applies even in the stipulations governing the most destructive of human activities, warfare. When laying siege to a city, the Israelites are told not to cut down the city's trees (Deut. 20:19). The reason given in the first instance is utilitarian: they ought to preserve the trees so they can eat what they produce. But a question is raised in this context that hints at a deeper truth: "Are the trees people, that you should besiege them?" It is one thing to make use of trees, even for siege works (v. 20); it is quite another to wantonly destroy them. To make war against other peoples may have its reasons and justifications, but there can be no justification for making war against other living things.

"The idea was that when faced with abundance one should consume abundantly—an idea that has survived to become the basis of our present economy. It is neither natural nor civilized, and even from a 'practical' point of view it is to the last degree brutalizing and stupid."

Wendell Berry[6]

The importance of restraint even in a context of overflowing abundance is one that Israel had already learned from the nation's time in the wilderness. Israel was saved out of the "iron-smelting furnace" of Egypt (Deut. 4:20), where a type of industrial economy prevailed in which the elite few controlled and managed the nation's land and resources for their own benefit at the expense of everyone else, including their Hebrew slaves.[7] Now, in the wilderness, God's people find themselves living in daily dependence on God's direct provision. Every day, except the Sabbath, God gives his people manna, bread from heaven, as much as—and more than—they need (Ex. 16:18–21). The temptation in the face of such bounty is to take extra, to store some for the future, perhaps to eat for oneself or to sell to others, to secure oneself against the risk of future scarcity. Yet, to do so in this instance would be to abandon trust in the God who saved them out of Egypt. It could lead the Israelites to forget their daily dependence on their creator and redeemer, and risk the temptation of returning to an economy based on scarcity, fear, disparity, and inequality. Thus:

6. v *The Art of the Commonplace*, 11.
7. Ellen F. Davis, *Scripture, Culture, and Agriculture: An Agrar-* *ian Reading of the Bible* (Cambridge: Cambridge University Press, 2009), 67–69.

This is what the LORD has commanded: "Everyone is to gather as much as they need. Take an omer for each person you have in your tent." The Israelites did as they were told; some gathered much, some little. And when they measured it by the omer, the one who gathered much did not have too much, and the one who gathered little did not have too little. Everyone had gathered just as much as they needed. Then Moses said to them, "No one is to keep any of it until morning.". . . Each morning everyone gathered as much as they needed, and when the sun grew hot, it melted away. (Ex. 16:16–21)

Even in Israel's later, settled life on the land, the principle that the provision of manna was intended to teach continues to be relevant:

He gave you manna to eat in the wilderness, something your ancestors had never known, to humble and test you so that in the end it might go well with you. You may say to yourself, "My power and the strength of my hands have produced this wealth for me." But remember the LORD your God, for it is he who gives you the ability to produce wealth, and so confirms his covenant, which he swore to your ancestors, as it is today. (Deut. 8:16–18)

In the parable of the rich fool, Jesus will later provide a dramatic example of the failure to remember God as the source and goal of all things: the apparently successful landowner of his parable stores up things for himself but fails to be "rich toward God" (Luke 12:21). It is not, to be clear, that planning for the future is ruled out for the people of God: witness the example of Joseph and even the need to collect enough manna on a Friday to have enough for the Sabbath (Ex. 16:22–27). And Deuteronomy 8:17–18 assumes that people's work on the land will in fact lead to the production of wealth. Yet the key insight is that this is no less the gift of God's grace than was the manna from heaven. And God's intentions for how his gifts are to be used remain the same.

Jacob Milgrom has argued that the odd restrictions in Israel's law code about not mixing creatures or sowing two seeds together (e.g., Deut. 22:9–11) reflect a cautiousness about not intruding on the divine (since the admixture of creatures was the provenance of the divine, as seen, e.g., in the cherubim and other decorations in the temple/tabernacle sanctuary). If this is right, then we also find here in Israel's law the principle of restraint at work.[8] This restraint derives from the recognition that God is God—and we are not—and that we harm others and ourselves if we forget the difference. It is in acknowledging and living within our creaturely limits that we find true abundance and fulfillment.

8. Jacob Milgrom, *Leviticus*, Continental Commentary (Minneapolis: Augsburg Fortress, 2004), 236–38. The point is developed by Davis, *Scripture, Culture, and Agriculture*, 86–87, 199, who argues that, in our own very different context, there are reasons to be cautious about the ways in which advances in genetics and technology enable us to manipulate life in novel, godlike ways with potentially unforeseen consequences, both for the creatures involved and for the integrity of the living communities of which they would be a part.

SABBATH AND JUBILEE

Living in constant awareness of their dependence upon God's abundant provision, exercising appropriate restraint, and embracing their role as God's people on the land are the commitments that also inform Israel's celebration of Sabbath and Jubilee. These distinctive features of Israel's life moreover reveal again something of the significance of the land itself. Already in Exodus, we learn that the seventh-day Sabbath rest is intended not just for Israelites, but for foreigners residing with them, and for their animals too (Ex. 20:10; cf. Deut. 5:14). In Leviticus, the commandment is expanded when God tells Moses, "the land itself must observe a sabbath to the LORD" (Lev. 25:2). Every seventh year, there is to be no sowing or pruning or reaping: the land itself is to have rest (vv. 3–7). Then, every forty-nine years, in the year of Jubilee, the land is to have its customary Sabbath rest, there is to be liberty for any who have become indentured, and the land is to be redistributed so that no one person or family gains excessive property and wealth at the expense of others (vv. 8–17).

The regular fallowing of fields can be a wise agricultural practice, of course, and the Jubilee regulations especially protect the ability of God's people to be sustained on the land and to ensure the reestablishment of equality in a world where injustices tend to arise over time. Yet the observance of Sabbath and Jubilee years for the land itself serves above all to remind Israel that God is the true owner and sustainer of the earth:

> Follow my decrees and be careful to obey my laws, and you will live safely in the land. Then the land will yield its fruit, and you will eat your fill and live there in safety. You may ask, "What will we eat in the seventh year if we do not plant or harvest our crops?" I will send you such a blessing in the sixth year that the land will yield enough for three years. While you plant during the eighth year, you will eat from the old crop and will continue to eat from it until the harvest of the ninth year comes in. (Lev. 25:18–22)

Such trust in God's provision and a ceasing from ordinary work requires Israel to remember her vocation and true purpose and to live in constant awareness that the land and its fruitfulness is a gift of God's grace. The land may have been given to the Israelites as their homeland, and thus in an important sense they can be said to belong to the land. But, as observance of the Jubilee years reminds them, the land does not belong to them: "The land must not be sold permanently, because the land is mine and you reside in my land as foreigners and strangers" (Lev. 25:23). The land belongs to God, and it is always and only by his grace and goodness that Israel resides there. The Israelite famer is thus a tenant farmer whose life and work is finally in the service of God himself as the owner and Lord.

The seriousness with which the biblical writers treat Sabbath rest can be inferred from the reminders and challenges to its faithful observance that appear occasionally in the prophets (e.g., Isa. 56:2–7; Jer. 17:21–27; cf. Neh. 13:15–22), as well as by the prominence of Sabbath controversies in the life of Jesus and the typological use of Sabbath rest by the author of Hebrews. Presumably because the practice of Sabbath rest for the land was honored more in the breach than in its observance, the Chronicler interprets the exile as a time when the land now finally enjoys its Sabbath rests (2 Chron. 36:21).

Here again we are confronted with the consequences of the failure of God's people to live as his people, to love and obey him in all things, including in how they treat the land. The result is brokenness, exile, and dispossession from the land. Such are the themes of the next chapter. Yet there is also hope, for God does not abandon his people or his creation. And the challenge and promise remain for God's people in all times to embrace who they are as limited human creatures, wholly dependent on their creator and redeemer, adopting practices that reflect his purposes for themselves and all of creation, and hence freed to experience the joy of the abundant life God intends for them.

SUMMARY

This chapter has explored ways in which Israel's life on the land reveals something of God's intentions for humanity in creation. Israel is reminded over and over again that, though the nation has been given the land as its homeland, it still belongs to God. Therefore, Israel's relationship to the land must reflect God's purposes for it, as he is its true owner and ruler. God's people are to live in ongoing awareness of their dependence upon God, to treat the land as a gift, to exercise restraint in their use of the land's resources and in their treatment of other living creatures, and to honor the land and its life as of value to God. In the sacrificial system, Israel is reminded of the nation's brokenness and need for redemption. The animals who stand in the people's place reveal the kinship that the people share with all of life, and they display God's grace in providing a means for the people's ongoing relationship with him. Above all, it is perhaps in the practice of Sabbath rest and Jubilee that Israelites are called to entrust themselves to God's good keeping and to reveal by their actions the reality of what they claim to believe about their Creator and Redeemer God.

RELEVANT QUESTIONS

1. What are the similarities and differences between the vocation of Israelites on the land in the Old Testament and the vocation of Christians on earth today?

2. What are some practical ways Christians could care for creation today that might serve to reveal to others the character and purposes of God, as was intended for Israel's life on the land?

3. List some practical ways in which the principle of restraint might apply to our treatment of the earth.

4. What relevance might Sabbath rest have for creation care today?

CHAPTER 6

A CREATION SUBJECTED TO FRUSTRATION

AN ENDURING GOODNESS

"The last word in ignorance is the man who says of an animal or plant, 'What good is it?' If the land mechanism as a whole is good, then every part is good, whether we understand it or not."[1] So claimed Aldo Leopold, the mid-twentieth century American scientist, author, and "father of conservation," as he has become known. Sixteen hundred years earlier, in a Lenten sermon series on the text of Genesis 1, the Cappadocian church father Basil of Caesarea made much the same claim: "Each of the things that have been made fulfills its own particular purpose in creation. . . . Not a single one of these things is without worth, not a single thing has been created without a reason."[2] In light of the goodness of all of creation, Basil encouraged his listeners to "recognize greatness even in small things, adding continually to your wonder and causing your love for the Creator to grow."[3] "In the rich treasures of creation," Basil claimed, "it is difficult to find what is most precious; it is too hard to bear the loss of what is omitted."[4]

For Basil, included among these "treasures of creation" are even those plants and animals that are harmful to human life: "Shall we give up acknowledging our gratitude for those things that are beneficial and reproach the Creator for those that are destructive of our life?"[5] Basil's wonder at creation encompassed all creatures, even the "scorpion's delicate stinger, which the Craftsman hollowed out like a pipe to throw venom into those it wounds. And let nobody reproach him on account of what he made, because he brought forth venomous animals, destructive and hostile to our life."[6] Even though these creatures sometimes cause harm to people, they nonetheless testify to God's creative goodness, in and of themselves.

---

1. Leopold, *A Sand County Almanac*, 190.

2. Basil, *Hexaemeron* 5.4. The translations (here and below) are my own, based on the Greek text in Basile de Cesaree, *Homélies sur L'Hexaéméron* (Paris: Les Éditions du Cerf, 1968). An English translation is available online at http://www.newadvent.org/fathers/1507. htm; I have also consulted the translation of Agnes C. Way, *St. Basil, Exegetic Homilies*, Fathers of the Church 46 (Washington, DC: The Catholic University of America Press, 1963), 71–72.

3. Ibid., 5.9.

4. Ibid., 5.4.

5. Ibid.

6. Ibid., 9.5. Basil compares the harm caused by dangerous animals to the use by a schoolmaster of a rod or whip to discipline students and keep order.

Basil avoids the temptation, indulged by so many later Christians, to dismiss whatever we do not understand in creation or whatever threatens human well-being as necessarily deficient, bad, or the result of humankind's fall. The only place where Basil allows himself to speculate like this is when he suggests that the thorns of roses came later "to remind us of sin, on account of which the earth was condemned to produce thorns and thistles for you."[8] At this point, Basil is no doubt thinking of Genesis 3:17–18: "Cursed is the ground because of you; through painful toil you will eat food from it all the days of your life. It will produce thorns and thistles for you, and you will eat the plants of the field." But Basil evidently does not consider this text to provide sufficient grounds to postulate a wider cosmic fall or to justify demeaning any particular plants or animals as inherently bad or the result of such a "fall." In fact, Basil's sermons are full of enthusiastic descriptions of plants and animals and what we might learn from them. His wonder at the diversity of life and his celebration of the goodness of all of creation, including predators and those creatures most harmful to human beings, reflect a perspective similar to that which we have identified in Scripture itself, especially in Genesis, Job, and the Psalms.[9] These biblical texts, taken together, ought to rule out for us, as they did for Basil, the notion that such things as predators or venomous creatures or any part of God's vast and wild creation are anything other than valuable parts of the goodness of the whole.

> "To keep every cog and wheel is the first precaution of intelligent tinkering."
>
> *Aldo Leopold[7]*

And yet, we know that all is not right. Scripture itself presumes that things are not as they ought to be. Human beings, God's image bearers, have rejected God and sin against him. Sin has consequences, and those consequences are experienced not just by human beings but by an entire groaning creation. "Cursed is the ground," God tells Adam in Genesis 3:17. The results of this curse are felt by every person who has ever lived and echo down through the Hebrew prophets and into the New Testament, where Paul describes the subjection of the entirety of creation to futility and its enslavement to "decay" or ruin (Rom. 8:20–22). In this chapter, we consider what the biblical writers might have in view when they describe this brokenness in creation, and we reflect on its potential significance for understanding our responsibilities in and for the rest of creation.

THE WORLD IS CHANGED

In the immediate context of Genesis 3, the cursing of the land is one of the series of curses that result from the disobedience of the man and woman in the garden

---

7. *A Sand County Almanac*, 190.
8. *Hexaemeron* 5.6.
9. At one point (ibid., 9.3), Basil observes that there could never be enough time to recount all the wonders of creation and in fact quotes Ps. 104:24: "How many are your works, Lord! In wisdom you made them all; the earth is full of your creatures."

of Eden. Taken as a whole, the curses suggest that the break that has occurred in the relationship between human beings and God results in brokenness and pain in the relations between man and woman, in the bringing forth of new life, and in the relationship between human beings and the earth. To be cursed is the opposite of being blessed. Thus, in contrast to the blessing of life in the garden of Eden, where good work presumably would always bear its expected good fruit, the curse on the land describes the difficulty and painful labor now involved in the cultivation of crops and the raising of food, work that will not always yield its hoped-for results: "Cursed is the ground because of you; through painful toil you will eat food from it all the days of your life. It will produce thorns and thistles for you, and you will eat the plants of the field" (Gen. 3:17–18). What has changed is fundamentally the relationship between human beings and the land. Humankind's vocation to "work and to keep" will now be done in a context of brokenness, hard labor, and potential fruitlessness.

The curse will be experienced especially by Cain, who, after killing his brother Abel, finds himself "cursed" from the ground, which has received his brother's blood (Gen. 4:11). The connections to the previous chapter suggest that this is the same curse pronounced in Genesis 3:17–18 but experienced in a particularly profound way by the murderer Cain. God tells him, "When you work the ground, it will no longer yield its crops for you. You will be a restless wanderer on the earth" (Gen. 4:12). As is hinted at in Genesis 3:17–18, not only will work be painful and difficult, it sometimes also will come up empty and end in futility. We have observed that the rest of Scripture clearly assumes that the earth "post-Fall" remains good and capable, by God's grace, of providing abundantly for the needs of people and other creatures alike. But humankind's rebellion against God means that the possibility of pain and fruitlessness always now hangs over human life on earth. The relationship between humankind and the earth is fraught, and the end, the *telos*, for which God created all things can no longer be reached—unless God acts to change the situation.

This thwarting of God's purpose is seen most clearly in the garden of Eden's emblematic tree of life, which held out to Adam and Eve the possibility of eternal life with God. The story implies that had the human couple lived in obedience to God and found in him their source of life and wisdom, rather than listening to the serpent, they then would have been able to take and eat from the tree of life. Incidentally, the story does *not* imply that human beings were created immortal. God expels them from the garden precisely to prevent Adam (and Eve) from living forever: "He must not be allowed to reach out his hand and take also from the tree of life and eat, and live forever" (Gen. 3:22). To live forever was a mere possibility, a condition of obedience, a possibility that is frustrated because of sin. To experience ongoing life now, in the context of sin and evil and apart from the intimate presence of God as experienced in the garden, would perhaps in any case be more a curse than a blessing. The restoration of the tree of life (Rev. 22) can come only in the context of a renewed humanity, made possible by the one who redeems and creates us anew and defeats the powers of sin and death that were unleashed by humankind's rebellion.

The point here is that the punishment for sin experienced by Adam and Eve involves at least in part the frustration of possibilities. To live forever with God in the garden of Eden is, after their disobedience, no longer possible, nor will it be possible for the life of Eden to be extended throughout the earth, a possibility that is hinted at in the Genesis narrative and which emerges more clearly in the light of the rest of Scripture.[11] The hope that the conditions of the temple-paradise of Eden might one day envelop the whole of the earth is, we will see, one that John develops in his vision of the new creation at the end of Revelation.

> "... upon men who, as animals, were essentially impermanent, he bestowed a grace which other creatures lacked—namely, the impress of his own Image.... But if they went astray and became vile, throwing away their birthright of beauty, then they would come under the natural law of death and live no longer in paradise, but, dying outside of it, continue in death and in corruption."
>
> *Athanasius* [10]

Yet Genesis already provides foretastes of the hope that God has not abandoned his purposes for his people or his creation. There is the enigmatic reference in Genesis 3:15 to the offspring of the woman who will crush the head of the serpent, a text early Christians saw as pointing to Christ's victory over Satan. Then, in the context of what may be the most dramatic outworking of God's curse of the land, the flood that he sends to "ruin" the earth that is being "ruined" by the violence and corruption of humanity, we learn that Noah will actually bring relief from the conditions of the curse: "He will comfort us in the labor and painful toil of our hands caused by the ground the LORD has cursed" (Gen. 5:29). How does this "comfort" come about? Perhaps, in part, Noah's saving of life through the waters of the flood is seen as a sign of the proper relationship that human beings are meant to have with the rest of creation, as an outworking of a proper relationship of love and obedience to God. But it is finally God's own promise and unconditional commitment to his creation after the flood that brings comfort and hope: "Never again will I curse the ground because of humans, even though every inclination of the human heart is evil from childhood. And never again will I destroy all living creatures, as I have done" (Gen. 8:21).

It is possible to read Genesis 8:21 as implying that the curse was a temporary one-time event that no longer applies in the context of God's cosmic covenant with all of creation that follows the flood. Yet it is in this same context that we learn of the fear that animals will have of human beings, who now are explicitly given animal life to eat alongside plants. So, clearly the brokenness between humankind and the

---

10. Athanasius, *On the Incarnation of the Word*, 1.3. (Grand Rapids: Christian Classics Ethereal Library). Available at http://www.ccel.org/ccel/athanasius/incarnation.html.

11. For a development of this theme, see G. K. Beale, *The Temple and the Church's Mission: A Biblical Theology of the Dwelling Place of God* (Downers Grove, IL: IVP Academic, 2004).

rest of creation remains. More likely what is meant in Genesis 8:21 is that God will not add to the conditions of the curse, nor will he ever again let loose the powers of chaos and allow the earth to be entirely handed over to destruction. Despite the evil of humankind and the ruin of all of creation that otherwise would be the inevitable result of human sin, God binds himself to the earth and its life, promising to sustain it in its regularity (8:22) and to bless it with fruitfulness and abundance (9:1, 7).

The curse on the land seems predominantly or exclusively to be directed at the relationship between human beings and the land. It does not seem to represent, for example, some sort of mysterious ontological change in the very makeup of creation itself. This has become a popular idea that nonetheless is contradicted by, among other things, the continuity in the portrayal of creation between Genesis 1 and the rest of Scripture.[12] What is most important for our purposes is to observe that the way the curse is enacted and experienced is in some sense dependent on humanity's ongoing relationship with God and how that is lived out in relation with others and the earth. This is seen most clearly in Israel's relationship with the land in the Old Testament. We have seen that blessings or curses of the people and the land together are held out to the nation as different possibilities dependent on the fundamental choice they make to follow the way of life held out in the Law or to reject God and follow in the way of death. And inasmuch as Israel's life on the land serves as a microcosm of humanity's life on earth, this same choice ultimately faces all of humankind.

In other words, to live in a post-Genesis 3 world is not to accept blithely the fact that the land is cursed. On the one hand, it does require that we acknowledge that our broken relationship with God has consequences for our relationships with each other and with the earth too, but on the other hand, it calls us to face the challenge of participating in the restoration of all of these relationships in light of the restored relationship with God that has been made possible in Christ. We are called, in other words, to join in the fight against the powers of chaos and destruction that human sin has unleashed. That these powers are real and that evil has become embedded not only in individual human hearts but in historical structures, societies, and institutions means, of course, that often an individual or community's experience of brokenness and the curse of the land may have much (or everything) to do with the general brokenness of humanity's relationship with God and the earth and little to do with their own actions or relationship to God. (We think, for example, of the dramatically unequal ways in which people in the majority world suffer the negative consequences of the rich world's exporting of its consumer waste or of the

---

12. Cf. John J. Bimson, "Reconsidering a 'Cosmic Fall,'" *Science and Christian Belief* 18 (2006): 63–81. For a strong defense of the contrary view, that the curse necessarily entails some sort of change in the very makeup of creation itself (though he does not specify precisely what this means), see Robin Routledge, "Cursing and Chaos: The Impact of Human Sin on Creation and the Environment in the Old Testament," in *As Long as the Earth Endures*, 70–91.

unequally distributed consequences of global climate change.) But, more hopefully, so too can people benefit from the effects of the righteous who have gone before them and from a wider context of faithfulness, responsibility, and appropriate care for the land. Above all, it ought to be in churches and Christian communities that it is possible to witness and experience something of the health and wholeness that God intends in our relationships with each other and with the earth too. This, after all, was Israel's calling: to be a nation where others could see in the blessings of life and fruitfulness of the land that the God of Israel was the one true God.

THE EARTH MOURNS

Sadly, of course, the experience of biblical Israel proves to be a recapitulation of the "fall" of Adam and Eve. The nation is described throughout the Old Testament as rejecting God's purposes, turning aside from the prescribed way of life, and experiencing brokenness as a result. The prophets try, over and over, to call the nation back to God's covenant, to wake the people up to the reality of their ruptured relationship with God and the consequences it is having for themselves, their land, and all of life.

As creation itself was a witness to the covenant God established with Israel, so again is all of creation called upon as a witness to testify against the people who have broken the terms of the covenant:

> Hear me, you heavens! Listen, earth! For the LORD has spoken: "I reared children and brought them up, but they have rebelled against me. The ox knows its master, the donkey its owner's manger, but Israel does not know, my people do not understand." (Isa. 1:2–3)

> Listen to what the LORD says: "Stand up, plead my case before the mountains; let the hills hear what you have to say. Hear, you mountains, the LORD's accusation; listen, you everlasting foundations of the earth. For the LORD has a case against his people; he is lodging a charge against Israel." (Mic 6:1–2)

Creation joins the prophets and God himself in bearing witness against the people's evil and injustice. (Notice too how in Isaiah 1 animals serve as a foil for the people; they "naturally" know and do what is required of them, whereas people too often do not.) Creation has a particular reason to join in the lawsuit, because it turns out that the land and its creatures now find themselves suffering due to the actions of God's people. As a result of the people's failure to honor God and keep his statutes, Isaiah says that, "Your country [or "land"; Heb. *erets*] is desolate" (Isa. 1:7). In Micah, too, the result of the people's injustice is desolation and famine:

> You will eat but not be satisfied; your stomach will still be empty. You will store up but save nothing, because what you save I will give to the sword. You will

plant but not harvest; you will press olives but not use the oil, you will crush grapes but not drink the wine. (Mic. 6:14–15)

We are reminded of Deuteronomy, of the blessings and curses Moses set before the people at the establishment of God's covenant. The Hebrew prophets apply the terms of this covenant to their own day, perceiving, as Hilary Marlow has shown, an intimate connection between faithfulness to God, the establishment of justice, and the health of the land.[13] In dozens of texts of the Hebrew prophets, then, the earth itself, and all of its life, is portrayed as suffering as a consequence of the people's sin and injustice. Consider the following examples, a small selection from many that could be cited:

Hear the word of the LORD, you Israelites, because the LORD has a charge to bring against you who live in the land: "There is no faithfulness, no love, no acknowledgment of God in the land. There is only cursing, lying and murder, stealing and adultery; they break all bounds, and bloodshed follows bloodshed. Because of this the land dries up [or 'mourns'], and all who live in it waste away; the beasts of the field, the birds in the sky and the fish in the sea are swept away." (Hos. 4:1–3)

I looked at the earth, and it was formless and empty; and at the heavens, and their light was gone. I looked at the mountains, and they were quaking; all the hills were swaying. I looked, and there were no people; every bird in the sky had flown away. I looked, and the fruitful land was a desert; all its towns lay in ruins before the LORD, before his fierce anger. This is what the LORD says: "The whole land will be ruined, though I will not destroy it completely. Therefore the earth will mourn and the heavens above grow dark, because I have spoken and will not relent, I have decided and will not turn back." (Jer. 4:23–28)

Why has the land been ruined and laid waste like a desert that no one can cross? The LORD said, "It is because they have forsaken my law, which I set before them; they have not obeyed me or followed my law. Instead, they have followed the stubbornness of their hearts; they have followed the Baals, as their ancestors taught them." (Jer. 9:12–14)

How long will the land lie parched [or "mourn"] and the grass in every field be withered? Because those who live in it are wicked, the animals and birds have perished. Moreover, the people are saying, "He will not see what happens to us." (Jer. 12:4)

---

13. Hilary Marlow, "Law and the Ruining of the Land: Deuteronomy and Jeremiah in Dialogue," *Political Theology* 14 (2013): 650–60; cf. idem, *Biblical Prophets and Contemporary Environmental Ethics*; Terrence E. Fretheim, *God and World in the Old Testament:* *A Relational Theology of Creation* (Nashville: Abingdon, 2005); Christopher J. H. Wright, *Old Testament Ethics for the People of God* (Downers Grove, IL: IVP Academic, 2011).

Many shepherds will ruin my vineyard and trample down my field; they will turn my pleasant field into a desolate wasteland. It will be made a wasteland, parched and desolate before me [or "it will mourn before me"]; the whole land will be laid waste because there is no one who cares. (Jer. 12:10–11)

The earth dries up [or "mourns"] and withers, the world languishes and withers, the heavens languish with the earth. The earth is defiled by its people; they have disobeyed the laws, violated the statutes and broken the everlasting covenant. Therefore a curse consumes the earth; its people must bear their guilt. Therefore earth's inhabitants are burned up, and very few are left. The new wine dries up and the vine withers; all the merrymakers groan. (Isa. 24:4–7)

In these texts, as in many others, drought, disease, ruined land, depopulation, and the death of other creatures are the consequences of human sin. In Isaiah 24:5, the problem is the people's breaking of the "everlasting covenant," likely a reference to the Deuteronomic covenant but also hinting at a more fundamental and universal breaking of the relationship between God, his human creatures, and the rest of creation. The reference may invoke the Noahic covenant and the establishment of a relationship between God and all of life that goes back to the creation narrative itself.[14] An echo of the creation narrative is certainly evident in Jeremiah 4, where the result of God's judgment is described as the undoing of the order established in creation. Darkness and ruin and chaos mean a return to the "formless and empty" state (v. 23) that existed before God called the world into being (Gen. 1:2). The sense here is that human evil and injustice lead, via God's judgment, to disorder and ultimately de-creation. In this context of cosmic upheaval, it is no wonder, then, that the earth itself is said to mourn (Jer. 4:28), lamenting the fate that has come upon her.

Notice how Jeremiah 4 and Isaiah 24 universalize Israel's experience on the land and apply it to the experience of all of creation. It seems necessary in these texts to translate, as the NIV does, the Hebrew *erets* as "earth" rather than just the "land" of Israel or Judah (which seems more narrowly to be the focus in some of the other texts cited above). The description of the plight of the cosmos is particularly vivid in Isaiah 24. The heavens along with the earth "languish" (or "wither/droop"), the land is "defiled" or polluted by its human inhabitants, and a "curse" consumes the earth. The word for "curse" is different than that used in Genesis 3, but what is described here is nonetheless, in some sense, an outworking of the effects of the curse pronounced in Genesis. Jeremiah's later description of God's judgment similarly seems to echo the language of the Genesis curse on the land: "They will sow wheat but reap thorns; they will wear themselves out but gain nothing" (Jer. 12:13). The Genesis

14. For a discussion of the options here, see Jonathan Moo, "Romans 8.19–22 and Isaiah's Cosmic Covenant," *New Testament Studies* 54 (2008): 74–89, here p. 85, n. 41.

curse on the land, particularized in the threatened curses of Deuteronomy, is now instantiated in the experience of God's people and is again universalized in the visions of Isaiah and Jeremiah. Israel's experience of God's judgment in drought and devastated land is a picture of the plight of the whole earth when its people live in injustice and violence and sin and fail to honor God as God.

The earth is portrayed in Isaiah 24:4 and many of these related texts as experiencing severe drought: it "dries up" and "withers." The Hebrew verb translated by the NIV as "dries up," however, is more often used to refer to mourning (as it is indeed translated by the NIV in Jer. 4:28, quoted above). In fact, the early Greek translators of Isaiah 24:4 understood the reference to be to the mourning of the earth itself, and probably this metaphorical sense should be maintained both here and, as suggested above, in Hosea 4:3, Jeremiah 12, and the various other prophetic texts where the earth or parts of the earth are described as "mourning" in the context of drought and devastation (Amos 1:2; Jer. 23:9–12; Isa. 33:7–9; Joel 1:5–20).[15] As in its role as a witness in the covenant lawsuit brought against God's people, the earth has its own voice, a voice that is raised in mourning and, like the ground that received Abel's blood, crying out for justice. The praise that all of creation offers to God, merely by being itself, has not ceased, but there are darker notes now too. Lament and sorrow have become an inevitable part of the earth's repertoire.

THE CREATION GROANS

The apostle Paul picks up on this motif. In keeping with the universalization of the plight of the land and the eschatological hope for new life that is already evident in Isaiah 24, Paul perceives that the entire creation is groaning in its current experience of subjection, futility, and ruin, even as it awaits a better future:

> For the creation waits in eager expectation for the children of God to be revealed. For the creation was subjected to frustration, not by its own choice, but by the will of the one who subjected it, in hope that the creation itself will be liberated from its bondage to decay and brought into the freedom and glory of the children of God. We know that the whole creation has been groaning as in the pains of childbirth right up to the present time. Not only so, but we ourselves, who have the firstfruits of the Spirit, groan inwardly as we wait eagerly for our adoption to sonship, the redemption of our bodies. (Rom. 8:19–23)

This is an important text for the way in which it highlights the inclusion of all of creation in the hope of the gospel, something which Paul rarely spells out as clearly

---

15. For another metaphorical use of the verb in this sense, and not in a context of drought, see Isa. 3:26: "The gates of Zion will lament and mourn." On the double meaning of the Hebrew word *abel* in Isa. 24 and related texts, see Katherine M. Hayes, *The Earth Mourns: Prophetic Metaphor and Oral Aesthetic* (Leiden: Brill, 2002), 12–18.

as he does here. We will therefore return to this passage in our discussion of Paul's vision of the new creation. For now, however, we are concerned more narrowly with the light this text sheds on the meaning of creation's "falleness."

What is evident first of all is that *something* is indeed wrong with creation now. Notice that the focus is on non-human creation: though the word used for "creation" here usually encompasses all created things, including human beings, in these verses, the "creation" is distinguished from and compared with the "children of God." So something like the so-called "natural world" must be particularly in view. Just as we presently "groan" as we wait for the resurrection, the "redemption of our bodies," so too does the rest of creation groan in longing for that day when God's children will be fully revealed for who they are. On that day, Paul says, all of creation will share in the freedom and glory that pertains to the resurrection life of the children of God. The "groaning" of creation in the meantime, as it is described here, picks up the language of mourning used in Isaiah and elsewhere to describe the plight of the earth when subject to human evil and injustice, by experiencing drought and ruin.[16] Paul also develops the eschatological thrust already implicit in the context of Isaiah 24–27: the groaning of creation is in anticipation of something better, like the birth pangs of a woman with child.

For the time being, though, creation finds itself subjected to "frustration" and in bondage to "decay." To be enslaved to "decay" might suggest the natural process of decomposition, disintegration, and death that perhaps will no longer apply or will look different in the new creation. Other texts certainly celebrate the time of resurrection and the new heavens and new earth as a time when death is no more (e.g., 1 Cor. 15:54 [citing Isa. 25:8]; Rev. 21:4). Paul himself uses the same word for "decay" elsewhere to contrast our present bodies that are sown in "corruption" (NIV "perishable") to our resurrection bodies, which will be raised "incorruptible" (NIV "imperishable"; 1 Cor. 15:42, 50). Yet the word for "decay" used here may also refer more generally to the "ruin" or destruction of the earth that is the result of human sin. It is the same word that the Greek translator of Isaiah 24:3 uses to describe the earth being "laid waste," and a related verb is used to describe the "ruin" of the earth by human beings that leads God to "ruin" the earth in the flood (Gen. 6:12–13; cf. Isa. 24:1). The word is often used for the moral corruption of humanity, and though the creation itself is not "corrupt" in this sense (being "subjected" against its own volition), it is likely that Paul sees its slavery to "decay" or "ruin" as intimately linked to the immorality of the human beings who are meant to be its rulers.

This is further hinted at in the description of creation's subjection to "frustration." To be subjected to "frustration" or "futility" is to fail to reach the ends for

---

16. For an extended argument that it is Isa. 24 that is particularly in view, see Jonathan Moo, "Romans 8.19–22 and Isaiah's Cosmic Covenant."

which God intended creation. There is a link here to the "futility" that human beings experience as a result of their failure to worship and glorify God, a situation Paul described earlier in his letter: "For although they knew God, they neither glorified him as God nor gave thanks to him, but their thinking became futile and their foolish hearts were darkened" (Rom. 1:21). This link is strengthened when we consider what Paul might mean by creation's "subjection" and humankind's role in it.

Who is the "one who subjected" creation? Given that the subjection was done on the basis of the hope that creation would then come to share in the freedom and glory of the children of God, it can be none other than God himself. He alone would have the power both to condemn creation to its present state and to ensure its glorious future. Yet, if we ask *how* God subjected creation to futility, we find that the only answer can be that God subjected creation to futility by subjecting creation to Adam and to all of humankind. In giving humankind dominion over creation, creation's fate became linked to ours. When Adam and all humankind turns away from the living God and our lives become empty and futile (all is "futile," says Ecclesiastes, using the same word [translated as "meaningless" in the NIV]), creation thus finds itself subject to our futility and emptiness. It suffers, as the prophets describe time and again, the consequences of human sin and injustice.

> "God subjected all things to Adam, and that included subjecting creation to fallen Adam, to share in his fallenness."
>
> James D. G. Dunn [17]

For Paul, as for the prophets before him, this suffering of creation could no doubt be discerned especially in times of severe drought and famine, in places where the land was being devastated by warfare, and perhaps in the loss of animals and the depopulation of ruined lands—all as much everyday realities in the first century as they are today.[18] What is different today is that such suffering of creation is on a truly global scale that only Paul's biblically trained imagination could have grasped, and the connection between creation's current suffering and human sin and ignorance has become much more evident. The Hebrew prophets focused especially on social injustice, failure to care for the poor and the weak, violence, bloodshed, and a general rejection of God and lack of knowledge of God as causes behind the ruin of the land. In our day, such connections are all the more evident, aware as we are of the inextricable connections between social and environmental justice, violence toward other people and our treatment of the land,

---

17. *Romans 1–8*, WBC 38a (Nashville: Thomas Nelson, 1988), 471.

18. It is sometimes suggested that Paul has in view such dramatic events as earthquakes and volcanoes, in keeping with the idea found in some other texts that such signs would precede the messianic age, but in our view, the messianic woes are not strictly in view in Rom. 8. The connections to Genesis (in the subjection of creation) and the prophetic tradition of the mourning earth (in the "groaning" of creation), as it experiences the ongoing effects of human sin, tell against the messianic woes interpretation. Paul does not, in this context at least, interpret the present suffering of the children of God or the groaning of creation as signs that the end is near; rather, he merely contrasts what is now generally the case (suffering, subjection to ruin, groaning) with the glorious freedom to come at the time of the resurrection.

and the cumulative, destructive effects of greed, corruption, and ignorance on the ability of the earth to sustain life.

But of course we live in a time when "ecological sin" in its own right has also become a sad reality, if we take seriously what Scripture reveals about God's purposes for his creation and our growing knowledge of the effects that many of our actions can have on other life. For an ancient Israelite, it was possible to choose directly whether or not to treat domestic animals well, whether or not to take the mother along with the eggs of wild birds being harvested, whether or not to fallow fields every seventh year, and whether or not to live life in general as if the land were a gift that belongs ultimately to God. The choices made could be a reflection of one's relationship to God, and the consequences of poor choices, of poor stewardship of the land, would eventually be felt directly too, at least on a small scale. But with the extraordinarily expanded possibilities in our day, linked to industrialization, globalization, technology, and a vastly larger human population, the choices we face individually and collectively have far greater weight and far more wide-reaching effects. Each of us in the wealthier parts of the world today has resources and possibilities open to us that only a king or queen would have had in ages past. Our access to cheap energy alone provides each American with the equivalent of hundreds of full-time human workers. Yet, because it is so easy for us to access such power, we understandably find it difficult to see that the use of this energy might entail significant responsibilities too. It is hard for us to grasp that our everyday decisions can have wide-reaching effects when they are so commonplace and easy to make.

GOD WEEPS FOR CREATION

The precise cause of creation's suffering is variously described in Scripture as the direct or inevitable result of human sin and as the direct result of God's judgment upon his sinful people.[19] That the earth should suffer from God's judgment through no fault of its own ("not of its own will," Paul says) may raise questions for us. Yet this is finally but an extension of the interrelatedness of humankind and the rest of creation and a sign of the far-reaching consequences of our sin. It is in any case instructive to observe God's own attitude toward the suffering of the earth. Notice, for example, in Jeremiah, how God himself laments for the land that experiences the effects of his judgment on human sin:

> I will weep and wail for the mountains and take up a lament concerning the wilderness grasslands. They are desolate and untraveled, and the lowing of cattle is not heard. The birds have all fled and the animals are gone. (Jer. 9:10)

---

19. It is also possible to identify the theme of creation's own fighting back against human evil, especially in the book of Revelation. In this case, it might be said that creation joins with the Creator and serves as an instrument in his judgment.

In this striking text, we get a glimpse of God's sorrow at the ruin of creation and the loss of animal life. Even if its proximate cause is God's own judgment upon human sin, this is not finally what he intends for his people and his earth. Indeed, in Romans we learn that God himself by his Spirit joins alongside us and all of creation in groaning, interceding for us in accordance with God's will (Rom. 8:26–27).

God's response provides some guidance for our own appropriate response to the ruin of the earth. Lament and mourning over human sin and injustice, as well as over the suffering of all of creation, is a necessary part of the life of the people of God. Yet out of our lament ought also come repentance. In the book of Joel, which describes a destructive locust plague of mythic proportions (echoing one of the threatened plagues described in Deuteronomy as a punishment of the people's sin), we find such a call for repentance:

> "Even now," declares the LORD, "return to me with all your heart, with fasting and weeping and mourning." Rend your heart and not your garments. Return to the LORD your God, for he is gracious and compassionate, slow to anger and abounding in love, and he relents from sending calamity. (Joel 2:12–13)

The result of repentance will be renewed blessing of the people and the land together, for "the LORD was jealous for his land and took pity on his people" (v. 18). What might such repentance, cries for God's mercy, and a return to justice and righteousness mean in our day for ourselves, our societies, and the earth itself?

OUR RESPONSE

If the land mourns, creation groans, and God himself weeps over the ruin of the earth, we surely cannot sit idly by when we see the destruction of creation. It remains possible for some people in some times and places to ignore creation's plight, to deny the reality of its groaning. There are today prominent Christians in well-off parts of the world who work hard to convince others that the sort of data we will present in chapter 13 about the state of the earth and its life is unimportant or of little concern to Christians. There are even some who claim that a good and gracious God would never let us or the earth experience major consequences from such apparently innocuous and otherwise beneficial things as burning fossil fuels, for example. Such Christians rightly recognize God's goodness and his commitment to preserve his creation, and they rightly celebrate human ingenuity, the many gifts with which the burning of fossil fuels provide us, for example, and the technologies that have benefited us all. Yet, to pretend that even good things cannot be poorly used or abused, or that a good and gracious God would not let us experience the consequences of our actions is to fail utterly to recognize the significant moral responsibility with which Scripture says God entrusts his human creatures. This line of thought sounds rather like the false prophets of Jeremiah's day who denied that anything was wrong or that God would ever act to judge the people's sin:

> But I said, "Alas, Sovereign LORD! The prophets keep telling them, 'You will not see the sword or suffer famine. Indeed, I will give you lasting peace in this place.'" Then the LORD said to me, "The prophets are prophesying lies in my name. I have not sent them or appointed them or spoken to them. They are prophesying to you false visions, divinations, idolatries and the delusions of their own minds." (Jer. 14:13–14)

Wearing blinders can enable us to ignore the consequences of our actions for other people and for all of life now and in the future, and conveniently can allow us to carry on with our current way of life and do whatever we like. Yet surely the God who calls us to justice and mercy and who weeps over ruined mountains and withered grasslands would have his people take seriously our responsibilities in and for his creation. Surely our call is to face social and environmental challenges squarely and honestly, and to work creatively to consider how our lives as God's children might even now begin to reflect God's purposes for us and his creation.

SUMMARY

This chapter has focused on the reality that creation is "fallen." Yet we have discovered that the "fallenness" of non-human creation as it is described in Scripture consists primarily or exclusively in its broken relationship with us. The non-human creation is inextricably bound up with humankind, and we with it. The whole earth therefore suffers the ongoing results of our broken relationship with God and our sinfulness, injustice, and failure to be the people God calls us to be. Yet our context is shaped not just by the fall but also by the power of the new creation, the kingdom of God inaugurated by Christ. So the "fallenness" of the world is not an excuse merely to accept the fact that creation suffers. As will become especially evident in later chapters, we are called to live now as members of God's kingdom, as new creations in Christ who live as those who have been reconciled to God in Christ and therefore are also being reconciled to others and to creation too, participating in the renewal of right relationships made possible in Christ.

Does this mean we ought to expect to bring in the conditions of the new creation in the present? The question assumes, of course, that we actually know what those conditions are. But, as we will see, even the Spirit-inspired imagination of the biblical writers can only begin to reveal something of what life in the presence of God in the new heavens and new earth will look like. So, as always, we must acknowledge our ignorance. Moreover, we must not neglect what we know from Scripture to be good in our pursuit of what we think may be better in the new creation. For example, it would be possible to conclude from passages that describe the end of death and suffering in the new age that such things as predation, decomposition, and animal death will one day be no more. Yet, even if this were true (and, again, we must at this point acknowledge our ignorance about precisely what the images and metaphors of Scripture point to), to think that we could bring in such a state now would be not only rather absurdly impossible but also would involve the denial of the very real goodness of the earth as God created it and as we still encounter it, in all of its wildness and diversity. This is why we began this chapter with a reminder of the goodness of all of God's creation: this world and all its creatures are valued by God and worthy of our care.

The whole point of Paul's argument about the groaning of creation in Romans 8 is that this is a temporary state, as is our own suffering. God himself has acted in Jesus Christ to redeem and reconcile all things back to himself, renewing human beings in his likeness so that we, as God's adopted children, may share in the freedom and glory of his Son. And since the rest of creation has been bound to us from the beginning, so too is it promised the same glorious future with us. Yet, for the time being, creation has not yet reached the end God intends for it, and, like us, it yearns for that future day of resurrection and new creation. In the next chapter, we begin to focus on that future hope as it has been inaugurated and made possible in and through the person of Jesus Christ.

RELEVANT QUESTIONS

1. What are the signs of creation's brokenness today? How do we avoid the temptation to claim that anything we don't like or understand is due to the "fall" and develop a more biblical understanding of the causes and results of creation's brokenness?

2. Suggest some implications of the possibility presented in this chapter that the "curse" involves in part the frustration of God's purposes for his people and his creation. What difference does the coming of Christ make to this situation?

3. If we acknowledge that creation will continue to suffer brokenness until the return of Christ, what is our goal in caring for creation now?

4. What does God's response to creation's suffering tell us about our appropriate response?

CHAPTER 7

JESUS AND CREATION

THE SIGNIFICANCE OF JESUS'S INCARNATION

The Word became flesh and made his dwelling among us. (John 1:14)

There is no more dramatic demonstration of the goodness of creation than the incarnation of Jesus Christ. That the one who is wholly other, the Lord of the universe, should take up the material stuff of this earth and enter into the earthy, dusty, sweaty, bloody life of this world is the most radical affirmation that the given world remains the arena of God's glory, however threatened by sin and corruption it might be. The ethos this act implies is more affirming of the integrity and value of created things than pantheism or, indeed, any other system of belief. All things are not gods: they have their own integrity, they are what they are. And yet in the goodness that material creation has by virtue of being the creation of a good and self-giving God, it has the potential to serve even as the vehicle of divine revelation. It is taken up by God in the incarnation to reveal himself to the world that is his own.

We might have expected the supreme revelation of the one who "lives in unapproachable light, whom no one has seen nor can see" (1 Tim. 6:16) to be an ineffable vision of light or fire, an unintelligible whisper or clap of thunder, a heavenly vision of otherworldly splendor. Yet the New Testament writers claim that to truly know God, we must look to Jesus, an embodied human person of flesh and blood, like us "in every way" (Heb. 2:17). The New Testament emphasizes that Jesus is included in the identity of the one God and in fact participated in the very act of creation itself: "Through him all things were made; without him nothing was made that has been made" (John 1:3; cf. 1 Cor. 8:6; Col. 1:16; Heb. 1:2).[1] Moreover, Jesus sustains the world, holding all things together by his power (Col. 1:17; Heb. 1:3). It is thus the most shocking claim of Christian Scripture that it is this same Jesus, the creator and sustainer of all that exists, who takes on flesh, becoming a part of his own creation.

> "So Jesus, in not clinging to the form of God but accepting the humility of the incarnation and the death of the cross, restores the glory of creatureliness. The incarnation affirms that creation is good, not that it is nice or beautiful, but that it is good because it is in this relationship of loving dependence on the self-giving of God."
>
> *Rowan Williams* [2]

---

1. On this theme and its implications, see especially Sean M. McDonough, *Christ as Creator: Origins of a New Testament Doctrine* (Oxford: Oxford University Press, 2010).

2. "Creation, Creativity and Creatureliness."

The incarnation rules out for Christians any philosophy that would deny the reality or goodness of the physical world. If God himself can take on the stuff of this earth, then the material stuff of this earth cannot be evil, a burden to be got rid of, or a hindrance to encountering God. The incarnation furthermore reveals a God who binds himself to all of his creation. And, as we will see, in Christ's physical resurrection from the dead, we are given a vision of creation's *telos*, its ultimate goal.

In keeping with the rest of the New Testament and the teaching of the early church, encapsulated in the creeds, Jesus is presented by the author of Hebrews as having been made like us "in every way" (Heb. 2:17). Jesus did not merely appear to be human. He was, without giving up his divine nature, fully a flesh-and-blood human being in every respect (except without sin; cf. Heb. 4:15). Given what we have learned from Scripture about what it is to be human, that we are earthy creatures, bound to and caught up with all of life on earth (see chap. 4), Christ's incarnation thus links God intimately to the entirety of his creation. We have already observed that creation's fate is connected throughout Scripture to God's image bearers, to his human creatures. Now its fate is bound up with and its hope assured in the one who is the true image of God, the one who is at once the exact imprint of the eternal God and fully a part of his created world, and the one who acts to renew the image of God in us too.

It has sometimes been asked whether God could have become incarnate in, say, a whale or a lion or a sparrow, rather than a human being. Given the inextricable connectedness of all of God's good creation, there is no *a priori* reason that God could not. In fact, such speculation helpfully reminds us of just how profound is Christ's humbling of himself. He did not consider equality with God something to be used for his own advantage but willingly took the very nature of a servant (Phil. 2:6–7). Being human ourselves, we find it difficult to grasp the depth of God's condescension in taking on our nature. We fail to consider that on the scale of God's descent to us, his incarnation in the form of an earthworm

"He is present both in the whole [of creation] and in the parts. What, then, is there incredible in His manifesting Himself through that in which He is? By His own power He enters completely into each and all, and orders them throughout ungrudgingly; and, had He so willed, He could have revealed Himself and His Father by means of sun or moon or sky or earth or fire or water. . . . Some may then ask, why did He not manifest Himself by means of other and nobler parts of creation, and use some nobler instrument, such as sun or moon or stars or fire or air, instead of mere man? The answer is this. The Lord did not come to make a display. He came to heal and to teach suffering men. . . . Moreover, nothing in creation had erred from the path of God's purpose for it, save only man. Sun, moon, heaven, stars, water, air, none of these had swerved from their order, but, knowing the Word as their Maker and their King, remained as they were made. Men alone having rejected what is good, have invented nothings instead of the truth, and have ascribed the honour due to God and the knowledge concerning Him to daemons and men in the form of stones. Obviously the Divine goodness could not overlook so grave a matter as this. But men could not recognise Him as ordering and ruling creation as a whole. So what does He do? He takes to Himself for instrument a part of the whole, namely a human body, and enters into that."

Athanasius[3]

---

3. *On the Incarnation*, 7.42–43.

would not be so very different. Yet, whatever the value of such speculation, the particularity of the incarnation finally matters. God did not become incarnate in just any creature, but as a human being. It was human beings, after all, who were uniquely created in the image of God. And God did not become incarnate in just any human being, but as a Jew in the line of David. These are not, moreover, incidental details; they are in fact central to God's redemptive purposes.

It is necessary that Christ be a human being if he, as the "Last Adam," is to reverse the curse and do what we could not do for ourselves, if he is to reveal to us what it truly is to bear God's image and reconcile us to God. It is necessary likewise that he be a Jew if Jesus is to bring redemption and fulfill God's purposes for his chosen people Israel, through whom he had promised to bless all peoples. It was moreover through God's chosen anointed king in the line of David that he promised to bring salvation to his people and to all of creation. So the particularity of the incarnation matters. And if Jesus reveals to us what it is to be truly human, to bear the image of God and to live as members of his kingdom, then it is not only the central events of his birth, death, and resurrection to which we must attend, but also to the particularities of his life and his teaching. In the rest of this chapter, then, we do just this, concentrating on those themes that are relevant for our purposes in exploring a theology of creation care.

THE PEACEABLE KINGDOM OF GOD'S MESSIAH

Jesus's identity as both the new Adam and new Israel is evident already in one of the first events of his ministry as narrated in the Gospels. In his temptation in the wilderness, we see Jesus facing a test like the one Adam and Eve faced in Eden and the one Israel faced in her wilderness wanderings. In fact, it is a form of the same temptation we all face. It is the temptation to refuse to acknowledge our dependence upon God, to look elsewhere for our source of life, and to reject our identity as human beings and the children of God.

Jesus has been fasting for forty days (no incidental number—recall Israel's forty years in the wilderness), and he is hungry (Matt. 4:2; Luke 4:2–3; cf. Mark 1:13). In this state of weakness and hunger, Jesus is tempted by the devil to fulfill his immediate desire for food and to do so by the easiest and most efficient means possible: use his divine power and turn stones into bread (Matt. 4:3; Luke 4:3). And Jesus can do this if he chooses; he and the devil are agreed on who he is and what power he has. (This is where the temptation Jesus faces is obviously different and on another scale than the ones we face!) Yet Jesus refuses to usurp God's purposes, to grasp the power that could be his and use it for his own ends. Instead, he voluntarily chooses restraint and the ordinary limitations of human life. So too with the following two temptations: Jesus will not put God to the test, taking advantage of the divine protection that is his, nor will he choose the easy way of inheriting the kingdoms of this world. Instead, God's anointed one accepts the limitations of creaturely life and heads down the path that leads finally to the cross.

Jesus does what we could not—what Israel, what Adam, what we all fail to do. He rejects Satan and shows us what it is to be truly human, to live wholly in dependence upon God. In Mark's version of the temptation story, we get a glimpse of the result of such obedience and faithfulness. Mark is much more concise than Matthew or Luke. Here is all he has to say about Jesus's temptation:

> At once the Spirit sent him out into the wilderness, and he was in the wilderness forty days, being tempted by Satan. He was with the wild animals, and angels attended him. (Mark 1:12–13)

Like Matthew, Mark describes the temptation as instigated by Satan and as ending with the ministering of angels. Satan is clearly the source of evil and stands opposed to Jesus in this passage. The angels, on the other hand, are there to support him; they stand clearly on the side of the Son of God. But in-between, Mark says that Jesus was "with the wild animals." Wild animals can of course be a threat and a danger to someone in the wilderness, so they potentially could be seen as part of the opposition and testing Jesus faces. But Mark says that Jesus was *with* the wild animals, and for Jesus to be "with" someone, or for someone to be "with" Jesus, is always a good thing in Mark's Gospel. To cite just a few examples: Jesus calls his disciples so "that they might be with him" (3:14); a man freed from demon possession begs Jesus that he might be "with him" (5:18); and Jesus says, "How can the guests of the bridegroom fast while he is with them? They cannot, so long as they have him with them" (2:19).

What could it mean then for Jesus to be "with the wild animals"? As Richard Bauckham has suggested,[4] we think that Mark is alluding in his typically brief and cryptic way to the way in which Jesus is ushering in the peaceable kingdom that Isaiah foresaw would be brought in by God's Spirit-anointed Davidic king (Isa. 11:1–9; cf. 65:25). Wild animals could and can be a threat in our broken world. But no longer in the kingdom of God. Jesus not only undoes the results of Israel's failure to be faithful for forty years in the wilderness of Sinai, he also undoes the results of Adam and all of humanity's rebellion against God. Jesus, the true image of God and faithful servant, is restoring the relationship between humanity and creation, pointing the way toward the peaceable kingdom of God. As the messianic king, Jesus can be truly "with" the wild animals, as God intended from the beginning. The enmity and brokenness that otherwise marks our relationship with non-human creation is being done away with.

---

4. Richard Bauckham, "Jesus and the Wild Animals (Mark 1:13): A Christological Image for an Ecological Age," in *Jesus of Nazareth: Essays on the Historical Jesus and New Testament Christology*, ed. Joel B. Green and Max Turner (Grand Rapids: Eerdmans, 1994), 3–21.

LOOKING TO JESUS TO LEARN WHAT IT IS TO BE HUMAN

We will consider further what life in God's kingdom looks like according to Jesus, but for the moment, it is important to observe how we discover in the temptation of Jesus a model for what it is to be truly human. We learn to be utterly dependent upon the God who provides and so to be free of the fear that leads us to look elsewhere for our fulfillment, to grasp always for more for ourselves, to reject our identity as God's children. Jesus's response to his testing in the wilderness helps us in fact to read the "fall" narrative in Genesis 3 again on its own terms.

It is often tempting to make the human protagonists in Genesis 3 into Promethean heroes, boldly standing up to the powers that be and wresting control of their destiny, whatever the consequences. We can't help but celebrate what seems to be their assertion of independence, seeing their defiance of authority as a necessary step on the way to maturity and adulthood, like the tragic heroes of Milton's *Paradise Lost*. We need to be reminded that this is not the perspective of the biblical writers. For them, the consequences of our failure to live in obedience to and dependence upon God are devastating. We find this hard to grasp because we cannot imagine anything but arbitrary authority. We always are making God into our own image, and we therefore see God as a bully, as someone whose demands are as arbitrary as those of any human ruler. We find it hard to accept a God who is truly transcendent, who needs nothing, and yet who is love and who out of love creates and enters into relationship with what he creates—a God who desires and actually knows what is best, who is the only source of life and love and being. The god we are often tempted to reject is not finally God at all.

Genesis suggests that when we seek to become a law unto ourselves and to become like God, we forget that we are earthly creatures who are sustained always and only in interconnected dependence upon each other, upon the earth itself, and ultimately upon our Creator God. Our hard-won independence thus results, according both to Genesis and the New Testament, not in genuine freedom but in an enslavement to sin that breaks all those relationships that otherwise sustain us. Our attempt to act like gods, to remake the world to suit only our own selfish ends, becomes only a naked will to power that finally separates us from each other and from our Creator. Such a separation is nothing other than death itself.

So in the story of Jesus's temptation, we are challenged again to find our identity and our life wholly in the God who reveals himself in Christ. And, as the rest of the Gospels reveal, we not only see in Jesus a model of what it is to be truly human but in him we are actually made able to share in his abundant life, the life that God intended for us from the beginning. Because Jesus remained obedient, even to death on the cross, he made possible the forgiveness of our sins and our reconciliation with God, the restoration and healing of all those broken relationships described in Genesis—including our broken relationship with the earth and other creatures. The image of God is thus renewed in us, and we are enabled to live as the children of God we were created to be, under the reign of God in Christ.

LOOKING TO JESUS TO LEARN WHAT IT IS TO RULE

It is this reign of God in Christ, his rule over all things, that is central to the meaning of the "kingdom of God" proclaimed by Jesus. Matthew calls it the "kingdom of heaven," meaning not a kingdom located in heaven but a kingdom whose ruler is in heaven ("heaven" being a way of referring to the presence of God, the place of his throne). Jesus famously tells Pilate that his "kingdom is not of this world" (John 18:36). We may be tempted to think Jesus means here that his kingdom has no real connection to the events going on around him, that somehow this heavenly kingdom remains forever ethereal and disconnected from the messy business of this life, of no possible threat to Pilate, the Roman Empire, or any other power structure of the day. But if we read the rest of the Gospels, we will not think this for long. His kingdom may not be *of* this world, but it is assuredly *for* this world.

If we attend to what Jesus actually has to say about the transformed life in the here and now and the reversal of priorities that God's kingdom ushers in, we will see that everything here on earth must change when his kingdom comes. In God's kingdom, it is the meek who inherit the earth (Matt. 5:5),[5] and it is the poor to whom the kingdom belongs (Luke 6:20). The signs of the kingdom's presence are moreover dramatic healing of the sick, physical restoration, raising to life, and liberation. All these are earthly reversals and physical manifestations of God's salvation, and they are inextricable from the good news that Jesus proclaims. This is a kingdom that transforms this world, that gives life and freedom. Finally, consider again that the kingdom of God comes precisely in the flesh and blood incarnation of Jesus, in the bloody and painful death on a cross that he is about to endure, and in his glorious bodily resurrection. These are earth-shattering events—in every sense of the word. No wonder creation itself responds to Jesus's death with earthquakes, splitting rocks, and a darkened sun at noon (Matt. 27:45, 51–53).

To return to John 18:36, it's worth observing that the Greek here suggests that Jesus's kingdom does not have its *origin* "from" (Gk. *ek*) this world. If it did, Jesus

---

5. It is possible to translate the Greek for "earth" in Matt. 5:5 as "land," meaning the "land" of Israel, which would be in keeping with its meaning in the same phrase as it appears in Ps. 37:11: "The meek will inherit the land and enjoy peace and prosperity." Jesus's first Jewish hearers may indeed have heard this as a promise (and politically relevant challenge) regarding to whom the land of Canaan would belong. Yet the universalization of the beatitudes and the good news of the kingdom, which encompasses Jew and Gentile together and is for all of creation, suggests that Jesus's blessing will necessarily have for later readers of Matthew's Gospel a wider referent that encompasses the whole of the earth.

says, his disciples would have used violence to fight back against his arrest, in the way of the servants of worldly kings. But Jesus's authority comes from elsewhere, from beyond the bounds of this creation, from the God of heaven who rules over all things. To encounter Jesus, then, is to experience already the kingdom of God come near (Mark 1:15), a kingdom that re-orders everything around its proper center: "The kingdom of the world has become the kingdom of our Lord and of his Messiah, and he will reign for ever and ever" (Rev. 11:15). Jesus is the true Lord and Ruler of all, God's anointed king, come to claim back his world for himself.

This sovereignty over all things challenges any other claimant to absolute power and authority, any other who would claim to be "Lord." Human beings may rule, as indeed all were created as God's image bearers, but only under the Lordship and authority of the true king. And if we are to know what our derivative rule in creation might look like, we must look first and last to Christ. The author of Hebrews cites Psalm 8's depiction of the exalted role of human beings within creation, which, as we saw in chapter 4, says that human beings have everything put "under their feet" (Heb. 2:8; Ps. 8:6). But the author of Hebrews observes that we don't actually see humanity ruling in creation like this; things are clearly not as they are meant to be. "But," the author goes on to say, "we do see Jesus, who was made lower than the angels for a little while, now crowned with glory and honor because he suffered death, so that by the grace of God he might taste death for everyone" (Heb. 2:9). The role ascribed by the psalmist to human beings is, according to Hebrews, fulfilled only in Christ.

> "We have a heavenly country, but in a sense it is too difficult to love, because we do not know it; above all, in a sense, it is too easy to love, because we can imagine it as we please. We run the risk of loving a fiction under this name. If the love of the fiction is strong enough it makes all virtue easy, but at the same time of little value. Let us love the country here below. It is real; it offers resistance to love. It is this country that God has given us to love. He willed that it should be difficult yet possible to love it."
>
> *Simone Weil*[6]

If we then look to Jesus to know what it is to rule as God's image bearers, what do we discover? We see one who has compassion on all who are helpless, ill, and suffering (Mark 6:34; Matt. 9:36; 14:14; 15:32; 20:34) and who acts to restore and heal them. We see one who refused to exploit his power and divinity, who laid down his life for others, who "made himself nothing" (Phil. 2:7) and went willingly even to death on a cross. We see the one who reveals to us what love is and who demonstrates God's own love for the whole of the cosmos (John 3:16). The example of Christ thus rules out any triumphalist, exploitative, domineering, or selfish exercise of our authority over others or over God's creation. We are called instead to live in the world, in all that we do (including our stewardship of creation), in love, as Jesus did: "This is how love is made complete among us so that we will have confidence on the day of judgment: In this world we are like Jesus" (1 John 4:17).

---

6. Simone Weil, *Waiting for God* (New York: Harper and Row, 1951), 178.

LOOKING WITH JESUS AT CREATION: CONSIDER THE LILIES . . .

We see in Jesus one who is deeply connected to and attentive to the natural world around him. In his life and teaching, we also discover that God's kingdom is one of abundance and overflowing life. Whereas Paul will borrow many of his metaphors and examples from the urban life of the cities where he spends much of his time, Jesus's teachings are deeply rooted in the soil of first-century rural Galilee. His parables most often use images of such things as farms and farmers, vineyards, seeds, fishing, trees, flowers, and birds; his teaching is mostly outside, along the seashore, on a boat, on a mountainside, on the green grass.

It is in fact instructive for those who teach or preach (or write!) to reflect whether our choice of illustrations and stories and metaphors are as attentive to our contexts as were Jesus's and Paul's. Moreover, following Jesus's example by drawing more of our illustrations from the natural world in particular might be a way of helping the church recapture a more fully biblical understanding of God's purposes in creation and redemption. It can help remind people of the beauty and richness of God's world, and might reconnect us with our true identity as created beings who are part of a marvelous creation under the sole sovereignty of God in Christ. So too can illustrations drawn from the world of creation (which, again, does not mean just wild nature but must include those parts of creation where we make our homes and grow our food, our cities and farms) be more inclusive of all whom we seek to reach; everyone, after all, is a part of creation and is intimately connected to and derives their life from God's creation, whether they acknowledge it or not!

In the Gospels, we get a glimpse of the value of the natural world for Jesus and the beauty he sees in it. For example, Jesus uses God's concern for sparrows to assure his disciples of the Father's care for them: "Are not two sparrows sold for a penny? Yet not one of them will fall to the ground outside your Father's care" (Matt. 10:29). If this is the sort of intimate knowledge and care God has for sparrows, how much more for us! So, yes, "you are worth more than many sparrows," Jesus says (10:31; cf. Luke 12:24), and we have here again a firm basis for recognizing the distinctive value of human life. But Jesus's whole point depends upon the fact that sparrows too have worth and significance before God and that each one is worthy of his care.

Jesus also turns to the beauty and abundance of nature to assure his disciples of God's provision for them. "Consider how the wild flowers ["lilies" in many English versions] grow. They do not labor or spin. Yet I tell you, not even Solomon in all his splendor was dressed like one of these" (Luke 12:27). Notice that followers of Jesus are here told to look at the natural world, to appreciate its beauty, and to draw conclusions from it—about the nature of the God who created it and what our response should be. In this case, the appropriate response is to give up our anxiousness for ourselves and not to worry: "If that is how God clothes the grass of the field, which is here today, and tomorrow is thrown into the fire, how much more will he clothe you—you of little faith!" (12:28).

The economy of God's kingdom is based not on scarcity, but on abundance. Jesus's example of the wildflowers and the ravens, earlier in the passage, whom God himself feeds (12:24), is intended to cast out the fear and anxiousness that so often lies behind our worry for ourselves, our grasping acquisitiveness, and our failure to be generous givers. In contrast, Jesus reminds his disciples that their Father in heaven knows all that they need and is able to provide abundantly: "But seek his kingdom, and these things will be given to you as well. Do not be afraid, little flock, for your Father has been pleased to give you the kingdom. Sell your possessions and give to the poor" (12:31–33). Such open-handed generosity in response to God's own generosity is how to store up treasure that will last, treasure that is kept safe for us in heaven, in the presence of God. This is what it is to live as members of Christ's kingdom, "for where your treasure is, there your heart will be also" (12:34).

In John's Gospel, Jesus says that, in contrast to all those who have come before and aimed only to steal and serve themselves, he has come so that his people "may have life, and have it to the full" (John 10:10). Life in God's kingdom is rich and full, overflowing with abundance. Yet to accept God's infinite ability to provide is not to sit back and neglect the very real responsibilities that God gives us, nor is it to squander the gifts he provides. The abundant life is not a profligate life; it is a life of gratitude, joy, and service in God's kingdom. In the *Didache*, a first-century Christian "instruction manual" of how to live as a follower of Christ, we learn that God desires to give his own gifts to everyone. Yet the means by which this is accomplished is actually through the generous giving of his own people (*Didache* 1.5).

When Jesus reveals his power and the abundance of God's kingdom in feeding the five thousand with nothing more than five barley loaves and two fish, he nonetheless tells his disciples, after all have eaten their fill, "Gather the pieces that are left over. Let nothing be wasted" (John 6:12). Even in a context of overflowing, apparently limitless abundance, the gifts of God's creation are not to be disdained, left to rot, or

> "I don't think it is enough appreciated how much an outdoor book the Bible is. It is a 'hypaethral book,' such as Thoreau talked about—a book open to the sky. It is best read and understood outdoors, and the farther outdoors the better. Or that has been my experience of it. Passages that within walls seem improbable or incredible, outdoors seem merely natural. This is because outdoors we are confronted everywhere with wonders; we see that the miraculous is not extraordinary but the common mode of existence. It is our daily bread. Whoever really has considered the lilies of the field or the birds of the air and pondered the improbability of their existence in this warm world within the cold and empty stellar distances will hardly balk at the turning of water into wine—which was, after all, a very small miracle. We forget the greater and still continuing miracle by which water (with soil and sunlight) is turned into grapes."
>
> *Wendell Berry*[7]

---

7. *Sex, Economy, Freedom and Community*, 103.

wasted. We are challenged here to see that, even if we faced no crisis in our use and distribution of resources or in the functioning of the earth's ecosystems, we would all the same be called as God's people to a carefulness and appropriate restraint that reflects our appreciation of the goodness both of our own limited creatureliness and of the gifts God provides.

LOOKING TO JESUS FOR CREATION'S GOAL: RESURRECTION AND NEW CREATION

We will consider in the next two chapters the present and future implications of the kingdom of God that Jesus inaugurates, the new creation that breaks into the old. It is worth observing briefly, even now, that any discussion of Christian eschatology and the fate of the cosmos must begin and end with the death and resurrection of Jesus. It is both the sign of the general resurrection and new creation to come, and the means by which it has been made possible. And, in keeping with what we might expect based on the miracle of the incarnation, the Gospels make it clear that Jesus's resurrection is a *physical* resurrection—not an abandonment of created existence, but a taking up and transformation of it.

The resurrected Jesus is indeed transformed: he is not always immediately recognized by his disciples, he manages to appear to them in locked rooms (though whether or not this has to do with the nature of his transformed body is impossible to say), and in his transformed body, he ascends back to the Father, one day to return. Yet the resurrected Jesus has flesh and bones; he is not a ghost (Luke 24:39). His body bears the marks of his crucifixion; his disciples can touch his hands and side. He cooks fish over a fire on the beach; he breaks bread and shares meals with his disciples. Even the emptiness of the tomb serves to illustrate the reality that the resurrection takes up and transforms the material stuff of this earth.

The physical resurrection of Christ is thus a sign—the only one we have—of what our own future resurrection might be like, of what life will be like at the time of what Jesus calls the *palingenesia*, the "renewal of all things" (Matt. 19:28). We see that God is not finished with our physical bodies, nor with the whole of his good creation. And it is Christ's death and resurrection, his victory over sin and death, that has accomplished this redemption of the entire world for himself.

CREATION'S RESPONSE TO JESUS

That Christ's death and resurrection has consequences for the entire cosmos is hinted at in the reverberations within the natural world that attend his death and resurrection. At his crucifixion, darkness covers the land at midday (Matt. 27:45; Mark 15:33); at his death, "the earth shook, the rocks split and the tombs broke open"

(Matt. 27:51–52); and at the resurrection, "there was a violent earthquake" (Matt. 28:2). The apostle Peter interprets all of these signs, and the coming of the Spirit at Pentecost, as fulfillment of Joel's prophecy of the "glorious day of the Lord," when God would "show wonders in the heavens above and signs on the earth below" (Acts 2:16–21). Creation responds to the coming of its king. Already in Jesus's ministry, he observes that if his disciples kept quiet about his coming as king, the stones themselves would cry out (Luke 19:40). And in the book of Revelation, we see that all of creation does indeed cry out in celebration at the coming of Christ.

In the Book of Revelation, creation is often portrayed as in upheaval, suffering from God's cosmic judgments, from the evil of those who are described as "those who destroy the earth" (Rev. 11:18), and from its own participation as God's instrument in the fight against those forces arrayed against his kingdom. Yet, as in the Psalms where the natural world is often described as offering hymns and praise to God, Revelation reveals that all of creation still goes on singing praises to God and Christ. This is seen in the four living creatures around the throne, who, as representatives of all of creation,[8] offer ceaseless praise to the Creator and Redeemer (4:8; 5:8, 14; 7:11; 19:4). Most dramatically, at the conclusion of John's magnificent description of the redemption wrought by the Lamb that was slain, he says, "Then I heard every creature in heaven and on earth and under the earth and on the sea, and all that is in them, saying: 'To him who sits on the throne and to the Lamb be praise and honor and glory and power, for ever and ever!'" (5:13).

As we will see in the next two chapters, all of creation is included in the benefits of Christ's redemption of his people. So it is no wonder that the entirety of creation should form a cosmic chorus of praise for Christ and what he has accomplished. It also makes it less surprising that, in the longer ending of Mark's Gospel (whether or not we treat this as Scripture), Jesus instructs his disciples to "Go into all the world and preach the gospel to all creation" (Mark 16:15). As Paul writes, it is precisely the good news of Christ's reconciliation of *all* things, "whether things on earth or things in heaven" (Col. 1:20) that "has been proclaimed to every creature under heaven" (Col. 1:23). The cosmic scope of this good news and its implications for a biblical theology of creation care will be explored in the next two chapters. For now it is enough to reflect on our own appropriate response to the revelation of God in Christ. We are surely called upon again to join alongside the rest of creation to offer ourselves in worship to our Creator and Redeemer.

---

8. As early rabbinic commentators suggested with respect to these beasts in Ezekiel, they are likely intended to be representatives of the entirety of animal life (one with a lion's head standing in for wild animals, an ox for domestic animals, an eagle for birds, and a man for humanity), just as the twenty-four elders in Revelation likely represent the fullness of God's people (twelve tribes plus twelve apostles).

SUMMARY

In the incarnation of Christ, we have the strongest confirmation possible of the goodness of creation—a theme that is found throughout the Old Testament. In Christ, we see the breaking in of God's kingdom on earth, a kingdom in which old enmities are abolished and peace is established between God and humanity, humanity and the earth, and human beings and each other. In Christ, we learn truly what it is to be human, to accept both our limitations as creatures who are not gods and also our high calling as obedient children of God. In Christ, we learn finally what it is to rule as God's image bearers, as those who in sacrificial love are willing to give of ourselves on behalf of those we rule. We also see in Jesus's teaching and life something of the priorities of God's kingdom, a kingdom of abundance and compassion and generous grace. In Christ's life and death and resurrection, we discover the breadth of God's concern and the cosmic scope of his love.

Above all, in Christ we encounter our Lord and Savior who alone can reconcile us to God, renew us in his image, and enable us to be his faithful servants—including in how we relate to and care for the earth that belongs to him. Some of the practical implications of this will be developed in the final chapter of the book. First, however, we must explore in the next two chapters more fully the meaning and significance of the new creation that God, by his Spirit, brings about in Christ, for us and for all the earth.

RELEVANT QUESTIONS

1. Would it be better to begin a biblical theology of creation with a focus on Jesus or on the Genesis creation narrative? What difference would it make?
2. How does what we learn from Jesus about what it is to be truly human apply to the practice of creation care?
3. What are the implications of Jesus's teaching about the abundance of God's kingdom for how we live in a world where there are many who are poor and do not have enough, and where many animals and plants are going extinct?
4. Why does creation benefit from the redemption brought about by Jesus?

CHAPTER 8

"WHAT COUNTS IS THE NEW CREATION"

THE PATTERN OF FULFILLMENT

As I begin this chapter, I (Doug) am sitting in a Starbucks coffee shop in a suburb of Chicago. On a hot and humid summer day, I have travelled here in an air-conditioned car from an air-conditioned house. As I write, I hear the noise of fellow customers plunking away on their laptops and talking (unnecessarily loudly, it seems to me) on their smart phones. A bit further away, baristas fill orders with a hiss of steam and clatter of cups. Yet further in the background is a constant hum of traffic from two busy highways, punctuated by the occasional blast of a horn or siren. The only sounds I hear are the sounds of human technology. The natural world seems very far away. To be sure, if I look closely, I can see the tops of some trees—but they are largely obscured by parked cars and a tangle of power lines.

I suspect that the "environment" of many readers of this book is similar to my Starbucks environment. Most of us are surrounded for much of our lives with the sights and sounds of our technological culture. I am the last to dismiss this technology as evil or entirely unwelcome—I remember sleepless nights tossing and turning on sweat-soaked sheets before we had air conditioning—but technology, for all the benefits it brings us, has the tendency to shove the natural world far from us. That world may be a place to which we retreat for a vacation, but it seems to have little to do with our everyday lives. For many Christians, this distance from the natural world impacts—and is impacted by—our reading of the New Testament. These twenty-seven books seem pretty unconcerned about the natural world. This especially seems to be true in the New Testament letters, which loom very large in the preaching of most churches and the reading of most Christians. The spiritual state of individuals and the life of the communities of those individuals is what these letters are "about." Talk about the environment is for tree-hugging New Agers or wilderness "freaks"—not for Christians.

Our purpose in this book is to correct this way of reading the Bible by showing that the created world remains important in God's purposes throughout the story of redemption. J. B. Phillips once challenged believers with the line "Your God is too small." We might paraphrase Phillips by challenging believers in our day: "Your redemption is too small!" In this chapter, then, we want to demonstrate that creation, while not often the focus of the New Testament letters, has a secure place in this climactic stage of God's redemptive plan.

Jesus's death and resurrection are the climax of the redemption story. These two events form the great pivot on which the plot of the story turns. The era of expectation gives way to the era of fulfillment. Jesus's triumphant cry "it is finished" (John 19:30) signals the end of one era, even as his resurrection and the pouring out of the Spirit on the day of Pentecost inaugurates another. Filled with the Spirit, Jesus's newly empowered followers boldly proclaim that the crucified Jesus is the resurrected one, installed as Lord over everyone and everything and the one in whose name salvation is offered to both Israel and the Gentiles (Acts 2:14–39; 4:8–12; 10:34–43).

The early Christians not only believed that they were living in a new act in the drama of redemption, they were convinced that they were living in the last act of that drama. The Old Testament, and especially the prophets of the Old Testament, had predicted that God would one day intervene to save his people and judge his enemies. They referred to this time as "the last days." Isaiah is typical:

> In the last days
> the mountain of the LORD's temple will be established
>   as the highest of the mountains;
> it will be exalted above the hills,
>   and all nations will stream to it.
> Many peoples will come and say,
> "Come, let us go up to the mountain of the LORD,
>   to the temple of the God of Jacob.
> He will teach us his ways,
>   so that we may walk in his paths."
> The law will go out from Zion,
>   the word of the LORD from Jerusalem.
> He will judge between the nations
>   and will settle disputes for many peoples.
> They will beat their swords into plowshares
>   and their spears into pruning hooks.
> Nation will not take up sword against nation,
>   nor will they train for war anymore. (Isa. 2:2–4)

Joel uses the language of "those days" to refer to the same time:

> And afterward,
>   I will pour out my Spirit on all people.
> Your sons and daughters will prophesy,

> your old men will dream dreams,
>   your young men will see visions.
> Even on my servants, both men and women,
>   I will pour out my Spirit in those days.
> I will show wonders in the heavens
>   and on the earth,
>   blood and fire and billows of smoke.
> The sun will be turned to darkness
>   and the moon to blood
>   before the coming of the great and dreadful day of the LORD.
> And everyone who calls
>   on the name of the LORD will be saved;
> for on Mount Zion and in Jerusalem
>   there will be deliverance,
>   as the LORD has said,
> even among the survivors
>   whom the LORD calls. (Joel 2:28–32)

The apostle Peter quotes from this passage in Acts 2 to explain to the Jews gathered in Jerusalem from all over the world how it is that they can all hear the disciples speaking in their own languages. The phenomenon is, he says, the fulfillment of Joel's prediction that the people of God would "prophesy," when God poured out his Spirit "in those days." The point is clear: Peter effectively proclaims that the "last days" have begun. Several other texts make this same point explicitly (e.g., 1 Cor. 10:11; Heb. 1:1–2; 1 John 2:18), while many others make it implicitly (e.g., by claiming, as Acts 2 does, that Old Testament prophecies about the "last days" are coming to pass in the life of the early church). We can, then, characterize the stage of the story inaugurated by Christ's death and resurrection as "eschatological" (a word that reflects the Greek *eschata,* "last things").

"Ethics is lived eschatology."
J. Richard Middleton [1]

Even as the early Christians rejoiced in the blessings of the last days, however, they also keenly anticipated even greater blessings in the future. For the "last days," initiated by the first coming of the Messiah, were yet to be consummated by his second coming. Paul makes this point by referring to two "appearances" in Titus:

> For the grace of God has appeared that offers salvation to all people. It teaches us to say "No" to ungodliness and worldly passions, and to live self-controlled, upright and godly lives in this present age, while we wait for the blessed

1. J. Richard Middleton, *A New Heaven and a New Earth: Reclaiming Biblical Eschatology* (Grand Rapids: Baker, 2014), 24.

hope—the appearing of the glory of our great God and Savior, Jesus Christ, who gave himself for us to redeem us from all wickedness and to purify for himself a people that are his very own, eager to do what is good. (Titus 2:11–14)

New Testament eschatology, then, falls into an "already/not yet" pattern. Many promises God made to his people concerning the last days have "already" been fulfilled, while many others have "not yet" come to pass and still others are fulfilled partially now but await complete fulfillment in the future.

GOD, HUMAN BEINGS—AND NATURE?

Most of us could compile a list of the blessings we enjoy because we live in the era of fulfillment. We are given God's Spirit as a permanently indwelling power, conforming us to Christ. We are justified, redeemed, saved, adopted into God's family, living in certain hope of ultimate resurrection. We suspect that the lists compiled would focus strongly and perhaps even exclusively on benefits enjoyed by human beings. This would not be surprising. The book of Acts and the letters of the New Testament concentrate on what God has done in Christ for people and how people should respond to the work of his grace in our lives. Indeed, the teaching and preaching in most churches is so concentrated in Acts and especially the letters that we are often quite unaware of this focus. Yet a moment's thought should raise some questions for us. As we have seen, the prophets in the Old Testament promise not just that God would bring blessings to people but they regularly predict that God's people would return to the land from which God had sent them because of their sin and that that land would be a place of abundance and safety. Ezekiel is typical:

> I will save my flock, and they will no longer be plundered. I will judge between one sheep and another. I will place over them one shepherd, my servant David, and he will tend them; he will tend them and be their shepherd. I the LORD will be their God, and my servant David will be prince among them. I the LORD have spoken. I will make a covenant of peace with them and rid the land of savage beasts so that they may live in the wilderness and sleep in the forests in safety. I will make them and the places surrounding my hill a blessing. I will send down showers in season; there will be showers of blessing. The trees will yield their fruit and the ground will yield its crops; the people will be secure in their land. They will know that I am the LORD, when I break the bars of their yoke and rescue them from the hands of those who enslaved them. They will no longer be plundered by the nations, nor will wild animals devour them. They will live in safety, and no one will make them afraid. I will provide for them a land renowned for its crops, and they will no longer be victims of famine in the land or bear the scorn of the nations. Then they will know that I, the LORD

their God, am with them and that they, the Israelites, are my people, declares
the Sovereign LORD. You are my sheep, the sheep of my pasture, and I am your
God, declares the Sovereign LORD. (Ezek. 34:22–31)

What has happened to these promises? Has the New Testament simply abandoned interest in the land? And does this lack of concern signal a broader disinterest
in the world of creation?

Interest in the world of creation is evident in the Gospels, as we have seen. Jesus
regularly interacts with the natural world around him and uses the agricultural world,
in which so much of his ministry took place, as the primary source for illustrations in
his teaching. However, while the natural world does not disappear in the ministry of
the apostles, it is much less evident. The "built environment," particularly the cities
of the eastern Roman Empire, becomes the focus of activity in Acts and the setting
for the letters. Moreover, direct teaching about the natural world is sparse indeed
in these books. It is therefore no surprise that the New Testament has been seen as
unconcerned with the world of creation. To be clear, the charge some have made that
the New Testament is anthropocentric is wide of the mark. The New Testament is,
rather, thoroughly God- and Christ-centered, but it is nevertheless the case that the
New Testament focuses on the relationship of human beings with God and Christ
and, derivatively, on the relationship of human beings with one another, especially
brothers and sisters in Christ.

Many environmental advocates fault this New Testament preoccupation with
human relationships for the ecological crisis we are now experiencing. The New
Testament letters have had an enormous influence on Christian theology and practice.
By putting humans in the center of the stage and shunting the world of creation to the
wings (or off the stage altogether), the New Testament, it is alleged, has contributed
significantly to the neglect of the environment in our day. Christians, as well as the
many cultures strongly influenced by the Christian worldview, have accordingly
fallen prey to a way of thinking that elevates humans and relegates creation to an
instrumental role—to be used, or exploited, in whatever way benefits what is thought
to be human good.

This way of thinking about the New Testament and its influence is, of course,
more than a bit of a caricature. On the one hand, other ideological influences are
at least as responsible for the unfortunate neglect of the world of nature in modern
cultures. Certain forms of Greek religion and philosophy, which have had an extraordinarily powerful influence on Western ways of thinking, are at least as important.
Also important is the heritage of the Enlightenment, with its renewed focus on
humans. And, on the other hand, most careful readers of Scripture will recognize
the kind of selfish anthropocentrism these writers accuse the New Testament of
propagating as foreign to the message of the New Testament.

With this being said, it remains the case that the letters of the New Testament say little about the world of nature, and these letters have an enduringly powerful influence on Christian theology and on the way Christians in general think about their faith. Consider, for instance, the proportion of sermons and Bible studies devoted to the letters in comparison with all other parts of Scripture. Preachers tend to neglect the Old Testament in their sermon series, propagating an ignorance of the "former testament" among their parishioners. Yet the Old Testament constitutes seventy percent of Christian Scripture, and its contribution to a robust theology of this earth should not be ignored. Because Christian preaching, teaching, and even theologizing are so heavily oriented toward the New Testament letters, there is a tendency to consider concern about the environment to be, at best, a side issue and, at worst, a dangerous temptation, leading Christians to neglect evangelism and discipleship.

The New Testament does indeed have a focus on humans and their relationships with God and fellow humans, but our purpose in this chapter and the next is to show that the larger natural world—which is so important in the Old Testament and the Gospels—has by no means disappeared in the New Testament letters. The occasional nature of the New Testament letters means that they deal primarily with pressing issues facing the fledgling communities of Christ-followers in the first century, but even these letters cannot finally be understood aright apart from the wider biblical story in which their authors considered themselves to be living. In fact, key concepts and passages reveal that the apostles, even when not focusing on this matter, endorsed the continuing significance of the world of nature in God's redemptive plan. God's new covenant work is as broad in its scope as the world he made. Following the eschatological pattern we described earlier, we focus in this chapter on the "already" of creation's redemption. In the next chapter, then, we will turn attention to the "not yet" aspect of God's redemption of creation.

The Land

We begin with an interesting and controversial matter: the place of the land of Israel in New Testament teaching. As we have seen, a particular piece of geography was one of the basic components of God's original promise to Abraham (Gen. 12:1–3). This land has a prominent role in the subsequent development of God's redemptive plan in the Old Testament. After their deliverance from Egypt and their testing in the wilderness, the people of Israel ultimately come to possess the land God promised to them. But, as we have seen, God makes clear through Moses that Israel would continue to enjoy that land only if they obeyed the law God gave them. If they failed to keep the law, God would remove them from their land. As early as the latter chapters of Deuteronomy, it becomes clear that Israel would indeed fail to maintain their covenant obligation and forfeit their possession of the land (Deut. 31:15–18).

Yet, even in the midst of these dire warnings and pessimistic predictions, a clear note of grace and God's continuing faithfulness is sounded: after the people's exile, God would bring his people back to their land again (e.g., Deut 30:1–5). This sequence outlined in Deuteronomy becomes a template for the long history of Israel and the land described in the Old Testament. The people fail to obey the law they were given; God expels them from their land because of their disobedience; and God promises that he will bring his people back from exile and settle them again in their land.

It might appear that the Old Testament ends with these promises fulfilled: under the leadership of Ezra and Nehemiah, the people of Israel return to their land, rebuilding their temple and establishing a degree of political autonomy. However, the situation of Israel in the land at the end of the Old Testament is a far cry from the picture the prophets predict. Only a minority of Jews are back in their land; the repeated wars and occupations by foreign powers make a mockery of the prophets' predictions of peace and security; and the people fail to display the spiritual vitality and faithfulness to God that was to characterize the Israel of the "last days."

At the time Jesus begins his ministry, then, it is fair to say that Israel is still "in exile," at least in some sense. Both Jesus and the apostles announce that God in Jesus is fulfilling prophecies about the restoration of Israel, thereby bringing Israel's exile finally to its true end. But how has that exile ended? The very word "exile" generally connotes some degree of geographical reference. An "exile" is a person who has emigrated from their native land, and returning from exile would thereby seem to suggest that one has moved back to their homeland again. Yet, as we have noted, the New Testament says very little about how all the Old Testament predictions about the land are being fulfilled through Jesus's end of the exile. Nevertheless, we have seen reason to think that Jesus reaffirms the land promises, even if he has transmuted them into a different shape. We now turn, then, to the Book of Acts and the letters to see what they contribute to our theme.

No New Testament text directly addresses the question about the way the Old Testament land promise is fulfilled in "the last days." This silence has opened the way for very different answers to the question. One trajectory stresses the need for continuity between Old Testament promise and New Testament fulfillment, insisting that the promise of a specific land to the people of Israel remains in force. This promise will be fulfilled when God turns from the Gentiles (his focus during this era) to the Jewish people after Christ's return in glory. On this view, usually associated with dispensational theology, the land promise will be "literally" fulfilled during the millennium, conceived as a period of time after Christ's return and before the final judgment. At the other extreme are various forms of a "spiritualized" fulfillment of the land promise. According to these theologians, following a pattern that dominates the New Testament reading of the Old Testament, it is Christ himself who embodies the fulfillment of the land promise. These interpreters note that Hebrews compares the "rest" promised to the people of Israel in the Promised Land to the "rest" enjoyed by believers in Christ (Heb. 3:7–4:11). Moreover, the language of "inheritance," closely tied to the land in the Old Testament, is used by New Testament authors to describe the believer's hope with God in Christ. For example, Peter writes: "Praise be to the God and Father of our Lord Jesus Christ! In his great mercy he has given us new birth into a living hope through the resurrection of Jesus Christ from the dead, and into an inheritance that can never perish, spoil or fade. This inheritance is kept in heaven for you . . ." (1 Peter 1:3–4: see also Eph. 1:14; Rom. 8:17; Rev. 21:7).

We do not have the space to adequately address this long-standing debate; although, of these two options, we think the second reflects a bit more accurately the basic direction of biblical-theological development. In his important study of this subject, W. D. Davies has captured at least part of the truth when he concludes, "In sum, for the holiness of place, Christianity has fundamentally, though not consistently, substituted the holiness of a Person; it has Christified holy space."[2] In the last analysis, however, neither of these two options does justice to the full spectrum of biblical-theological teaching on the issue. It is perhaps fair to say that a degree of *Christifying* or *spiritualizing* the Old Testament land promise occurs in the New Testament. But, more important is the way that Jesus and the apostles suggest that the land promise has been *universalized*. That is, building on what we have argued in our discussion of the Old Testament and the Gospels, we find evidence in the New Testament letters that the Old Testament promise of a specific land, where God's people dwell securely in fellowship with him, is expanded in the New Testament to "a new heaven and a new earth," a thoroughly renewed cosmos where believers will enjoy complete security and fellowship with God. Some of the relevant texts focus exclusively on the future, the "not yet" side of fulfillment, and we will consider them in the next chapter. In the rest of this chapter, we will look at passages that suggest some degree of a present—"already"—element of fulfillment.

The "Land" Becomes the "World"

In Romans 4, Paul cites the experience of Abraham to buttress two key points that he makes in 3:21–31: that justification comes through faith, not "works"/"works of the law" and that Gentiles are being brought into the kingdom as equals with Jews. Abraham, as Genesis 15:6 implies, was put right with God by faith—before he was circumcised (Rom. 4:9–11; see Gen. 17) and apart from the law (Rom. 4:13–15). Because Abraham put his trust in God and was justified without being circumcised and apart from the law, he becomes the "father" of Gentile believers as well as Jewish believers (4:11–12). It is in this context that Paul says something relevant to our

---

2. W. D. Davies, *The Gospel and the Land: Early Christianity and Jewish Territorial Doctrine* (Berkeley: University of California, 1974), 385.

concern: "It was not through the law that Abraham and his offspring received the promise that he would be heir of the world, but through the righteousness that comes by faith" (4:13). In the Old Testament, the "inheritance" of Abraham and the people of Israel is often identified with the land of Israel (see, e.g., Ex. 32:13; Lev. 20:24; Num. 14:24; Deut. 4:21; Ps. 78:55). Paul's reference in this verse to the "world" (Gk. *kosmos*) is therefore noteworthy. "Inheriting the world" is Paul's shorthand way of summarizing the three elements of the promise God made to Abraham: that he would have an immense number of descendants, embracing "many nations" (Gen. 12:2; 13:16; 15:5; 17:4–6, 16–20; 22:17), that he would possess "the land" (Gen. 13:15–17; 15:12–21; 17:8), and that he would be the means of blessing to "all the peoples of the earth" (Gen. 12:3; 18:18; 22:18). Of course, the context makes clear that Paul's focus is on the first of these aspects of the promise—the inclusion of Gentiles within the spiritual family of Abraham is what this part of Romans 4 is all about. But Paul would never have chosen the combination of "inherit" and "world" if he wanted to say only this. Reference to the geographical element of the promise is unmistakable. And by speaking of the "world" rather than the "land," Paul implies a universalizing of the geographical promise.[3] The Old Testament itself plainly hints at an expansive "seed" of Abraham, requiring an expansive place for them to live. God's promise to Abraham ultimately has in view not just one nation living in one area, but "many nations" (Rom. 4:18) inhabiting the whole world. For our purposes, then, it is especially important to note that Paul sees the fulfillment of the promise as including the whole of creation.[4] One might object that we should not make too much of this reference since Paul is not really talking about the created world in this context. But we argue that this makes his reference all the more telling, for it suggests that early Christians were naturally including the created world as participating in the fulfillment of God's redemptive plan in Christ. Reference to the "new creation" (Gal. 6:15; 2 Cor. 5:17) reinforces and carries further this focus on the created world in the redemptive work of God. But before we turn to these texts, we need to treat briefly one other reference in Paul to the "land."

Long Life on the Earth

In Ephesians 5:21–6:9, Paul instructs believers about responsibilities within the typical ancient household, treating in sequence wives and husbands (5:22–33),

3. Paul reflects certain tendencies in the Judaism of his day. For instance, the author of the intertestamental Jewish book *Jubilees* attributes these words to God, renewing the promise to Jacob when his name was changed to "Israel": "I am the LORD who created heaven and earth, and I shall increase you and multiply you very much. And there will be kings from you; they will rule everywhere that the tracks of mankind have been trod. And I shall give to your seed all of the land under heaven and they will rule in all nations as they have desired. And after this all of the earth will be gathered together and they will inherit it forever" (32:18–19; translation from James H. Charlesworth, ed., *The Old Testament Pseudepigrapha*, 2 vols. [New York: Doubleday, 1985], 2:117–18).

4. Paul's insistence on this point may indirectly challenge the pretensions of the Roman Empire, which was increasingly claiming its own worldwide significance. See, e.g., M. Forman, *The Politics of Inheritance in Romans*, SNTSMS 148 (Cambridge: Cambridge University Press, 2011).

children and parents (6:1–4), and slaves and masters (6:5–9). Addressing children in 6:2–3, he quotes from the Decalogue: "'Honor your father and mother'—which is the first commandment with a promise—'so that it may go well with you and that you may enjoy long life on the earth [ESV "land"].'" In the Greek that Paul is probably quoting, both versions of the commandment promise that those who obey it will enjoy "good" and "long life in the land" (Ex. 20:12; Deut. 5:16). They also describe the land as "[which] the LORD your God is giving you." This makes clear that the reference is to the land of Israel. The commandment reflects a widespread Old Testament pattern, according to which a rich and long life in the land of Israel is promised to those who obey the law (see, e.g., Deut 5:33; 6:2; 11:9; 32:7).

What, then, does Paul mean when he promises children that obeying their parents will lead to "long life on the earth"? First, we need to comment on the translation. "Earth," the NIV reading, is only one possible meaning for the Greek word here (gē), which can also mean "land" (which is what the ESV, for instance, chooses). In the context of Exodus 20:12 and Deuteronomy 5:16, as we have seen, the word (which in the Greek translation of the Old Testament is the same Greek word Paul uses) clearly means "land." If we retain this translation in Ephesians, then Paul might be quoting the promise in a kind of typological fashion. "Long life on the land," the Old Testament form of blessing for covenant obedience, would have something else as its New Testament counterpart. What might this be? Following a pattern of "spiritualizing" that some see as basic to the New Testament interpretation of the Old Testament, the reference could be to spiritual life or the kingdom of God (for the latter, see, e.g., 1 Cor. 6:9; Gal. 5:21).[5] Some think that Paul's use of "inheritance" (a word, as we have seen, related to the land) in Ephesians supports this interpretation. However, the word is actually used in Ephesians as a very general way of depicting all that God has promised his people (1:14, 18; 5:5), so insisting that 6:3 must have a spiritual meaning because these earlier texts do can end up being a case of circular reasoning. It is in any case necessary to remember that one important blessing God has promised his people is quite physical indeed: a resurrection body.

Whatever we decide about these other texts, however, the main problem with a "spiritual" interpretation of Ephesians 6:3 is that the reference to "living long" is simply not a concept that is easily translated into a so-called "spiritual" benefit. Probably what Paul is promising is quite simply that obedient children will live a long and good life. The promise, as with all proverbial promises of this kind, speaks of what is generally true, not of what will be true in every situation. In any case, the NIV is probably correct to translate "earth" here, since this is how Paul uses the

---

5. The Jewish philosopher/theologian Philo, a near contemporary of Paul's, interprets the Old Testament "live long in the land" as immortality (*Special Laws* 2.262).

word elsewhere.[6] Paul is here working from the same universalizing hermeneutic that we saw at work in Romans 4:13. The "land" promised to the people of God, focused on (but never confined to!) Palestine, has in the last days been extended to the universal dimensions intended by God all along. As believers share with Abraham the inheritance of the "world," so obedient children are promised long life on the "earth." And, of course, this conception has explicit antecedent in the teaching of Jesus, who promised that the "meek" would "inherit the earth" (Matt. 5:5).

We think, then, that Paul understands the promise accompanying the commandment about obedient children to involve living for a long time on the earth, interpreted as a physical reality. One important question remains: When does Paul think this promise will be fulfilled? Most interpreters think Paul is here reflecting the widespread Old Testament teaching, found especially in Proverbs, that promises blessings to God's faithful people in this life. Obedient children will do "well" and enjoy a long life in this present world. However, it is also possible that Paul is promising a long life, not necessarily in their present life on earth, but in the "new heaven" and "new earth." Obedient children, like all faithful believers, can look forward to a "long life"—indeed, an "eternal" life!—in a renewed and transformed world. Which of these options we should choose is unclear, but the ambiguity reminds us that, for Paul, we live in the overlap of the ages, in the tension of the "already" and "not yet."

NEW CREATION

If Romans 4:13 and Ephesians 6:2–3 hint that the entire created world continues to be important in the age of fulfillment, Paul's claim that the "new creation" has arrived would appear at first glance to confirm the matter. Paul uses the phrase twice only, and he is the only New Testament author to use it:

> Neither circumcision nor uncircumcision means anything; what counts is the new creation. (Gal 6:15)

> Therefore, if anyone is in Christ, the new creation has come: The old has gone, the new is here! (2 Cor. 5:17)

Unfortunately for our purposes, these texts are not as clear as they might seem. A quick check of other versions shows that 2 Corinthians 5:17, for example, could be taken to refer to the individual believer rather than to creation generally. Thus, for instance, the NASB translates it, "Therefore if anyone is in Christ, he is a new creature; the old things passed away; behold, new things have come." The ESV renders it, "Therefore, if anyone is in Christ, he is a new creation. The old has

---

6. The word *gē* occurs fourteen times in Paul's letters. One refers to the earth in terms of its physical makeup ("dust"—1 Cor. 15:47), but the others all clearly mean "earth," not "land." See also our brief discussion of Matt. 5:5 in chap. 7.

passed away; behold, the new has come." Many interpreters think that Galatians 6:15 also refers to the believer as a "new creature" or "new creation." The NASB rendering "creature" is, it should be acknowledged, quite possible, since the Greek word involved, *ktisis*, can refer either to an individual created thing—"creature" (though Paul never unambiguously uses it this way)—or to the created world in general. And the context of each of these verses certainly has relevance to the individual believer. Nevertheless, as we will see, a compelling argument can be made for a more expansive interpretation: that "new creation" is Paul's shorthand expression for the radically new state of affairs that Christ's coming has inaugurated—a state of affairs that includes renovation of the created world itself.

The Roots of New Creation

Because "new creation" is used only twice in the New Testament and in contexts that provide no clear definition of the phrase, its use in literature outside the New Testament becomes important for determining its meaning. Writers and speakers will often use language that their readers or listeners are familiar with, and when they don't take the time to define it, they are usually assuming the standard meaning of that language. So what does our evidence from the ancient world suggest that Paul would have meant by the phrase?

The actual phrase "new creation" (in its equivalent in other ancient languages) occurs in only two or perhaps three Jewish texts before Paul. One of those texts is in the first-century Jewish book called *Jubilees*, where the reference clearly encompasses the entire earth:

> For the Lord has four [sacred] places upon the earth: the Garden of Eden and the Mount of the East and this mountain which you are upon today, Mount Sinai, and Mount Zion, which will be sanctified in the new creation for the sanctification of the earth. On account of this the earth will be sanctified from all sin and from pollution throughout eternal generations. (4:26)[7]

A similarly cosmic sense of the phrase is found in the Dead Sea Scroll of the "Hymns" (1QH 13:11) and in the Jewish apocalyptic book *1 Enoch* (72:1; the date of this text is uncertain, so it may or may not predate Paul).

This evidence is significant, but it is also of course true that two or three occurrences do not constitute anything like conclusive evidence for the meaning of the phrase "new creation." Probably even more significant, then, is the likelihood that both Paul and these Jewish texts are reflecting a concept found in the latter chapters of Isaiah. Creation language is pervasive in Isaiah 40–55, where it is sometimes used to emphasize the "new thing" God will do when he brings his people back from their exile. Isaiah

7. Charlesworth, *Old Testament Pseudepigrapha*, 2:63.

43:18–19, to which Paul is probably alluding in 2 Corinthians 5:17, is a good example: "Forget the former things; do not dwell on the past. See, I am doing a new thing!" The "former things" are God's past acts of deliverance, especially the rescue of his people from Egypt at the time of the exodus. Isaiah's point is that the new deliverance that God will accomplish for Israel is so much greater, so decisive, and so far-reaching that it will be as if they have been created anew. As the book of Isaiah develops, this idea of a "new creation" is expanded even further, so that it ultimately embraces the entire cosmos: Israel's restoration will take the form of nothing less than a "new heavens and a new earth" (Isa. 65:17–22; cf. 66:22–24). The probable background from which Paul draws the language of "new creation," then, suggests that it would include reference to a total renovation of the universe: a "new creation" as extensive as the "old" creation.

The background of the phrase "new creation" thus suggests that it refers to a restoration of God's people that extends to the cosmos itself. Does this sense fit the contexts in which Paul uses the phrase?

Galatians 6:15

"New creation" occurs first at the end of Paul's letter to the Galatians: "Neither circumcision nor uncircumcision means anything; what counts is the new creation" (6:15). The reference to circumcision touches on Paul's central concern in Galatians: to convince the newly converted Gentile Christians in Galatia to renounce a false gospel being propagated by people he calls "agitators" (5:12). These agitators were claiming that Gentiles could be considered true children of Abraham (3:6–9, 15–29) and recipients of God's blessing (3:9, 14), only if they placed themselves under the law of Moses (2:16; 4:21; 5:4)—a condition marked above all by the rite of circumcision (5:3; 6:12). Paul responds to this false teaching by stressing the decisive change that occurred with the death and resurrection of Christ. Paul makes this point at the very beginning of the letter, referring to God the Father as the one who "raised [Jesus Christ] from the dead" (1:1) and to Christ as the one "who gave himself for our sins to rescue us from the present evil age" (1:4). The cross was at the very heart of Paul's original preaching in Galatia: "Before your very eyes Jesus Christ was clearly portrayed as crucified" (3:1). Through Christ's death God "redeems," "buys people out of," their condemned status under the curse of the law (3:13; cf. 4:5). And, as Christ's death effects the transfer from "old age" to new, so, as believers identify with Christ, they find themselves transferred from the old age to the new. Paul, speaking of his experience as representative of other believers, claims that he has "been crucified with Christ," and so lives a totally new life (2:20). Similarly, he claims that he will boast only about the cross of Christ, because it is through Christ that "the world has been crucified to me, and I to the world" (6:14).

This last text, which immediately precedes the verse we are looking at, is particularly interesting. Here Paul stresses that being "in Christ" means a dramatic shift in one's whole worldview. The "world" refers to the fallen and sinful world, with particular focus on the value system of that world. "New creation" in verse 15 is the counterpart to that world and its values. In a move typical of Paul's polemics in Galatians, he associates God's old covenant requirement of circumcision with this worldly system of values that has now been judged and ended by Christ's death and resurrection. Significantly, it is not only circumcision that has no value in this new "world," but uncircumcision as well. This pair of terms reminds us forcefully of a similar claim Paul makes earlier in the letter: "There is neither Jew nor Gentile, neither slave nor free, neither male nor female, for you are all one in Christ" (3:28). People who are "in Christ" enter a realm in which the distinctions of ethnicity, social class, and gender that are determinative for this world no longer matter.

The background of the phrase and the context in which it occurs in Galatians combine to suggest that "new creation" refers broadly to the totality of the new state of affairs introduced by the climactic events of Christ's death and resurrection. On this reading, the phrase includes, but is not limited to, two other interpretations: the transformed individual believer, as well as the new community in which "there is neither Jew nor Gentile, neither slave nor free, nor is there male and female" (3:28). "New creation" refers to the entirety of God's redemptive work in Christ. Paul typically stresses the application of this work to individual humans, brought out of their dead state because of sin into new life, and to the new covenant community, where the barriers erected by the structures of this world are overcome. But we have every reason to conclude that a redeemed creation must also be included in this work of "new creation."

2 Corinthians 5:17

As we have seen, the only other occurrence of "new creation" in the New Testament comes in 2 Corinthians 5:17. Reference here to an individual believer appears at first sight to be the natural interpretation, since "new creation" follows a clause that refers to "anyone . . . in Christ." Most English versions therefore translate in a way similar to the ESV: "if anyone is in Christ, he is a new creation." In fact, however, the case for an application of the language only to individuals is not as strong as it first appears.

The Greek of the verse has nothing corresponding to the "he is" of the ESV in the second part of the verse. As is often the case, the Greek is quite elliptical, leaving it up to the reader to fill in the blanks. A straightforward English rendering would be something like, "If anyone is in Christ, new creation!" The "anyone" in the first clause gives some basis for inserting the language "he [or 'that person,' CEB] is." But the NIV rendering, "new creation has come" is also quite possible (see also CEB, "that person is part of the new creation").[8] Indeed, we think this rendering is better than the alternative.

8. Some interpreters insist that the subject and verb of the protasis—"if anyone is in Christ"—must be carried over to the apodosis—"that person is a new creation." But there is nothing in the syntax of the verse that requires this. See 1 Cor. 10:27 for an example of a significant shift in subject and verb from protasis to apodosis: "If an unbeliever invites you to a meal and you want to go, [you] eat whatever is put before you without raising questions of conscience."

The main reason will again be the likely background of the phrase and the concept to which it points in the Old Testament (particularly Isaiah) and Jewish apocalyptic writings. Indeed, as we have seen, the second part of verse 17 directly alludes to a key "new creation" passage in Isaiah (43:18). Another reason for preferring to see a broad reference in "new creation" is the comparison with Galatians. It is logical to think that Paul gives this rare phrase the same meaning in both its occurrences in his letters. Of course, one could respond that this is a circular argument: we are just reading the uncertain and debated meaning of Galatians into 2 Corinthians. A lot depends on how strong a case we have made for the broader meaning in Galatians. But the context in 2 Corinthians also suggests the likelihood of a broad meaning similar to what we have seen in Galatians because the two texts are focused on similar issues. In Galatians, Paul uses the reality of the "new creation" to remind his readers that they are living in a new age with a new set of values. If they follow this guidance, they will reject the false teaching of the agitators, who insist that the law of the old covenant era must apply in the new as well. Paul is also arguing for a fundamental reorienting of values in 2 Corinthians.

As in Galatia, some teachers have come to Corinth and argued that the Corinthian believers should follow them rather than Paul (10:10–12; 11:4–5, 12–15, 19–23; 12:11). They are questioning Paul's ministry credentials and procedures. Paul refers to these rivals in our context: "We are not trying to commend ourselves to you again, but are giving you an opportunity to take pride in us, so that you can answer those who take pride in what is seen rather than in what is in the heart" (5:12). Elaborating on the criteria by which the Corinthians should evaluate these matters, Paul in verses 14–15 cites the death of Christ as the great turning point in human history—just as he does in Galatians. Christ's death means that people should live by a new standard: no longer "for themselves" but "for him who died for them and was raised again." Paul goes on to spell out the consequences of this new perspective for the way in which he and other Christians view others, and especially Christ: "From now on we regard no one from a worldly [or 'fleshly'; *sarx* in Greek] point of view. Though we once regarded Christ in this way, we do so no longer" (v. 16). Paul's contrast in this verse between "once" and "from now on"/"no longer" alludes to the key framework he uses to interpret the redemptive plan of God: the contrast between "this age" and "the age to come." He is saying that people who live in this new age must evaluate everything from the standards fundamental to this new age. The claim about "new creation" in verse 17 relates to both verses 14–15 and verse 16. A person who is "in Christ" belongs to the new age of redemption—the "new creation"—in which he or she lives for Christ and not for themselves (vv. 14–15) and no longer evaluates anything by the "worldly" standards of the old age that is passing. To belong to the new creation means a "total re-orienting of one's values and priorities away from the world (self) and toward the cross

(Christ, others)."[9] "New creation" functions here, as in Galatians, to indicate broadly the new age, the new state of affairs that Christ has inaugurated, as the crucial context for a Christian system of values.

Creation and New Creation

We can now draw conclusions from our study of "new creation." In both texts where Paul uses this phrase, he *applies* the language to the current situation of Christian believers. But the phrase *refers to* the ultimate state of affairs God will bring into being as a result of his redemptive and transformative work through Christ. Herman Ridderbos puts it like this: "When he [Paul] speaks here of 'new creation,' this is not meant merely in an individual sense (a 'new creature'), but one is to think of the new world of re-creation that God has made to dawn in Christ, and in which everyone who is in Christ is included."[10] As he often does, Paul appropriates a key theme from Isaiah, who stresses the radical and far-reaching nature of God's promised redemption by referring to it as a "re-creation." Those who are "in Christ" (2 Cor. 5:17; see Gal. 3:28) belong, though they still live in the world, to this newly created world, a world that awaits its full establishment but which is experienced even now by faith.

On the one hand, then, those who use the concept "new creation" as if it simply designates the renewal of the whole of the material universe are guilty of restricting the scope of the phrase in one direction. But, on the other hand, those who restrict the phrase only to spiritual realities are equally guilty of inappropriately restricting its scope in the other direction. "New creation" is Paul's way of summarizing the unlimited scope of God's redemptive plan, a plan that ultimately encompasses "new heavens and a new earth."

Interpretation of Scripture in the West has suffered from a dualism, inherited from the Greeks, that tends to remove the material world from the sphere of God's ultimate purposes. But we cannot remove creation from "new creation." Those who use the phrase to refer only to the future transformed universe and those who confine it only to present spiritual realities separate what Paul ultimately wants to keep together.

RECONCILING ALL THINGS

The cosmic scope of God's redemptive work in Christ, alluded to with Paul's language of "new creation," is made even more clear in Colossians 1:20. This verse, which brings to a glorious climax one of the great theological passages in the New Testament

---

9. Victor Paul Furnish, *II Corinthians*, AB 32A (Garden City, NJ: Doubleday, 1984), 322.

10. Herman Ridderbos, *Paul: An Outline of His Theology* (Grand Rapids: Eerdmans, 1974), 45.

(vv. 15–20),[11] celebrates the universal reach of God's redemptive work in Christ. Through Christ, Paul asserts, God is working "to reconcile to himself all things, whether things on earth or things in heaven, by making peace through his blood, shed on the cross." Paul usually uses the language of reconciliation to refer to the establishing of peaceful relations between God and human beings.[12] Some interpreters attempt to restrict the reference here to the reconciliation of human beings who respond to the invitation to be reconciled.[13] But Paul's explicit reference to "all things," a key motif throughout this passage, along with his specific inclusion of things both on earth and in heaven, makes this kind of restriction only to humankind unlikely. Far more likely is that the description of God's reconciling all things to himself here is a way of claiming that God will ultimately bring everything in the universe into its appropriate relationship with himself. Paul's claim that this reconciliation takes the form of "making peace" through the cross of Christ reinforces this idea. This language reflects the widespread Old Testament expectation that in the last day God would establish universal *shalom*, "peace," or "well-being."[14] While some theologians may exaggerate the implications of verse 20 in the service of an unbiblical universalism that fails to account for Paul's equally strong emphasis on the need for individuals to have the gospel proclaimed to them and to respond to Christ in faith, this passage does, indeed, assert a thoroughly biblical universalism: that God's work in Christ has in view a reclamation of the entire universe, tainted as it is by human sin (cf. Rom. 8:19–22). The New Testament makes human beings the prime objects of this reconciliation; note in this context Colossians 1:21–23. But the text simply does not allow us to limit this "reconciling" work to human beings. At the very heart of Colossians 1:15–20 is the motif of universality: that nothing in the universe falls outside the scope of God's creative and redemptive work in Christ. The peace that God seeks is a peace that

> "Unless the reference and the power of the redemptive act includes the whole of man's experience and environment, straight out to its farthest horizon, then the redemption is incomplete."
>
> *Joseph Sittler* [15]

not only applies to humans in their relationship to God, but also to humans in their relationship with one another (with implications for our treatment of other people), and to humans in their relationship with the natural world (with implications for our treatment of the material world). Thus Colossians 1:20 rightly features as one of the key New Testament supports for the claim that reclamation of the world of nature must be included in God's new creation work of transformation.[16]

---

11. Most scholars think that Col. 1:15–20 reproduces (or, more likely, is based on) an early Christian "hymn." The evidence for this view is not as strong as some think, but in any case, nothing in our argument depends on a decision one way or the other.

12. Rom. 5:10, 11; 11:15; 1 Cor. 7:11; 2 Cor. 5:18, 19, 20; Eph. 2:16; Col. 1:22.

13. I. Howard Marshall, "The Meaning of 'Reconciliation,'" in *Unity and Diversity in New Testament Theology: Essays in Honor of*

George E. Ladd, ed. Robert A. Guelich (Grand Rapids: Eerdmans, 1978), 126–27.

14. See esp. Isa. 52:6–10; and also, among other texts, Isa. 9:7; 26:3, 12; 27:5; 52:7; 55:12; 66:12; Jer. 29:11; 30:10; 33:6, 9; 46:27; Ezek. 34:29; 37:26; Mic. 5:5; Hag. 2:9; Zech. 9:10.

15. Joseph Sittler, "Called to Unity," *Pulpit Digest* 42 (1962): 12.

16. It is possible, but probably unlikely, that Paul refers to a similar notion in 2 Cor. 5:19a: "God was reconciling the world to

SUMMARY:
THE WORLD OF NATURE IN THE "LAST DAYS"

Many Christians never even consider that their faith might have a bearing on their thinking about and interaction with the natural world. And they might well cite the New Testament itself to justify this neglect. References to nature in the Book of Acts and the New Testament letters are few and undeveloped. The apostles never make the natural world the main focus of their theological teaching. Nor do they directly exhort believers about their responsibilities to respect and care for the natural world. The "triangle of relationships" we have found in the Old Testament—humans and God, humans and other humans, humans and the natural world—might appear to have lost one of its sides. On this view, sadly very widespread, a concern with nature is part of the Old Testament story that has been left behind in the New Testament, as material concerns give way to spiritual ones.

What we have seen in this chapter, however, contradicts this all too common way of viewing the New Testament. The apostles, appropriating keywords and concepts from earlier stages in the story, show that the natural world continues to have an important role in this new phase of the story of redemption. Our texts, however, do not say much about the exact nature of this role. And two matters make it especially challenging to say anything more specific about the issue. First, the texts we have considered in this chapter refer to the natural world with very general language that remains undeveloped in each context: Abraham and his spiritual descendants inherit "the world"; faithful children are promised long life on this "earth"; Christ's coming inaugurates a "new creation"; God is reconciling "all things" to himself.

Second, whatever role the natural world might have in the ongoing story must be understood within the framework of the larger story. As we have seen, the distinctly New Testament part of this framework is marked by the tension between the "already" and the "not yet." The "last days" have been inaugurated, but we await their culmination. In the next chapter, we will look at texts that focus on the "not yet" side of creation's role in redemption, and these texts helpfully fill out some of the specifics in our very general picture. The texts we have looked at in this chapter are much harder to classify. The promise of "long life on the earth" (Eph. 6:2–3), as we have seen, could refer either to the present world or to the one to come. The other texts, precisely because they are so general, probably refer to both "already" and "not yet." The "world" that Abraham's spiritual descendants inherit may refer primarily to the future, when the new earth and new heaven become a reality. But Paul surely

---

himself in Christ." The many parallels between 2 Cor. 4–5 and Col. 1:15–20 suggest that "world" could refer to the cosmos (see, e.g., Joseph Fitzmyer, "Reconciliation in Pauline Theology," in *No Famine in the Land: Studies in Honor of John L. McKenzie*, ed. James W. Flanagan and Anita Weisbrod Robinson [Missoula, MT: Scholars, 1975], 161–62; Furnish, *II Corinthians*, 319). However, the pronouns in the second part of v. 19 seem to suggest that "world" here, as it often does in the New Testament, refers to the world of humanity.

envisages a current fulfillment of this promise also, as the extension of spiritual benefits beyond Jews to the Gentiles requires at the same time the extension of the "land"
to include the "world" where these Gentiles live. "New creation" also participates
fully in Paul's framework of inaugurated eschatology. Just as the Kingdom of God
can be both presently enjoyed (e.g., Col. 1:13–14) and yet will be inherited in the
future (e.g., Gal. 5:21), so "new creation" refers to the totality of God's redemptive
and transformative work, experienced now in renewed individuals and renewed
relationships and to be climaxed in the eschaton in a renewal of "all things" (Acts 3:21;
cf. Col. 1:20). "Paul's image of 'new creation' stands . . . as a shorthand signifier for
the dialectical eschatology that runs throughout the New Testament."[17] To be sure,
the renewal of the world of nature included in God's "new creation" program may
be mainly a future expectation. As we will see in the next chapter, it is at the time of
Christ's return that the creation is ultimately set free. And it is true that the initial
fulfillment of God's redemptive plan has not led to any objective transformation
of creation. As John Reumann puts it, "the grass is not any greener, the sunsets no
more colorful than in pagan days."[18] From another angle, however, believers who
have come to understand that this world is the creation of the God they worship will
find new and deeper meaning in the world they observe and experience. Moreover,
as the "second Adam," Jesus Christ restores the full sense of "image of God" that was
marred in the fall. We who belong to Christ can therefore again "image God" well
by ruling creation in the wise and benevolent way God first intended. As redeemed
"image bearers," God enlists his people in the work of prefiguring and preparing for
the work of ultimate transformation that he will accomplish in the last day. Therefore,
perhaps more as a matter of working toward rather than divine accomplishment, the
transformation of the natural world inherent in "new creation" has a present aspect.

In a similar way, the "already/not yet" pattern of New Testament eschatology
must be applied to Colossians 1:20. While secured in principle by Christ's crucifixion
and available in preliminary form to believers, universal peace is not yet established.
It is because of this work of universal pacification that God will one day indeed be
"all in all" (1 Cor. 15:28) and that "at the name of Jesus every knee should bow, in
heaven and on earth and under the earth, and every tongue acknowledge that Jesus
Christ is Lord, to the glory of God the Father" (Phil. 2:10–11).

In the Old Testament, a restoration of people to the land and the renewal of the
land itself figures prominently in God's promise to Israel. We have argued in this
chapter that this focus on the material world is not abandoned in the New Testament.

17. Richard Hays, *The Moral Vision of the New Testament: Com-munity, Cross, New Creation: A Contemporary Introduction to New Testament Ethics* (San Francisco: HarperSanFrancisco, 1996), 198. For a wide-ranging analysis of New Testament theology along these lines, using the overall image of "new creation," see also Greg Beale, "The Eschatological Conception of New Testament Theology," in *"The Reader Must Understand": Eschatology in Bible and Theology*, ed. K. E. Brower and M. K. Elliott (Leicester: Inter-Varsity, 1997), 11–52.

18. John Reumann, *Creation and New Creation: The Past, Present, and Future of God's Creative Activity* (Minneapolis: Augsburg, 1973), 97–98.

While not nearly as prominent as it is in the Old Testament, God's provision of "space" for his people remains a clear component of the eschatological fulfillment we experience in Christ. That space is no longer tied to a particular piece of terrestrial geography; it now encompasses the entire earth. This "earthly" component in the pattern of fulfillment must be factored into our vision of what God is now doing in the world and also into our hope for the future.

> "While the New Testament's theology of place is refocused, it is just as materialist as that of the Old Testament."
>
> *Craig G. Bartholomew*[19]

RELEVANT QUESTIONS

1. How is God's fulfillment of his plans for "new creation" working itself out in the "already" of your own time?
2. What are you hoping for when you die or when the Lord comes again? How does your hope shape your living as a Christian today?
3. How does the biblical "pattern of fulfillment" inform the way you become involved in creation care today?

---

19. Craig G. Bartholomew, *Where Mortals Dwell: A Christian View of Place for Today* (Grand Rapids: Baker, 2011), 244.

CHAPTER 9

"I AM MAKING EVERYTHING NEW!"

The 1968 movie *2001: A Space Odyssey*, based on an Arthur C. Clarke short story, is regarded by critics and filmmakers as one of the greatest and most influential films ever made. But I never liked it (the date of the movie will furnish the alert reader with a clue about the identity of the author who is writing this sentence). I did not like it because I could never figure out the ending. I don't think I am alone in being frustrated with this kind of uncertainty. Most of us want to know how the plot ends.

Are we in similar doubt about the end of creation's story? Many Christians are uncertain about it. And there is reason for this uncertainty: Scripture itself, at first sight at least, appears to sketch slightly different scenarios for creation's end. Some passages seem to stress discontinuity: we might label this the "replacement" model. According to this model, the present universe we live in will be destroyed and replaced by a new one: "the new heavens and a new earth." Perhaps included under this general rubric is the view that our present creation will be replaced with a purely spiritual existence "in heaven" (a view that has surprisingly little support in Scripture but that nonetheless remains popular). Other parts of the Bible, however, appear to teach that this creation, while changed in certain ways, will endure into eternity. We call this view the "transformation" model.

We will argue in this chapter that the transformation model best summarizes the varied teachings of the Bible about the future of creation. But we want to make an important point about the significance of our argument at the outset. There is no doubt that a belief that our present creation will continue in some form into eternity provides a stronger basis for creation care than the alternative "replacement" model. The longer we think something is going to last, the more we tend to care for it. I take much better care of a valuable book I hope to pass on to my children than the morning newspaper, destined for the recycle container within a few hours. But even if we should think that the Bible teaches that our present creation will be replaced with a new one, care for our created world would still be imperative. For one thing, the eventual destruction of this creation would not negate or in any way detract from the clear teaching of Scripture that God has given humans the responsibility to care for this world—however long it may last or whatever its destiny might be. For another thing, the realization that something may be destined for destruction does not entail a lack of concern for its present condition. Suppose I were to be given a revelation from God that the house I am currently living in is destined to be destroyed one day (as, indeed, all houses will be, if this world lasts long enough). Should I therefore neglect its upkeep? Should I not rather work to make it as comfortable and enjoyable a place for me and my family to live in as long as it lasts? We may believe that creation is destined for destruction—that, as the popular saying has it, "it's all going to burn"—but we should not therefore conclude that we can treat it any way we want in the meantime.

Nevertheless, we think Scripture teaches something different: that this creation will continue, in a transformed state, into eternity. Our God is not a God who discards what he has made, who is defeated by sin and evil. Our God is a redeeming God, a God who is determined to reclaim his fallen world, setting it free from its enslavement to corruption and bringing it to a final state of glory. As we saw in the last chapter, God has already initiated this program of cosmic redemption. In this chapter, we turn from the "already" to the "not yet," as we outline what the Bible says about the last act in the story of creation.

CREATION'S DESTINY: LIBERATION

Paul's letter to the Romans is famous for its brilliant and sustained explanation of the "good news" (Rom. 1:16). After detailing the dilemma that humanity finds itself in because of sin (1:18–3:20), Paul recounts the way in which God has acted to provide human beings a way out of the terrible consequences of their choosing to go their own way. In Christ, God reveals his "righteousness"—his acting to put people in the right before him (3:21–26). And this righteousness is available not just to the historical people of God, Israel, but to all people who believe as Abraham did (3:27–4:25). This is the heart of the good news that Jesus Christ has made available to the world.

But the good news goes further than this. In Christ, believers are put right before God, but we are also guaranteed ultimate salvation on the day that God summons everyone before him for judgment (chaps. 5–8; see esp. 5:9–10). Neither sin (chap. 6) nor the law (chap. 7) can stand in the way of God's saving work among his people, for they are "in Christ," whose death and resurrection rescues us from the condemnation that Adam's sin has brought upon us (5:12–21; 8:1). In the first part of chapter 8, Paul shows how the Spirit confers on believers the new life Christ has won for us—life that we enter into now and which will be finalized in the resurrection of our bodies. And it is just at this point that we see clearly reflected again the "already/ not yet" tension that gives distinctive shape to the New Testament depiction of the work of God for us. As believers, we cry out even now "*Abba*, Father," celebrating our adoption into the family of God (8:14–16). But as children, we are also heirs, waiting for the ultimate revelation of our status as God's children when our bodies are redeemed (8:23). In the second half of Romans 8, then, Paul's purpose is to assure us that, even in the face of suffering, we who are now God's children can look forward with complete confidence to being "glorified" (8:18, 30): nothing "will be able to separate us from the love of God that is in Christ Jesus our Lord" (8:39).

It is in this context that we encounter the most important passage in the New Testament about the future of creation: Romans 8:19–22. We have dealt with certain aspects of this passage earlier, but we now need to return to it for other purposes. It is important to set these verses in their context, so we cite Romans 8:18–25:

> I consider that our present sufferings are not worth comparing with the glory that will be revealed in us. For the creation waits in eager expectation for the children of God to be revealed. For the creation was subjected to frustration, not by its own choice, but by the will of the one who subjected it, in hope that the creation itself will be liberated from its bondage to decay and brought into the freedom and glory of the children of God.
>
> We know that the whole creation has been groaning as in the pains of childbirth right up to the present time. Not only so, but we ourselves, who have the firstfruits of the Spirit, groan inwardly as we wait eagerly for our adoption to sonship, the redemption of our bodies. For in this hope we were saved. But hope that is seen is no hope at all. Who hopes for what they already have? But if we hope for what we do not yet have, we wait for it patiently.

As the context reveals, Paul brings creation into the picture to make a point about believers. Like the created world in general, believers "groan," suffering and eagerly anticipating the completion of God's plan. And, like the created world, believers will one day enjoy release from decay and enjoy the freedom and glory that are given in the finale of God's kingdom work.

Paul introduces "creation" in this text to make a point about believers' experience of suffering and hope. Verses 19–22 support verse 18 in two ways. Believers should not be surprised at the need to wait patiently in the midst of suffering, because this is the experience of the wider creation also. And believers should indeed be eagerly anticipating their ultimate glory because their glorification will mean the liberation of the created world itself. Because Paul's focus in Romans 8 is on human beings, some interpreters have minimized the significance in the reference to creation here. However, we think the point to take away from this passage is just the opposite. By introducing the created world into what has been called "the inner sanctuary [Romans 8] within the cathedral [Romans] of the Christian faith," Paul makes clear that the cosmic dimension of God's redemptive work continues to be basic to early Christian thinking—just as it should be basic to ours. Like Paul, our proclamation of the gospel, while focused on the good news that sinful human beings can be brought into relationship with the God of this universe, must also include the good news that God is bringing his entire creation into the perfect state that it now falls so far short of because of human sin. How are we to understand this good news for creation? What is its destiny according to this passage? What implications might its destiny have for believers here and now? We turn to some details of the text to answer these questions.

The first issue to be tackled is basic to everything else: What is Paul talking about in verses 19–22? The main topic of these verses is clearly the entity expressed by the Greek word *ktisis*: it occurs once in each verse. All modern English versions translate this word as "creation," and this unanimity is quite justified: "creation" is the usual meaning of *ktisis* in both Paul's letters and the New Testament in general. Paul can use the word to refer either to the act of creation (1:20), an individual "created thing" (1:25), or to the created world in general (8:39). The content and context of Romans 8:19–22 make clear that a general reference to "creation" is intended here. A more difficult question is whether Paul intends the word to include the entire created universe or some more limited part of the creation. Noting that the creation is said here to "hope" (v. 20) and "groan" (v. 22), some interpreters insist that the reference must include human beings. However, the transition from verses 22 to 23 makes it very hard to think that "creation" here includes believers. And Paul would hardly credit unbelievers with the kind of hope he speaks of here. Most interpreters therefore conclude, rightly, that Paul is using "creation" to refer to the nonhuman creation.[1] The apostle reveals here his debt not only to the content, but also to the style of the Old Testament: in proclaiming God's purposes for the cosmos, psalmists and prophets often attributed human emotions and activities to creation (e.g., Ps. 65:12–13; Isa. 24:4; Jer. 4:28; 12:4).

In keeping with his "big picture" approach in Romans 5–8 (e.g., Adam vs. Christ in 5:12–21), Paul in these verses gives us a broad outline of the history and destiny of creation. To be sure, Paul says nothing explicit here about the original state of creation, but his claim that it has been "subjected to decay" certainly implies that its original state was without such decay. The original "good" creation of Genesis 1 is assumed here. In keeping with his concern to help believers understand their own movement from suffering to glory (8:18), Paul's focus is on the contrast between the "fallen" state of creation and its destined liberation from decay. In an earlier chapter, we assessed what Paul and the rest of Scripture says about the "fallenness" of creation and discovered that the emphasis is on the brokenness of the relationship between human beings and the earth. This brokenness goes back to Adam and is instantiated in the continuing sin of human beings, who, turning aside from God, focus on what

---

1. Many would argue that "sub-human," while a somewhat questionable way of referring to the created world, might be more accurate—if, that is, Paul is excluding angels from the creation he describes here.

they (mistakenly) consider to be their own good to the detriment of the good of others and of the created world. The "groaning" of creation (8:22) is in fact an apt and poignant description of the state of the created world—the "environment"—in our own day. By abusing our role as stewards of creation, we have contributed to the "frustration" of that creation, preventing it from achieving its ultimate end of glorifying God by being what God intended it to be.

Our concern now is with what this passage teaches about the future of creation. Paul does not go into detail, but he does provide us with three general points. First, we can assume that the "frustration" to which creation is now subjected will be removed in the future. The word translated "frustration" often connotes the worthlessness associated with idols or ungodliness in general (see, e.g., Ps. 4:2; Paul uses the cognate verb in Rom. 1:21 to refer to the futile thinking of sinful people). Human sin has prevented creation from reaching the goal God had set for it: to function harmoniously with humans and to glorify God. This will change, Paul implies, when the children of God are revealed. Creation will then function as God intended; people will no longer feel estranged from it, and it will thereby glorify God.

The second description of creation's future is more explicit: "The creation itself will be liberated from its bondage to decay" (Rom. 8:21). "Bondage" or "slavery" (Gk. *douleia*) is a typical Pauline way of characterizing the state of believers before coming to Christ (Gal. 5:1; Rom. 8:15; cf. Gal. 4:24). Indeed, the apostle makes clear that all humans are "enslaved" to some power. What distinguishes Christians is that they are no longer enslaved to idols (Gal. 4:8; 1 Thess. 1:9) and sin (Rom. 6:6), but to Christ (Rom. 14:18; Col. 3:24). The "slavery" of creation described here, however, continues: creation's being set free falls on the "not yet" end of the eschatological agenda. As we observed in chapter 6, the "decay" to which creation is now enslaved is difficult to identify, since the word can also be translated "corruption" (e.g., ESV; cf. Eph. 4:22), "ruin," or "destruction" (Gal. 6:8). In light of the Old Testament texts to which Paul is alluding (Gen. 3 and Isa. 24–27), this is Paul's summary word for the condition of creation after the fall into sin. While not itself "guilty" of sin, creation suffers because of the sin of human beings. The sin of Adam brought God's curse on creation, a curse that focuses on a new estrangement between humans and creation (Gen. 3:17). Continuing human sin "corrupts" creation in various ways. We selfishly and mindlessly consume its resources; we pollute it with unsafe manufacturing processes; we accelerate potentially harmful atmospheric changes by pouring greenhouse gases into the air. Simply put, the "decay" of creation means that it is used and abused in ways God never intended, preventing it from being what it was designed to be and thereby hindering its ability fully to glorify God.

Paul's third description of the future of creation is closely related to the second: creation, Paul claims, will be "brought into the freedom and glory of the children of God" (Rom. 8:21). The NIV suggests that creation will itself experience "glory."

However, the text is not so clear about this. The Greek here could be paraphrased "the freedom that accompanies the glory that the children of God will experience." God's purpose ultimately to "glorify" his people is the overarching theme of Romans 8:18–30, mentioned at the beginning and the end of the section. It is, in fact, one of the key overarching themes of chapters 5–8 (see 5:2). Creation, Paul is clear, will share in the freedom that will accompany this glory. If, as Haley Goranson has argued, the "glory" in view here is linked to the glory associated with God's rulers, it might be said that creation finds its freedom precisely when God's human creatures rule within creation as they were created to.[2] But in any case, what Paul does explicitly attribute to creation's future is "freedom." He uses the word absolutely, without specifying just what creation is freed from. Paul uses this word in this absolute way elsewhere to characterize the benefits people enjoy in Christ (1 Cor. 10:29; 2 Cor. 3:17; Gal. 2:4; 5:1, 13). However, that from which believers are set free is often clear from the context (e.g., the law in Galatians), and so here also Paul has just mentioned "decay" or "ruin" as one of those things from which creation is set free. Nevertheless, it is possible that Paul intends "freedom" to serve as a kind of summary word for all the good things God is going to do for creation in the future.

Romans 8:19–22, in final analysis, is tantalizingly vague about just what the future of creation will look like. But it does make two vital points. First, this creation does, indeed, have a future. There can be no doubt that Paul is referring throughout this paragraph to the created world we now see all around us. It is *this creation* that is "in bondage to decay," that "groans," and that will one day enjoy "the freedom that accompanies the glory that the children of God will experience" (v. 22). This text, then, makes clear that creation has a secure role in the continuing drama of redemption. The fulfillment of God's redemptive plan has taken a form that is not always clearly revealed in the Old Testament itself: there are "mysteries" in the Old Testament revelation of that plan that are only revealed in the New Testament. But this text makes clear that the created world has a secure place in the scope of New Testament fulfillment. The New Testament has not replaced a material focus in the Old Testament with a "spiritual" one. As in the Old Testament, the New Testament reveals that God's redemptive plan encompasses the whole of reality—physical as well as spiritual. Humans, nature, the spiritual realm, the universe itself—nothing will be left out of God's final redemptive work. As we contemplate the terrible strain that creation is under in our time, we badly need to recapture this grand vision of God's redemptive plan.

Second, Romans 8:19–22 also makes clear that it is God who will transform creation and that he will do it at the culmination of redemptive history. The one who

---

2. Haley Goranson, "'Image' and 'Glory' Redefined: Keys to the Puzzle of the Presence of Adam in Romans" (paper, Society of Biblical Literature International, St. Andrews, Scotland, July 2013).

both "subjects" creation to frustration and sets it free from decay is God. Creation's waiting in eager expectation "for the children of God to be revealed" (v. 19) implies that it is at this time that creation will be transformed. In this context, the "revelation" of the children of God must refer to that moment when "the glory . . . will be revealed in us"—when believers are publicly disclosed as the glorified people of God, an event that accompanies Christ's own final revelation (1 Cor. 1:7; 2 Thess. 1:5–10; 1 Peter 4:13). Creation's ultimate hope lies in something only God can do. On the one hand, this truth should encourage us: there is, indeed, hope for creation! And this hope "does not put us to shame" (Rom. 5:5). We know the one who has promised; he will do it. Yet this truth also reminds us of our human limitations. No human effort, no government program, no Christian ministry will transform creation. As long as sinful humans populate creation, it has no hope for ultimate transformation.

> "If we accept the diagnosis that human wrongdoing is responsible for ecological degradations, it follows that those who are concerned to live according to God's will for his world must be concerned to avoid and to repair damage to God's creation as far as possible. Like the coming of the Kingdom of God, we cannot achieve the liberation of creation but we can anticipate it."
>
> *Richard Bauckham* [3]

Christians must therefore resist various forms of "green utopianism": the idea prevalent among some environmentalists that our own programs, if only fully implemented, will usher in environmental nirvana. The story of creation in the Bible begins and ends with an act of God. On the other hand, however, our distinctive Christian hope does not mean we should fall prey to a pessimistic "what good can we do anyway?" passivity. It is God who ultimately transforms his creation. But this does not mean we have no calling or role in working to bring creation closer to the goal God has set for it. The revelation of God's purposes carries with it a calling to participate in those purposes. And while our role ultimately cannot be to transform creation, we do have a role in bringing creation closer to that goal. We cannot create Eden on earth; only God can—and will! But God expects us, indeed commands us, to anticipate to the best of our ability that final state. "Always give yourselves fully to the work of the Lord, because you know that your labor in the Lord is not in vain" (1 Cor. 15:58). We live "between the times" as people who rejoice in having been adopted as God's children (Rom. 8:14–17) and eagerly anticipate our ultimate inclusion in God's family when our bodies are raised (Rom. 8:23). So we work in the sober realization that our best efforts will always fall short of the glorious outcome God intends for us and the world. Yet we also work in confidence because God supplies his Spirit to guide and empower us. And we work in hope because we know we are aligned with the purposes of the God of this universe. In this way, also, we give others a chance to catch a glimpse of what is coming.

---

3. *The Bible and Ecology*, 100.

CREATION'S DESTINY:
A PLACE "WHERE RIGHTEOUSNESS DWELLS"

Romans 8 paints a clear picture: the story of creation ends with its liberation, freed from its "bondage to corruption," as it finally becomes the kind of place God has always intended that it should be. Romans 8, to use the terms we introduced above, teaches a "transformation" view of creation. The continuity between this creation and the next that we see in this text resonates with the trajectory of teaching about creation in the Old Testament and the Gospels. Yet anyone familiar with their Bible will know that other passages at first sight do not seem to present the same kind of end for creation. The clearest and most important of these comes in the third chapter of Peter's second letter. We quote here the relevant section of this chapter in full:

> Above all, you must understand that in the last days scoffers will come, scoffing and following their own evil desires. They will say, "Where is this 'coming' he promised? Ever since our ancestors died, everything goes on as it has since the beginning of creation." But they deliberately forget that long ago by God's word the heavens came into being and the earth was formed out of water and by water. By these waters also the world of that time was deluged and destroyed. By the same word the present heavens and earth are reserved for fire, being kept for the day of judgment and destruction of the ungodly.
>
> But do not forget this one thing, dear friends: With the Lord a day is like a thousand years, and a thousand years are like a day. The Lord is not slow in keeping his promise, as some understand slowness. Instead he is patient with you, not wanting anyone to perish, but everyone to come to repentance.
>
> But the day of the Lord will come like a thief. The heavens will disappear with a roar; the elements will be destroyed by fire, and the earth and everything done in it will be laid bare.
>
> Since everything will be destroyed in this way, what kind of people ought you to be? You ought to live holy and godly lives as you look forward to the day of God and speed its coming. That day will bring about the destruction of the heavens by fire, and the elements will melt in the heat. But in keeping with his promise we are looking forward to a new heaven and a new earth, where righteousness dwells.
>
> So then, dear friends, since you are looking forward to this, make every effort to be found spotless, blameless and at peace with him. (2 Peter 3:3–14)

At first glance, this passage appears to teach a "replacement" model of creation's end: Christians look forward to a "new heaven and a new earth" that will be put in place after the existing heavens and earth are destroyed. It is this text that Christians have especially in view (whether they know it or not) when they think of the present creation in terms of the slogan "it's all going to burn."

Setting this text alongside Romans 8 presents thoughtful Christians with a dilemma—one that arises with respect to many theological and practical issues. God has chosen to reveal his Word to us in a diverse set of sixty-six books, written over the course of a millennium or more. We believe that these sixty-six books together make up one book, "*the* Bible," inspired by God and therefore ultimately unified in its teaching on any given subject. Yet this unity is not always easy to discover—witness the many disagreements among committed Christians on a variety of topics. The end God intends for this present creation is one of those. It is not enough simply to cite Romans 8 or Colossians 1:20 and conclude that Scripture teaches that creation will be transformed. Nor can we simply quote 2 Peter 3 and conclude that creation will be destroyed. The view we ultimately adopt as "the biblical view" must be able to integrate the teaching of all these passages.

The process of relating the various texts of the Bible on any given topic has been compared to putting together a puzzle. In this case, however, we don't have the box to tell us what the final picture is supposed to look like, nor do the puzzle pieces have a clear shape. We ourselves shape them as we interpret the texts they represent. The task before us, then, is to fit together the Romans 8 and 2 Peter 3 pieces of the "end of creation" puzzle in a way that respects each of these key texts and at the same time yields a coherent picture. Of course, we must acknowledge that our starting point can affect the outcome. We may be accused of fixing the shape of Romans 8 and then forcibly shaping 2 Peter 3 (and other relevant texts) in order to match its contours. We run the risk, in other words, of forcing 2 Peter 3 into the mold that we have already established for Romans 8. Had we started with 2 Peter 3 and read Romans 8 in its light, it might be objected, our conclusions would be quite different. The force of this point must be acknowledged. Yet we have to begin somewhere. We have to start with some pieces of the puzzle. What is important is that we be willing to go back and reshape Romans 8 if we simply can't fit new pieces of the puzzle into the shape we have already given it. Because the Bible comes to us in many different books, with different forms and emphases, there will be times when we will struggle to fit every passage on a topic into a neat pattern. When that happens, we want to make sure we are constructing a picture that does most justice to all the texts—even if, as sometimes happen, some texts don't fit as naturally as others into that overall picture

As we have seen, the New Testament, while not saying a lot about the created world, claims that it will be "reconciled" (Col. 1:20) and "liberated" (Rom. 8:21). This vision for the creation does not appear to be compatible with the idea of creation's destruction. What, then, is 2 Peter 3 teaching? How can this critical puzzle piece be fit into the larger picture of creation's transformation? We will argue that, despite first appearances, 2 Peter 3 is not teaching that the present creation will be annihilated and replaced with a totally new one. Rather, Peter is teaching that the present creation will be radically renovated by God so that it might become a place "where righteousness dwells" (v. 13), cleansed of sin and evil.

Let's begin with the context. Peter's second letter is laser-focused on false teachers. Peter describes and warns about these teachers in chapter 2, but he also has them in view in some things he says in both chapters 1 and 3. Note 1:16: "For we did not follow cleverly devised stories when we told you about the coming of our Lord Jesus Christ in power. . . ."[4] The focus we see here on what we might call "eschatological skepticism" is mirrored at the beginning of the passage we have quoted above in chapter 3: "Above all, you must understand that in the last days scoffers will come, scoffing and following their own evil desires. They will say, 'Where is this "coming" he promised? Ever since our ancestors died, everything goes on as it has since the beginning of creation'" (vv. 3–4).

As an appropriate response to these mockers, then, Peter says quite a lot about the cosmos in this passage. This focus is signaled by the way he pairs "heaven" and "earth" throughout the text.

"the heavens came into being"/"the earth was formed" (v. 5)
"present heavens and earth" (v. 7)
"the heavens will disappear"/"the elements will be destroyed"/
     "the earth . . . will be laid bare" (v. 10)
"destruction of the heavens"/"the elements will melt" (v. 12)
"a new heaven and a new earth" (v. 13)

"Heavens" or "heaven" takes its meaning from its opposite, "earth."[5] It denotes all the created universe apart from planet earth. The phrase "heavens and earth" is what we call a "merism," a literary device that pairs two or more parts of an entity to denote the entity as a whole. As in the familiar Genesis 1:1, then, "heaven(s) and earth" denotes the entire created universe.

This focus on the cosmos, however, is not for its own sake. The false teachers probably combined skepticism about a future judgment with the immoral lifestyle for which Peter condemns them in chapter 2. What does it matter what we do, they may have reasoned, since there is no day of judgment we have to worry about?

---

4. Second Peter 1:16 refers to the Transfiguration, but the language Peter uses to describe it suggests he views it as an anticipation of the final coming of Christ.

5. The Hebrew word for "heaven" is plural in form but singular in meaning. How to carry over the meaning of the Hebrew in English is debated, and various English versions follow different patterns. The NIV tends to use "heaven" when the reference is to the place where God dwells and "heavens" when the reference is to the part of the cosmos distinct from the earth. Hence the NIV uses the plural throughout this text, following the lead of the Greek, which also uses *ouranos* in the plural throughout. The exception is the phrase "a new heaven and a new earth," in v. 13, where the singular is used because of the technical nature of the phrase (see Rev. 21:1).

In response to this, Peter reminds them that the history of the cosmos has not been a uniform, uninterrupted history. God has regularly intervened. Indeed, the created world has not always been here: God brought it into being at a certain point in time (3:5). That same world was "destroyed" by God in the judgment of the flood (v. 6). And, as the heavens and the earth had a beginning, so they have an end: they are "reserved for fire, being kept for the day of judgment and destruction of the ungodly" (v. 7). Peter assures his readers that God will keep his promise to send his Son back to judge the earth—but in his own time (vv. 8–9). He then goes on to describe what the coming of the "day of the Lord" will look like. Our text, then, responds to the false teachers by warning them of the reality of judgment to come.

But Peter's purpose is not only negative—to counter the skepticism of the false teachers—but positive as well. In the middle of his description of the end, he asks the searching question: "What kind of people ought you to be?" (v. 11). The ultimate fate of creation should remind us of the importance of leading "holy and godly lives." Living this way will commend us to Christ at his return (v. 14), but it will also, Peter claims, "speed" the coming of that day (v. 12). While there is understandable debate about just how our godly living might bring the day closer, this allusion reminds us again that human response to God is not unrelated to his own plans for the created world. We again see that thinking about creation's end should not engender passivity but a renewed and energetic devotion to do the work of God's kingdom now.

A second step in our interpretation is to establish the text we are working with. Manuscripts of the Greek New Testament have different words at the end of verse 10, and a decision about the right text has significant bearing on what this passage as a whole is teaching. Several variations exist, but three deserve consideration.

1. "will be burned up"—translating *katakaēsetai*
2. "will be found"—translating *heurethēsetai*
3. "will not be found"—translating *ouch heurethēsetai*

The first option has a venerable history in the English Bible, being reflected in the KJV and also lying behind the renderings in the NKJV, RSV, NJB, and NASB. But it is questionable because it uses the language of "burning" that appears elsewhere in our text—leading us to suspect that scribes might have added it because it seemed to fit well in the passage.

Nearly all recent commentators and English translations have adopted the second option. A fundamental principle in evaluating textual variants is that "the more difficult reading should be preferred." This principle reflects the tendency of scribes to simplify and clarify the texts they were copying. And it is difficult at first glance to understand what the earth and everything being "found" might mean. It is probably this difficulty that led the editors of the latest edition of the Nestle-Aland *Greek New Testament* (28th ed.) to adopt the third option. The editors apparently thought that, despite its sparse support (it has no Greek support at all, but is conjectured on the basis of some ancient translations), it made best sense of the verse. But a text without any Greek support should be considered only if all the extant Greek options simply make so sense. And this is not the case.[6] The second option, "will be found," is certainly difficult. But it has the support of some early and reliable Greek manuscripts, and we can make sense of it when we recognize that the verb "find" can sometimes have the sense of "expose." Hence the translation adopted in most English translations: "will be laid bare" (NIV; NET); "will be exposed" (ESV; CEB); "will be disclosed" (NRSV; HCSB). Peter would be claiming that the day of the Lord will expose both "the earth" and "the things done in the earth." Faced with divine scrutiny on the day of judgment, the tendency of human beings is to cover over their deeds, recognizing how far short from the divine ideal they fall. "People will flee to caves in the rocks and to holes in the ground from the fearful presence of the LORD and the splendor of his majesty, when he rises to shake the earth" (Isa. 2:19; see also Rev. 6:15–16). But there will be no hiding from God on that great day: all will be "laid bare" before God so that he might judge fairly and equitably. See, for example, Isaiah 26:21: "See, the LORD is coming out of his dwelling to punish the people of the earth for their sins. The earth will disclose the blood shed on it; the earth will conceal its slain no longer." Peter himself seems to suggest this same general idea in his first letter: "These [trials] have come so that the proven genuineness of your faith—of greater worth than gold, which perishes even though refined by fire—may result ["be found to result in"] in praise, glory and honor when Jesus Christ is revealed" (1:7).

With these two preliminary points in place, we are in position to evaluate the way Peter views the relationship of this creation to the "new heaven and a new earth." We begin with the contrast that Peter draws between "the present heavens and earth" (2 Peter 3:7) and "a new heaven and a new earth" (v. 13). Peter undoubtedly bases his prediction on Isaiah, whose prophecy about a "new heavens and a new earth" is the climax of his prophetic utterances.

> See, I will create new heavens and a new earth. The former things will not be remembered, nor will they come to mind. (65:17)

> "As the new heavens and the new earth that I make will endure before me," declares the LORD, "so will your name and descendants endure. From one New Moon to another and from one Sabbath to another, all people will come and bow down before me," says the LORD. "And they will go out and look upon the dead bodies of those who rebelled against me; the worms that eat them

---

6. No English translation has adopted this reading. For some pertinent comments on the new 28th ed. of the Nestle-Aland text, see Peter Head, "*Editio Critica Maior*: An Introduction and Assessment," *TynBul* 61 (2010): 131–52 (he comments on 2 Peter 3:10 on pp. 145–46).

will not die, the fire that burns them will not be quenched, and they will be loathsome to all mankind." (66:22–24)

The context of the first prophecy refers to a series of blessings, among them very long life ("the one who fails to reach a hundred will be considered accursed"—Isa. 65:20), the enjoyment of the fruits of one's work ("my chosen ones will long enjoy the work of their hands"—v. 22), and the establishment of peace between wild and domesticated animals ("the wolf and the lamb will feed together, and the lion will eat straw like the ox"—v. 25). These changes might imply a radically different creation than the one that we know—a world in which people live much longer lives than now and in which wolves and lions are no longer carnivores. But we must also be sensitive to the poetic nature of prophetic language and note that the emphasis here (as in the related text, Isa. 11:6–9) is on the end of untimely death, the reversal of the futility of the curse, and the removal of strife between wild creatures and the human, domesticated world. In Isaiah as a whole, the focus of future hope is consistently on *restoration* and the transformation of this world, which may suggest that Isaiah's vision of the future even in chapters 65 and 66 is not of a new universe replacing the one we now live in but of a renewal and transformation of the present world. In the final analysis, it might be that neither Isaiah nor 2 Peter 3 provides enough evidence on their own to determine whether a "replacement" model or a "transformation" model best represents the biblical perspective; certainly neither text eliminates the "transformation" option from consideration.

Peter's three references to "fire"/"burning" with respect to the present cosmos might nonetheless appear to be more decisive:

"the present heavens and earth are reserved for fire" (v. 7)
"the elements will be destroyed by fire" (v. 10)
"the destruction of the heavens by fire" (v. 12)
"the elements will melt in the heat" (v. 12)

Some interpreters think Peter depends here on a widespread idea in his own culture that history would culminate in a world conflagration, a conflagration out of which would emerge a new and transformed world. But more likely the primary background for Peter's imagery is the Old Testament, where "fire" often connotes God's judgment. Note, for instance, this passage from Isaiah, which immediately precedes the "new heavens and a new earth" text we cited above:

See, the LORD is coming with fire,
    and his chariots are like a whirlwind;
he will bring down his anger with fury,
    and his rebuke with flames of fire.

> For with fire and with his sword
>> the LORD will execute judgment on all people,
>> and many will be those slain by the LORD. (Isa. 66:15–16)

Isaiah very often uses the imagery of fire to refer to God's judgment (Isa. 1:31; 4:4; 5:24; 9:5, 19; 10:16–17; 26:11; 27:4; 29:6; 30:27–33; 31:9; 33:11, 14–15; 47:14; see also, e.g., Nah. 1:6; Zeph. 1:18; 3:8; Mal. 4:1).

Note also Micah 1:3–4:

> Look! The LORD is coming from his dwelling place;
>> he comes down and treads the heights of the earth.
> The mountains melt beneath him
>> and the valleys split apart,
> like wax before the fire,
>> like water rushing down a slope. (See also Ps. 97:3–4; Isa. 63:19–64:1 LXX)

Old Testament prophetic texts are full of this kind of imagery. And imagery it is. We make fundamental mistakes in interpretation if we don't understand the "language game" in which particular words are being used. "Hail Mary" means one thing in religious language; it refers to something quite different in football commentary. Thus, if I were to cite, for example, Revelation 5:6—the "Lamb" who has been slain—as evidence that my Savior is a beast rather than a human, I would be mistaking the "language game" John is playing. To be sure, there is considerable controversy over just how literally we should take such passages. But the "language game" of apocalyptic-style prophecy features vivid references to physical destruction in order to convey the terrifying reality of God's intervention to judge a sinful and rebellious world. We suspect that Peter, in dependence on the prophets, is making a similar point to his readers and, indirectly, to the false teachers: the day of the Lord will be an "earth-shattering" event.

At this point, it is important to recall the larger point Peter is making in chapter 3 of his second letter: that everyone needs to take into account the terrifying reality of God's intervention to judge the world of human beings. The flood, to which Peter refers in verse 6 as the "destruction" of the world, was of course intended to cleanse the world of human sin and evil. Peter suggests the parallel future "destruction" of the heavens and the earth has a similar focus, since he describes that day as one of "judgment and destruction of the ungodly" (v. 7). The same concern is reflected in his reference to God's delay of the end because of his desire that no one should "perish" (v. 9). On the other hand, positively, the "new heaven" and "new earth" will be a place "where righteousness dwells" (v. 13). We don't deny that Peter speaks about the destiny of the cosmos in this passage. But what happens in the cosmos here is significant not simply for its own sake, but because of what it says about God's purposes for humans. Much of the imagery about the cosmos, then, is intended (as in its OT background) to convey the awesome nature of this final judgment.

But the claim that "the elements will melt in the heat" (v. 12) raises yet another question: What are these "elements" (see also v. 10)? Since the Greek word translated "elements" (*stoicheia*) was often used in the ancient world to refer to the fundamental building blocks of the universe, many interpreters think Peter uses the word to refer generally to the physical universe. However, this same word was sometimes used more narrowly to refer to "heavenly" bodies: the sun, moon, planets, and stars.[7] In verse 12, then, as in verse 10, Peter may not be referring to the destruction of the physical universe generally, but, more narrowly, to the removal of the heavenly bodies. This more specific meaning of "elements" would fit very well into the scenario that Peter seems to be presenting here. We noted earlier that the end of verse 10 is best rendered something like "the earth and everything done in it will be laid bare." But in order to "lay bare" the earth and "everything done in it," God needs to strip away those things that might obscure his view: the "heavens" (perhaps referring especially to the outer parts of the heavens) and the "elements" (the inner parts of the heavens).[8]

This interpretation of "elements" is very attractive, but we cannot finally be sure if it is right (and in fact the authors of this book are divided over its meaning!). "Elements" as a reference broadly to all the basic components of the physical universe was very common in Peter's day, and in verse 12, the pairing of "elements" with "heavens" might suggest it has this broader sense in this context. What is finally most important for our purposes, however, is to see that whether "elements" means the components of the physical world or the heavenly bodies, their "melting" does not clearly connote destruction.

Yet one might respond to all this that we are trying to avoid the obvious. All this exegetical quibbling cannot change the brute fact that Peter plainly predicts, not once, but three times, the "destruction" of the existing cosmos (vv. 10, 11, 12). Yet it is not at all clear that this language is, in fact, intended to describe the total physical annihilation of the cosmos. And we don't have to look further than the immediate context to make this point. Peter uses this same language in verse 6 to describe what happened to "the world" in Noah's day.[9] As every Bible reader knows, however, the flood did not annihilate the existing world; it cleansed it of evil (and especially of evil people), but the earth survived intact and renewed.[10]

---

7. We cannot point to any text predating Peter's letter that uses *stoicheia* in this sense. But the word is used in this sense in texts shortly after Peter's day, so there is good reason to think this usage was available to Peter.

8. See esp. Moo and White, *Let Creation Rejoice*, 121–22. As an image related to fire and heat, "melting" also refers to judgment in the OT. See the text from Mic. 1:3–4, cited above, as well as, e.g., Ps. 46:6; 68:2; 97:5; 147:18; Ezek. 22:20–22; Amos 9:5; Mic. 1:4; Nah. 1:5.

9. Peter employs two different Greek "word groups" to connote "destruction" in our text: *lyō* in vv. 10, 11, and 12 and *apollymi* (a verb) and *apōleia* (a noun) in vv. 6 and 7.

10. A few interpreters have argued that "world" in this verse refers to human beings. But the sequence in our passage—creation of the "heavens and the earth" (v. 5), destruction of "the world of that time," "present heaven and earth" to be destroyed—makes clear that "world" here is equivalent to "heavens and earth."

It is also worth observing that the words Peter uses to describe "destruction" can be used elsewhere to describe what happens to ointment that is poured out wastefully and to no apparent purpose (*apōleia* in Matt. 26:8; Mark 14:4); to wineskins that can no longer function because they have holes in them (*apollymi* in Matt. 9:17; Mark 2:22; Luke 5:37); or to a coin that has been "lost" (*apollymi* in Luke 15:9). In none of these cases do the objects cease to exist; they cease to be useful or to exist in their original, intended state.

When we look carefully at the meaning of Peter's keywords and take into account the "language game" of apocalyptic prophecy that Peter is playing, the idea that he is predicting an eventual annihilation of the universe by fire is not so evident. To be sure, this *could* be what the text means. We still think, taken on its own terms, that this is not the most obvious meaning of the passage. But when we turn back to the larger biblical-theological issue and seek to fit the puzzle piece of 2 Peter 3 into the overall picture provided by the rest of Scripture, this interpretation becomes even less attractive. We think it is reasonable, therefore, to conclude that 2 Peter 3 does not intend to describe the annihilation of the universe on the day of the Lord. Rather, as the parallel with the flood suggests, Peter is predicting that God will "destroy" this world by judging evil, establishing justice and peace, and radically transforming the creation into a place where "righteousness makes its home," reflecting God's original intentions for it from the beginning.

CREATION'S DESTINY: "A NEW HEAVEN AND A NEW EARTH"

We might naturally expect to find more specifics about the future of creation in the Book of Revelation. And it is indeed the case that the natural world has a larger place in Revelation than in any other New Testament book; however, the focus is usually on the present rather than the future. The bulk of Revelation contains a series of visions that describe the tribulations and judgments of a world in upheaval and under God's judgment; other scenes portray all of creation gathered around the throne in endless praise to God and Christ. But at the end of the book especially, we do get a tantalizing glimpse of what John, like Isaiah and 2 Peter, describes as "a new heaven and a new earth." As in the parallel we have just studied in 2 Peter 3:13, this phrase clearly refers to the entire created world.[11] And, as in 2 Peter 3, interpreters sometimes argue that John is predicting the destruction of this creation and its replacement with a different one. But this is even less clear here than it is in 2 Peter.

11. As in 2 Peter 3:13, the NIV uses the singular "heaven" (which corresponds here to the Greek). Indeed, Revelation, except in 12:12, always uses *ouranos* in the singular. "Heaven and earth" occurs elsewhere in Revelation in 20:11; other pairings of heaven with earth in Revelation are found in 5:3 (with "under the earth" added); 10:6 (with "the sea"; cf. also 12:12; 14:7, with both "sea" and "springs of water"); 5:13 adds both "under the earth" and "on the sea."

Like the Old Testament prophetic books that John so often echoes and alludes to, and other Jewish apocalypses before him, John makes extensive use of symbolism, metaphor, and poetic language to convey the message of his Revelation. Readers are invited into a world of stories and images that are intended to communicate truth about God and his purposes but which are not intended—and in fact make no sense—if they are read as straightforward depictions of physical phenomena. Consider again the central images of the book: Christ as a slain lamb, and Jesus's portrayal elsewhere in the book as a lion, a rider on a white horse, and Daniel's exalted "son of man." All of these images call for serious study and reflection to understand what is being revealed about the identity of Christ, but a so-called "literal" interpretation of the images would miss John's point entirely. As we observed earlier, we have to be aware of the "language game" we are playing. The difficulty of pinpointing the referents in John's language renders very difficult any kind of certainty about just what John's vision is saying about the relationship between this creation and "a new heaven and a new earth." Several texts need to be considered.

Immediately after the promise of a new heaven and a new earth, John goes on to say, "for the first heaven and the first earth had passed away." While a different Greek verb is used, this prediction is very similar to Peter's claim that "the heavens will pass away with a roar" (2 Peter 3:10 ESV).[12] This "passing away" could refer to the destruction of the present world. But it could equally suggest that God intends to judge and annihilate the sinful elements in this universe—without destroying it.[13] Another verse in the context claims that, with the advent of the Great White Throne judgment, "the earth and the heavens fled from [God's] presence" (Rev. 20:11). Again, this imagery might suggest the destruction of the universe.[14] More likely, however, the language describes the depths of the fear of the entire created world in the face of God's coming for judgment.[15] Equally unclear is the last part of this verse: "and there was no place for them." Does this refer to destruction[16] or to judgment?[17] Or, and this seems most likely, does it refer to the fact that no place is found for them to hide from the judgment of God? In fact, Revelation 11:18

---

12. Other NT texts say something similar (using, however, a different Greek verb, *parerchomai*). Jesus describes the "passing away" of the heaven and the earth (Matt. 5:18; 24:35//Mark 13:31// Luke 21:33; 16:17). Paul claims that the new creation is preceded by the passing away of the "old" (2 Cor. 5:17).

13. The standard Greek lexicon of the NT (BDAG) classifies the meaning of the verb here (*aperchomai*) under the heading "to discontinue as a condition or state."

14. Grant Osborne, *The Book of Revelation*, BECNT (Grand Rapids: Baker, 2002), 721 (he compares 16:20).

15. The closest parallels to Rev. 20:11 are Ps. 104:5–7: "He set the earth on its foundations; it can never be moved. You covered it with the watery depths as with a garment; the waters stood above the mountains. But at your rebuke the waters fled, at the sound of

your thunder they took to flight"; and Isa. 17:13: "Although the peoples roar like the roar of surging waters, when he rebukes them they flee far away, driven before the wind like chaff on the hills, like tumbleweed before a gale."

16. David Aune, *Revelation 17–22*, WBC 52C (Waco, TX: Word, 1998), 1101, 1117 (he compares *1 Enoch* 96:16).

17. The closest biblical parallel to John's language is found in Theodotion's version of Dan. 2:35, where the materials of the great statute in Nebuchadnezzar's dream are carried away by the wind, and "no place was found for them" (*kai topos ouch heurethē autois*). The immediate reference (within the parameters of the dream) is to a material phenomenon, but the meaning has to do with judgment. See also Rev. 12:8.

suggests that God stands firmly against the destruction of his creation: according to this verse, the final judgment involves not destroying the earth but "destroying those who destroy the earth."

If some of these texts leave us uncertain about the fate of the created world, other passages in this context suggest more strongly that the "new heaven" and "new earth" does not replace the existing universe but transforms it. The Greek word for "new" that John uses in 21:1—*kainos*—generally connotes a renewal of what already exists rather than something that is totally new (which is usually connoted with *neos*). Significant also is the summarizing proclamation of God in Revelation 21:5: "I am making everything new!" He does not proclaim "I am making new things." "Making everything new" rather suggests the renewal of what exists, not its replacement with something else. The voices from heaven in Revelation 11:15 proclaim, in words made famous by the "Hallelujah Chorus," "The kingdom of the world has become the kingdom of our Lord and of his Messiah, and he will reign for ever and ever." The concern in these visions is with the need to transform the existing sinful world into a world in which the reign of God and his Messiah is fully realized. "Babylon" (Rev. 17–18) must be replaced with the New Jerusalem (21:9–22:5). John's description of this New Jerusalem, which is closely tied to the "new heaven" and "new earth" of 21:1, is also suggestive. The text is full of references to the original creation, a place where the kings of the earth bring their splendor into it (21:24), implying that John intends to portray "the reverse of the curse," a return to the conditions of Eden and, more than this, the realizations of God's purposes for creation from the beginning, taking it to the end he always intended for it.

CREATION TRANSFORMED

So what does the picture of the end of creation look like now that we have tried to fit together some of the key puzzle pieces? The pieces of 2 Peter 3 and Revelation 21–22 could certainly be shaped in a way that seems to support a "replacement" model. But, as we have argued, a closer look at both passages, sensitive to their style and the metaphorical nature of their language, raises serious doubts about this conclusion. On the other hand, at least two other puzzle pieces—Romans 8:19–22 and Colossians 1:20—can only fit a picture of creation's transformation. We add to this exegetical support for a transformation model an important theological point: the resurrection of the body. The destiny of God's people is to live forever in resurrected bodies; "our bodies will be *changed* (1 Co 15:51), not *replaced*."[18] And this permanent embodiment demands a significant continuity of some kind

---

18. Michael Horton, *The Christian Faith: A Systematic Theology for Pilgrims on the Way* (Grand Rapids: Zondervan, 2011), 916.

between this world and the next. In fact, the analogy of the human body, as many interpreters have suggested, may offer the best way to resolve the tension between destruction and transformation with respect to the universe. Here also, we find a puzzling combination of continuity and discontinuity. Jesus, in his resurrection body, is able to appear to his disciples in a locked room, and his resurrection body is not always immediately recognizable: it is, as Paul puts it with respect to the resurrection body in general, a new kind of body, suited for existence in the spirit-dominated eternal kingdom (1 Cor. 15:35–54). Yet there is continuity in the body: in some sense, the body that was in the grave is the same as the body that appears to the disciples after the resurrection. This "transformation within continuity," as Colin Gunton puts it, furnishes an apt parallel to the future of the cosmos.[19] It also provides part of the ethical basis for our care for creation. Paul says that it matters how we treat our physical bodies now, because we have been "bought at a price" (1 Cor. 6:20). So too does it matter how we treat the rest of creation, if it too shares in the hope of the "freedom and glory of the children of God" (Rom. 8:21).

> "Without an element of continuity, the story of the eschaton would simply be a second story, with no coherent connection with the presently unfolding story of this creation. . . . Without an element of discontinuity, however, that second story would simply be a redundant repetition of the first. This duality of sameness and change is implied in the Christian tradition by the use of phrases such as 'the new creation' and 'the resurrection of the body.'"
>
> *John Polkinghorne*[20]

If then, "everything is going to burn," the fire must be a refining not a destroying fire. The imagery we should have in our minds is not a log consumed in our fireplace but the piece of ore turned into a precious piece of metal.

WHAT ABOUT HEAVEN?

Reference to the future embodied state of believers leads us naturally to one final issue in our discussion of the future of creation: heaven. Among the Christians I am familiar with, "going to heaven" when one dies is by far the most common way of referring to the believer's hope. And, considered on its own, this language has biblical roots. To be sure, as many interpreters have pointed out recently, few if any New Testament texts speak in terms of believers "going to heaven" after death.[21] Our ultimate inheritance is "kept in heaven" for us (1 Peter 1:4), but it is not said that we go to heaven to get our inheritance. The text that comes closest to saying this is, perhaps, John 14:2–3: "My Father's house has many rooms; if that were not so, would I have told you that I am going there to prepare a place for you? And if

---

19. *Christ and Creation*, 31. See also Murray J. Harris, *Raised Immortal: Resurrection and Immortality in the New Testament* (Grand Rapids: Eerdmans, 1983), 168–70; and, on the biblical tension between destruction and renovation, Paul Williamson, "Destruction or Transformation? Earth's Future in Biblical Perspective," in *As Long as the Earth Endures*, 124–45.

20. John Polkinghorne, *The God of Hope and the End of the World* (New Haven: Yale University Press, 2002), xxiii.

21. See, e.g., N. T. Wright, *New Heavens, New Earth* (Cambridge: Grove Booklets, 1999); Middleton, *A New Heaven and a New Earth*, 211–37.

I go and prepare a place for you, I will come back and take you to be with me that you also may be where I am." If the Father's "house" is in heaven, then we would here have a promise that Jesus is preparing a place for us in heaven. However, this is not at all clear. Interpreters variously think that Jesus's coming refers to his presence with the disciples through the Spirit after his death, to his coming for believers at death, or to his second return in glory. And having a "place" in the Father's house could refer generally to the believer's "abiding" with the Father.[22]

Nevertheless, a certain logical argument for the idea of the believer's being in heaven after death does have some cogency. In John 14, and in a few other passages, we are promised that believers will be "with Christ" or "where he is" when they die (see also, e.g., Luke 23:43; Phil. 1:23). Yet the New Testament is explicit about the resurrected and ascended Christ being in the presence of God, "in heaven" (e.g., Acts 1:11; 3:21; Phil. 3:20; Col. 4:1; 1 Thess. 1:10; 4:16; 2 Thess. 1:7; Heb. 4:14; 8:1; 1 Peter 3:22; Rev. passim). So we seem to be justified in thinking that believers do, indeed, "go to heaven" after they die. However, what is important to stress is that this great blessing, to be with Christ in heaven after death, is nevertheless not the greatest blessing. As Paul perhaps implies in 2 Corinthians 5:1–10, the "intermediate state" of being with Christ before his return in glory is a temporary and somewhat ambiguous state. For the ultimate hope of the believer is to live in a resurrected body. The biblical view of human beings is that embodiment is a fundamental aspect of who we are as persons. To be without a body—even when "with Christ"—is less than ideal. So while we may be justified in speaking of heaven as our (temporary) destiny when we die, it would be better to speak as the New Testament does of being "with Christ." And it is, above all, important for Christians to broaden their horizons about the future and focus more significantly on our ultimate state, when we live again in bodies—resurrected and transformed.[23] The destiny of humanity in Revelation is that we should reign "on the earth" (5:9–10).[24] And, as we suggested above, eternal life in a material body would appear to require an equally material environment: not heaven, but the new heaven and new earth.

Why is this issue worth bothering with? As we have seen, "going to heaven" may not be an inappropriate way to speak of the believer's hope after death; the problem is when Christians view going to heaven as their ultimate hope, and this seems to be the case for most who speak in these terms. The danger is that this way of expressing the Christian's hope tends to buy into an unbiblical dualism that the

---

22. For two quite differing views, see, e.g., D. A. Carson, *The Gospel According to John*, PNTC (Grand Rapids: Eerdmans, 1991), 488–90; Craig S. Keener, *The Gospel of John: A Commentary*, vol. 2 (Peabody, MA: Hendrickson, 2003), 937–39.

23. Richard Cartwright Austin warns about the tendency in Christian history to spiritualize images of future restoration (*Hope for the Land: Nature in the Bible* [Atlanta: John Knox, 1988], 214).

24. Some Christians, of course, think that this reign focuses on a millennial period after Christ's return (as is thought to be depicted in Rev. 20). However, it is difficult to think that Rev. 5:9–10 envisages anything less than the ultimate purpose of God for his people, especially since the ultimate portrayal of this reign in Revelation comes in the context of the whole new creation, in Rev. 22:5.

church has had to fight throughout its existence. The idea that being embodied is a bad thing is deeply rooted in Greek thinking and has had an enormously strong influence on philosophy and theology—an influence that has shaped the views of ordinary believers. Separation from the body, with all its unruly passions (to have sex with the wrong people, to eat too much) and weaknesses (felt more and more the older one gets) is often seen as the ideal. And, of course, the more we think of our eternal destiny in terms of the soul liberated from the body, the more we will think of our eternal home as some kind of "place up there" without any kind of material reality. In other words, focusing on "heaven" as our ultimate home leads us to lose concern for the material world around us.

> "The final goal is not the destruction of creation but rather the unification of heaven and earth such that the renewed earth itself becomes Yahweh's throne room. We are not going to heaven. Heaven is coming here."
>
> *Rikk E. Watts* [26]

Better, then, to think of our eternal home as "a new heaven and a new earth." This is the "home of righteousness," where Christ rules and where we rule with him. Adjusting our perspective in this way will help us appreciate the significance of the rest of creation too. [25]

SUMMARY: A MATERIAL ETERNITY

My (Doug) third son recently lived in a house that was going to be torn down and replaced. At the risk of creating bad habits for the future, he and his wife pretty much let their children run wild. They could draw pictures on the walls, wear any shoes they chose indoors, and open and shut doors as violently as they wanted. They could treat the house so badly because they knew it was not going to be around much longer. Indeed, it seems to be a natural human reaction not to take much care of things we know are transient or temporary. So it is with our world. If we think our planet is doomed to be destroyed in a fiery cataclysm (perhaps before too long), we will have less incentive to treat it well. If, however, as we have argued in this chapter, creation in fact has a future, we have more reason to care for it. Of course, this whole line of thinking has to be qualified. For instance, if my son's family knew their house was going to be inhabited by one or more families after them before it would be destroyed, they would have had reason to care for it. Similarly, even if we knew the earth was to be destroyed one day but that generations of people would still live on it before then, we would have reason to care for it. Our overall point in this chapter, however, is that the future of creation reminds us of its importance and

25. Note, for instance, Richard John Neuhaus, "Christ and Creation's Longing," in *Environmental Ethics and Christian Humanism* (Nashville: Abingdon, 1996), 129: "One of the problems [in creating interest in the environment], I suspect, is that contemporary Christians do not take as seriously as we should our human embodiment and our hope for the resurrection."

26. Rikk E. Watts, "The New Exodus/New Creational Restoration of the Image of God: A Biblical-Theological Perspective on Salvation," in *What Does It Mean to Be Saved? Broadening Evangelical Horizons of Salvation*, ed. John G. Stackhouse, Jr. (Grand Rapids: Baker Academic, 2002), 36.

value in God's eyes—an attitude that should have considerable influence on how we view the world and how we treat it.

What is ultimately important is that we adjust our thinking about the material world in accordance with what Scripture teaches about it. The Bible, in both the Old Testament and New Testament, is marked by a holistic outlook that marries the spiritual and the material. I plan to spend eternity not as a disembodied spirit floating up in the air among the clouds but as an embodied person dwelling on the renewed earth. To think this way is important for a whole host of issues we face today. Others have developed the significance of embodied, physical redemption for our view of sex (as Paul does in 1 Cor. 6:12–20) and for how we understand the gospel to address people's physical and material needs. In this book, we are seeing that we must also factor into our thinking the earth itself, as God's creation, if we are to learn fully what it means to "live a life worthy of the Lord and please him in every way" (Col. 1:10).

RELEVANT QUESTIONS

1. How have you and other people you know contributed to the present "groaning" of creation? What might you do to minimize your own negative effect on creation?
2. How can we hold together the biblical tension between the continuity and discontinuity in creation as it moves from this age to the next? How does the future of our bodies help us to visualize this tension?
3. How does the New Testament suggest we should read Old Testament promises about Israel's land? What implications would this reading have for our understanding of the flow of biblical teaching and the present state of creation?

PART 3

REFLECTING ON RELEVANCE

CHAPTER 10

THE GOSPEL AND CREATION CARE

Do not conform to the pattern of this world, but be transformed by the renewing of your mind. Then you will be able to test and approve what God's will is—his good, pleasing and perfect will.

Romans 12:2

In this well-known verse, the apostle Paul highlights the fundamental role played by our minds: Christians are transformed when their minds are renewed, when their basic pattern of thinking about everything is changed from an orientation to this world and its values (see Rom. 1:28) to one informed by biblical truth brought home by the Spirit. We hope that the story of creation summarized in the previous chapters has fostered a renewed and profoundly biblical way of thinking about the world we live in. Creation is not just the stage on which the story of redemption takes place; creation is a key actor in that story.

As Romans 12:2 makes clear, however, the renewing of Christian minds has a purpose that extends beyond our thinking. A renewed mind, Paul makes clear, will be one that can "approve" the will of God: that is, both assent to God's will and put it into practice. As we come to appreciate afresh the role of creation in God's plan, then, we should be moved to deeper worship of the God who made this beautiful world we live in and also to a firmer commitment to care for this world he has entrusted to our care. In this final section of this book, "Reflecting on Relevance," we will suggest some specific ways that a renewed commitment to care for creation can be implemented.

Many, perhaps most, Christians are happy to endorse "creation care" in principle. Indeed, to oppose it might seem like arguing against motherhood or apple pie. "Of course we should take care of God's creation!" The problem comes in translating a vague value (the world we live in is God's good creation and destined to be redeemed) into a motivating source of action. One of the reasons so many Christians do not make this transition is ignorance. We don't truly appreciate the effect that many of our lifestyle choices have on the wider created world around us. In the last two chapters, we hope to bring to Christians' attention some of the specific ways that we can put our creation care value into action.

We can also be hindered in our commitments by a failure to understand how the story of creation we have outlined fits into larger biblical themes and concerns. In an average church service, I am bombarded with all sorts of good things to get involved in: serving in my local homeless shelter, volunteering at a life-affirming counseling center, helping in the church nursery, participating in short-term mission trips, singing in the choir, visiting the homebound, etc. Add to this ever-growing list our fundamental need to be discipled through worship, Bible study, and prayer, and it is little surprise that activities involving creation care end up far down the list—if they are on the list at all. We acknowledge the challenge. However, as we will argue below, becoming involved in genuine creation care need not be a time-consuming endeavor. Some are certainly called to devote much of their energy to the task, just as some are called to devote themselves full-time to evangelism, discipleship, justice, or care for the poor—and we as the church should support those who are so called. But for most of us, much can be done simply by reflecting on and making better everyday choices about things we already do. We may need to shift our priorities for how we use our time and money. As we have seen, to be human means to be in relationship with the earth. The only question is how that relationship will look for each of us and how we decide to live as those who "work" and "keep" the earth for God's glory. But the possibilities that are open to us in this calling can be missed if we see creation care as merely one thing on a crowded list of priorities. What happens all too easily is that creation care gets shoved to the bottom of the list—or pushed off the list altogether.

In order to assess where creation care stands in our array of Christian responsibilities, it will be helpful to ask about how creation care relates to a central New Testament and contemporary Christian concern: the gospel. We make two points: creation care is part of the gospel itself, and creation care can never be separated for Christians from the transformation of people that is central to the gospel.

CREATION CARE AS PART OF THE GOSPEL

We have seen that the created world has a future in the plan of God: it is not going to be destroyed but renewed. We have also seen that it is God himself who will ultimately renew the world. God has also promised to renew humans by giving them bodies fit for life in the Spirit (1 Cor. 15:44). But it is only those humans who respond positively to the gospel in this life who will enjoy this positive transformation, and it is through our sharing the gospel that they will be moved and enabled to respond. Paul outlines this sequence in a series of questions: "How, then, can they call on the one they have not believed in? And how can they believe in the one of whom they have not heard? And how can they hear without someone preaching to them?" (Rom. 10:14). Believers must preach the gospel so that people can hear, believe, and be saved. Caring for creation might therefore seem to be a distraction, taking believers away from our central mandate, to preach the gospel.

We can understand why some Christians object on these grounds to any kind of serious commitment to creation care. We agree that evangelism is at the core of our mission as Christian believers. We also recognize that it is possible to focus on issues such as creation care for the wrong reasons. For example, some believers might be drawn to creation care because it is popular in some cultural circles—whereas sharing the gospel, now and always, is "foolishness" in the eyes of people in our culture (cf. 1 Cor. 1:23). Nevertheless, we are convinced that the antithesis of creation care versus the gospel is a false one.

The key issue is what we mean by "gospel." We suspect that many evangelical Christians would answer something like this: "the gospel is 'good news' because it is the message that God in Christ offers sinful human beings the opportunity to be saved from their sins and enjoy eternal life with God. 'Sharing the gospel' means telling other people what God has done for them and inviting them to respond in faith." This way of thinking about the gospel finds support in many texts. One of them is the well-known theme statement of Paul's letter to the Romans: "For I am not ashamed of the gospel, because it is the power of God that brings salvation to everyone who believes: first to the Jew, then to the Gentile" (Rom. 1:16). Paul is committed to preaching the gospel (see vv. 14–15) because he knows that God uses the gospel to save human beings who respond in faith. However, if we consider some verses that are not as well-known as Romans 1:16, we begin to sense that the gospel is more than we first thought. In the verse that immediately precedes 1:16, Paul says he wants to "preach the gospel also to you who are in Rome." The "you" in this verse makes it clear that Paul is referring to the Roman Christians. The fact that he wants to preach the gospel to people who are already believers suggests that there is more to the gospel than an invitation to salvation. The wider scope of "gospel" is implied again in the next chapter. In 2:16, Paul says that God "judges people's secrets through Jesus Christ, *as my gospel declares*" (emphasis added). Here the gospel is not an invitation to be saved but a message that warns about judgment. "Through Jesus Christ" in this verse is a key pointer to what Paul means by the gospel. The "good news" is fundamentally about Christ. The claim that the gospel mediates salvation (Rom. 1:16) is preceded by assertions that the gospel is "about [God's] son" (1:9; see 1:1–4).[1]

We find a similar christological focus in gospel language elsewhere in the New Testament. Mark tells us that his book about the deeds and teaching of Jesus is "good news about Jesus the Messiah, the Son of God" (1:1). In a passage in which Jesus

---

1. See also Rom. 15:19; 16:25; 1 Cor. 9:12; 2 Cor. 2:12; 4:4; 9:13; 10:14; Gal. 1:7; Phil. 1:27; 1 Thess. 3:2; 2 Thess. 1:8.

announces his mission, he borrows language from Isaiah to say that he has come "to proclaim good news to the poor" (Luke 4:18). The "good news" is that the "year of the Lord's favor," the eschatological Jubilee, when people would be released from their oppression, prisoners would be set free, and the blind would see, has arrived (vv. 18b–19). As his narrative unfolds, Luke shows how Jesus is beginning to fulfill these expectations: he restores a man's withered hand (6:10); he releases a woman "bound" by her illness (13:12–16); he pronounces a blessing on the poor (6:20). Luke, of course, does not ignore the spiritual side of Jesus's ministry: as he reveals in his interaction with Zacchaeus, Jesus "came to seek and to save the lost" (19:10; see also, e.g., 15:1–32). But Luke shows that the "good news" that Jesus announces is more than the invitation to have one's sins forgiven. The "good news" is focused on the kingdom that is inaugurated in the first coming of Jesus (Matt. 4:23; 9:35; 24:14; Luke 4:43; 8:1; 16:16; Acts 8:12). And, of course, the kingdom Jesus proclaims includes all that God is doing to bring all of his creation under his benevolent reign.

The good news that God has sent his Son as Israel's long-awaited Messiah and the world's Savior has particular relevance to human beings who are oppressed by Satan and condemned by their sins. And so it is not surprising that this aspect, or implication, of the gospel is featured prominently in the New Testament. Salvation for humans from sin is the "cutting edge" of the gospel, and the church must remain passionately committed to communicating this aspect of the gospel message. Nevertheless, if we restrict the gospel only to an invitation to receive Christ as Savior, we will miss the breadth of the gospel message. For Paul especially, "gospel" is shorthand for *all* that God has done in Christ. Paul urges his converts in Philippi to live "in a manner worthy of the gospel of Christ" (Phil. 1:27), to conduct their lives in ways that are in keeping with the message about who Christ is and what he has done.

The breadth of the word that we see in its New Testament occurrences makes good sense in light of the way the language was being used in New Testament times. As so often is the case, "gospel" language has its background both in the Old Testament and in the Greco-Roman culture in which the early Christians were immersed.

In the Old Testament, the Hebrew verb that underlies most occurrences of "good news" language in English, *basar*, means basically "announce news"—whether that news is good or bad (1 Sam. 4:17; 31:9)—but it usually has the connotation "proclaim good news," as when the psalmist invites praise of the Lord:

> Sing to the LORD, praise his name;
>> proclaim [tell the good news of] his salvation day after day.
> Declare his glory among the nations,
>> his marvelous deeds among all peoples. (Ps. 96:2–3)

Passages in the prophets, especially Isaiah, where this language is used to describe God's future intervention on behalf of his people, are particularly significant for the New Testament use of "good news" language (Isa. 40:9; 41:27; 52:7; 61:1; Nah. 1:15; see also Joel 3:5 [2:32 in English versions] in the Septuagint). Isaiah 40:1–11 and 52:1–12 function as "bookends" around a significant series of prophecies in Isaiah.[2] "Good news" language is found in both. Compare:

> You who bring good tidings to Zion, go up on a high mountain. You who bring good tidings to Jerusalem, lift up your voice with a shout, lift it up, do not be afraid; say to the towns of Judah, "Here is your God!" (Isa. 40:9)

> How beautiful on the mountains are the feet of those who bring good news, who proclaim peace, who bring good tidings, who proclaim salvation, who say to Zion, "Your God reigns!" (Isa. 52:7; see also Nah. 1:15)

The New Testament writers are undoubtedly influenced by these passages. In fact, Paul quotes Isaiah 52:7 in Romans 10:15. And Jesus himself summarizes his ministry with the words of Isaiah 61:1, where "good news" is again a central idea: "The Spirit of the Lord is on me, because he has anointed me to proclaim good news to the poor. He has sent me to proclaim freedom for the prisoners and recovering of sight to the blind, to set the oppressed free" (Luke 4:18; cf. 7:22; Matt. 11:15). The "good tidings" that Isaiah announces is that God would not leave his people in their state of exile. He would return as the powerful, reigning God to rescue his people and make them his own again. John Oswalt's summary of the "good news" announced in Isaiah 52:7 fits quite nicely the broader Old Testament and New Testament significance of "gospel":

> It [the good news] entails a condition where all things are in their proper relation to each other, with nothing left hanging, incomplete, or unfulfilled (*peace, shalom*); it entails a condition where creation purposes are realized (*good, tob*; cf. Gen. 1:4, 10, etc.); it entails a condition of freedom from every bondage, but particularly the bondage resultant from sin (*salvation, yeshua*).[3]

In the Old Testament, then, "good news" refers broadly to God's promise to exert his kingly power on behalf of his oppressed people. This focus on God's powerful intervention on behalf of his people is reinforced by the way the language was being used in the wider New Testament world. Particularly interesting are texts that refer to the ruling power of the Roman emperor as "good news." The most famous is an inscription that was apparently widely displayed in the Roman world of the New

---

2. John Oswalt, *The Book of Isaiah 40–66*, NICOT (Grand Rapids: Eerdmans, 1998), 367; J. Alec Motyer, *The Prophecy of Isaiah: An Introduction and Commentary* (Downers Grove, IL: InterVarsity Press, 1998), 419.

3. Oswalt, *The Book of Isaiah 40–66*, 367.

Testament period. The most complete form was discovered in Priene in Asia Minor and so is usually called the "Priene Inscription." In this inscription, the birth of Emperor Augustus is heralded as "good news" (Greek *euangeliōn*) for the world (see the sidebar).

The evidence from the Roman world justifies the conclusion of Graham Stanton: "In the Greco-Roman world of Paul's day, 'glad tidings' were associated regularly with the new hope, the dawn of a new era, the 'good news' brought about by the birth, the accession, or the return to health of a Roman emperor."[5] Some recent interpreters thus think that Paul and other New Testament writers apply the language of "gospel" to Jesus in deliberate contrast to the way people in their day were applying it to the emperor. The implicit message they were sending was "Jesus is Lord, Caesar is not."[6] We think it quite likely that the first readers of the New Testament would have heard this nuance in some of the references to gospel, but we must be cautious about pressing this point too far. The evidence from the ancient world does not appear to justify the conclusion that "good news" was a technical term associated with the imperial cult, and "good news" continued to be applied to a variety of situations. But the proclamation of Jesus as Lord challenges any and all other claimants to that title, and in the first century, that necessarily meant challenging, among other things, the cult of the emperor.

We draw two important consequences for creation care from this somewhat long discussion of gospel. First, there is no conflict between gospel and creation care. In fact, care for the created world is a necessary implication of the gospel. The "good news" that the New Testament proclaims is that through Jesus Christ, Son of God and Messiah of Israel, God has brought to its climax his plan to reestablish his reign over all creation. Jesus's incarnation, death, resurrection, and ascension inaugurate God's kingdom. Jesus is Lord—good news! To do justice to the New Testament focus, we must add that a special emphasis in this good news is the offer of salvation to sinful human beings. As Paul summarizes for the Corinthians, "Christ died for our sins," and it is "by this gospel" that "you are saved" (1 Cor.

The full text of the "Priene" inscription:

It seemed good to the Greeks of Asia, in the opinion of the high priest Apollonius of Menophilus Azanitus: "Since Providence, which has ordered all things and is deeply interested in our life, has set in most perfect order by giving us Augustus, whom she filled with virtue that he might benefit humankind, sending him as a savior, both for us and for our descendants, that he might end war and arrange all things, and since he, Caesar, by his appearance (excelled even our anticipations), surpassing all previous benefactors, and not even leaving to posterity any hope of surpassing what he has done, and since the birthday of the god Augustus was the beginning of the **good tidings** for the world that came by reason of him," which Asia resolved in Smyrna.[4]

---

4. Translation from M. E. Boring, K. Berger, and C. Colpe, *Hellenistic Commentary to the New Testament* (Nashville: Abingdon, 1995), 169. The Greek text can be found in W. Dittenberger, ed., *Orientis Graecae Inscriptiones Selectae*, 2 vols. (Leipzig: S. Hirzel, 1903–5; repr. Hildesheim: Olms, 1960), 2.48–60 (= OGIS 458).

5. Graham Stanton, *Jesus and Gospel* (Cambridge: Cambridge University Press, 2004), 34.

6. See esp., e.g., N. T. Wright, "Gospel and Theology in Galatians," in *Gospel in Paul: Studies on Corinthians, Galatians and Romans for Richard N. Longenecker*, ed. L. Ann Jervis and Peter Richardson, JSNTSup 108 (Sheffield: Sheffield Academic Press, 1994), 223–32. Wright appears to opt for a more inclusive view in his more recent *Paul and the Faithfulness of God* (Minneapolis: Fortress, 2013), 916.

15:3, 2). Nevertheless, the gospel is "the power of God that brings salvation" (Rom. 1:16) only because it is, more basically, the story of the Son of God, who entered into our state as David's descendant (that is, the Messiah) and who was raised to become "Son of God in power" and Lord of all (Rom. 1:2–4). To use the language we used earlier in referring to redemption, we must say to many believers that "your gospel is too small." The good news is about the whole of the created world. It reveals the way in which God's purpose for all of creation is accomplished in Christ, the means by which a world wrecked by sin and corruption is renewed and restored to its Creator.

As we have seen, the creation that God brought into being has not been abandoned by God. He continues to care for it and is determined to liberate it from its "bondage to corruption." This liberation is part of God's great rescue operation that we call "good news." Believers are called to live "gospel-shaped" lives. Becoming a disciple of Christ means adopting the values and habits that are in keeping with the "good news" story. That story recounts God's extraordinary grace in providing forgiveness for rebellious, selfish sinners—and so we tell fellow sinners about this astonishing good news. The story also speaks of God's purpose to reconcile people to one another, as Paul makes clear in Ephesians 3:6: "This mystery is that through the gospel the Gentiles are heirs together with Israel, members together of one body, and sharers together in the promise in Christ Jesus." And so we work for reconciliation between ethnic groups and races and social classes. The story speaks of "good news for the poor." And so we reach out to the poor and the outcasts in our society. And the story speaks of creation being set free. And so we seek ways to begin that work of liberating creation.

> Creation care is a "gospel issue within the lordship of Christ."
> *Lausanne Movement[7]*

> Informed and inspired by our study of the scripture—the original intent, plan, and command to care for creation, the resurrection narratives and the profound truth that in Christ all things have been reconciled to God—we reaffirm that creation care is an issue that must be included in our response to the gospel, proclaiming and acting upon the good news of what God has done and will complete for the salvation of the world. This is not only biblically justified, but an integral part of our mission and an expression of our worship to God for his wonderful plan of redemption through Jesus Christ. Therefore, our ministry of reconciliation is a matter of great joy and hope and we would care for creation even if it were not in crisis.
> *Lausanne Study Group[8]*

TRANSFORMED BY THE GOSPEL

A second important implication of gospel for creation care is more indirect—but quite important. The story of the gospel is designed to transform our basic way of thinking about the world in which we live. As Alister McGrath says, "The gospel transforms our view of reality, enabling us to see things as they really are."[9] The gospel

7. From the Statement of the Third Lausanne Congress, 2010, *The Cape Town Commitment*, part I.7.A.

8. Lausanne Study Group on Creation Care, St. Ann, Jamaica, November 2012. The full statement can be found at https://www.lausanne.org/content/statement/creation-care-call-to-action.

9. "The Doctrine of Creation," 17.

is not just something we believe or proclaim, it is something that we are to live. The "renewing" of the mind that Romans 12:2 speaks of is accomplished as believers dwell on (and in) the good news story and allow it to shape our view of reality. Responding rightly to the story of creation that we have outlined will only take place as we adopt for ourselves the values that the Bible's story of creation teaches. The challenge is especially strong for those of us who live in the affluent West. Again, we quote Alister McGrath:

> Lynn White is completely right when he argues that human self-centeredness is the root of our ecological crisis, but quite wrong when he asserts that Christianity is the most anthropocentric religion the world has seen. The most self-centered religion in history is the secular creed of twentieth-century Western culture, whose roots lie in the Enlightenment of the eighteenth century and whose foundation belief is that humanity is the arbiter of all ideas and values.[10]

Wolfhart Pannenberg makes a similar point. Referring to White's thesis, he notes that it was only at the beginning of the eighteenth century that the dominion command was interpreted in terms of absolute human power over nature—just at the time "when modern humanity in its self-understanding was cutting its ties with the creator God of the Bible."[11]

For too many of us, the "story" that gives rise to our values is the story of our materialistic and self-focused culture. It is only as we dwell on and inhabit the story of God's plan, the good news, that we will take on the mindset of Christ and the values of his kingdom. We must struggle against a strong current in our culture that whispers to us, "Sure, talk about creation care; even recycle. But don't let a concern about God's creation interfere with your lifestyle or pursuit of economic gain." The gospel reminds us that God's purposes for us and the earth we live in go far beyond our present reality. He wants us to become faithful Christ followers, looking ahead to and anticipating the day when our bodies will be raised. He wants us to become caring stewards of the world we live in, viewing our world as God's creation, which he cares for and is planning to redeem.

SUMMARY: THE EYES OF FAITH

Creation care, then, is both part of the "good news" we share with the world and also the lens through which, with the eyes of faith, we can see the world around us from God's perspective. Alister McGrath, whom we have already quoted in this chapter, fittingly concludes our discussion of this point:

---

10. *The Reenchantment of Nature*, 54.
11. Wolfhart Pannenberg, *Anthropology in Theological Perspective* (Philadelphia: Westminster, 1985), 78.

Put simply, it is an invitation to see nature in a new way. Not simply to look at it, but to behold it, to appreciate it for what it really is, and to act accordingly. This is about stripping away delusions and misunderstandings—such as any idea that nature is an autonomous entity, with which we may do as we please. You can see the obvious ethical implications of this. This is not our world, over which we have sovereignty; it is God's, and we are his stewards, appointed and called to tend his world as something that has been entrusted to us.[12]

RELEVANT QUESTIONS

1. When is the last time you preached or heard a message on creation care? What does your answer say about the "wholeness" of the gospel in your church?
2. How can individuals and churches avoid becoming imbalanced in their speaking about and acting on the various aspects of the gospel?
3. Reflect a bit on what your own role in proclaiming the good news about God's care for creation might be.

---

12. McGrath, "Doctrine of Creation," 40. As Michael Northcott puts it: "Green consumerism, ecocracy, even environmental protest movements, ultimately cannot succeed in radically changing the direction of modern civilisation so long as they avoid the moral and spiritual vacuum which lies at its heart" (*The Environment and Christian Ethics*, 312). See also (from outside the faith), Kate Soper, who argues that if we are serious about helping nature, we need to be willing to take a hard look at the material preoccupation that typifies so many believers: ". . . we need to re-think hedonism itself. . . . An eco-friendly consumption would not involve a reduction of living standards, but rather an altered conception of the standard itself" (Kate Soper, *What is Nature? Culture, Politics and the Non-Human* [Oxford: Blackwell, 1995], 268–69).

CHAPTER 11

HUMANS AND CREATION: UNDERSTANDING OUR PLACE

As we have surveyed the biblical story of creation, our attention has been particularly on what we may call the "non-human creation"—as is appropriate for the purpose of this book. "Creation care," as we and most others use the phrase, refers to the way Christians are to be involved in caring for the world around us—nature, our "environment." But of course the story of creation can hardly be told without including humans beings. We have seen that humans are central players in the biblical drama of creation and redemption. Only they were made "in God's image." Humans, far more than any other creature, have the potential to impact seriously the earth. It is humans who have used their God-given abilities to develop earth's resources for the good of both humans and the earth. And, sadly, it is humans, in their selfishness and greed, who have led to the "groaning" of creation. At the same time, it is for the full redemption of human beings that all of creation waits, when it will share in the liberation that accompanies the revealing of the children of God (Rom. 8:19–20). The script for the drama of creation gives human beings a prominent—indeed, a central—role in the story. Ultimately, then, we must ask about the place of humans in "creation care." We might divide our focus into two parts, active and passive. From the active side, we must ask further about the role of human beings in doing the "caring"—specifically, how should we Christians understand ourselves in light of our call to care for creation? From the passive side, we must inquire about the role humans play in the creation for which we are caring—specifically, how should Christians balance their obligation to care for creation with their obligation to care for humans?

STEWARDS OF CREATION

In what became a famous (or infamous) remark, Edward Abbey once claimed, "I'd rather kill a *man* than a snake."[1] Though Abbey was probably engaging in a bit of hyperbole to make a point, Abbey's preference for the snake over the human has its

---

1. Edward Abbey, *Desert Solitaire: A Season in the Wilderness* (New York: Touchstone, 1968), 17.

roots in a radical ideology associated with some environmentalists. They argue that it is precisely the assumption made by humans that they are superior to the rest of creation that has led to environmental crisis. They label this assumption "speciesism," the view (misguided, in their estimation) that sees the human species as superior to all others. To heal the planet, these thinkers argue that we must rid ourselves of this arrogant assumption of superiority. We must, rather, cultivate a view of the natural world in which humans find a place alongside, and not above, other animals and elements of nature.

It must be acknowledged that few people, including environmentalists, go this far in advocating for complete equality between human beings and other animals. Quite apart from any Christian, religious, or philosophical considerations, the view seems for most people to be contradicted by reality. The very fact that human beings are uniquely responsible for damaging the earth in a way no other species has ever done suggests that humans have, at the least, unique power to affect their environment and perhaps—especially given our unique ability to think and reflect on these effects—also unique responsibilities. Nonetheless, speciesism does raise some questions that we need to address. The central tenet of modern ecological science is the realization that everything is connected. We live, like it or not, in a single, interconnected biosphere. Moreover, from the standpoint of Christian theology, humans are created beings. We owe our existence to a Creator, and we exist as part of—not apart from—the thing we call creation. At the same time, humans, uniquely, have been created in the image of God. And, however we define that image, the Scriptures and our own experience make it clear that humans have unique relational and intellectual abilities—in degree if not in kind—that give us a distinct place within that created world.

If, then, some radical environmentalists have exaggerated the degree to which humans are simply a part of creation, it seems to be the case that many people in the West, including many Christians, have neglected to see the degree to which we are bound up with creation. A balance that follows the teaching and story line of the Bible is essential and is directly relevant to how humans "care for" creation.

On the one hand, then, we need to appreciate the special role humans have within the created order. As we have seen in our discussion of Genesis 1, humans are given the charge to "rule over" the animal kingdom (vv. 26 and 28) and to "subdue" the earth (v. 28). The Hebrew verbs behind "rule over" and "subdue" are strong ones and not only justify but *mandate* a significant degree of human intervention in the created world. Indeed, as Fred van Dyke has pointed out, the very nature of human beings means that we will be involved in managing creation.[2] A biblical environmental ethic

2. Fred van Dyke, "Beyond Sand County: A Biblical Perspective on Environmental Ethics," *Journal of the American Scientific Affiliation* 37.1 (1985): 47.

will avoid the uncritical hostility toward technology that characterizes some of the more extreme forms of environmentalism, recognizing that God has given human beings the mandate to use their unique abilities creatively to work in the natural world.[3] Genesis 1 provides a biblical basis for the scientific enterprise, as humans explore the world for which they have been given significant responsibility and work to discover ways to rule in and care for it wisely and effectively.

The question, then, is not *whether* humans will "rule" the earth, it is *how* they are to do it. Again, we recall our discussion of Genesis 2, where the "ruling" mandate of chapter 1 is unpacked in terms of caring for the temple-like place of God's presence in the world. God placed Adam in the garden "to work it and take care of it" (v. 15), suggesting that humans are to rule and subdue the earth by carefully tending it. "Ruling" is qualified by "serving." As theologian Colin Gunton puts it:

> To image the being of God towards the world, to be the priest of creation, is to behave towards the world in all its aspects, of work and of play, in such a way that it may come to be what it was created to be, that which praises its maker by becoming perfect in its own way. In all this, there is room for both usefulness and beauty to take due place, but differently according to differences of activity and object.[4]

As the story of the Bible unfolds, the task of ruling well on behalf of God is short-circuited by sin. We have argued that being created in the "image of God" (Gen. 1:26–28) refers especially to the ability of humans to form appropriate relationships—between humans and God, among humans, and between humans and creation. The fall did not obliterate the image in human beings, but it did introduce a fatal selfishness and corruption into the way the relationships that form that image are carried out.[5] By being incorporated into Christ, who is himself the image of God (e.g., Col. 1:15), human beings can be restored to a right, God-glorifying way of living within all those relationships that make up the image of God. What the first Adam bent into a focus on the self, the second Adam turns back into a focus on God. The application to our relationships to the world of nature should be obvious. As Henri Blocher has said, "If man obeyed God, he would be the means of blessing to the earth; but in his insatiable greed, in his scorn for the balances built into the created order and in his short-sighted selfishness he pollutes and destroys it."[6] The restoration of the image enables Christians to become the master-pleasing stewards we were meant to be. In Christ, then, believers can become the serving rulers of creation that God first intended us to be. We rule as God's royal representatives.

A popular way of capturing this vital balance between "ruling" and "serving"

---

3. See, e.g., Osborn, *Guardians of Creation*, 129–40.

4. *Christ and Creation*, 121.

5. See, e.g., ibid., 103–8.

6. Henri Blocher, *In the Beginning: The Opening Chapters of Genesis* (Downers Grove, IL: InterVarsity Press, 1984), 184.

is the language of stewardship. Application of the stewardship metaphor to human beings' relationship with nature was popularized by the seventeenth-century theologian Matthew Hale[7] and is now ubiquitous in evangelical writing on the environment.[8] The final words of the programmatic Evangelical Declaration on the Care of Creation are, "We make this declaration knowing that until Christ returns to reconcile all things, we are called to be faithful stewards of God's good garden, our earthly home."[9] To be sure, no passage of Scripture explicitly applies the actual language of stewardship to the human interaction with the natural world. Nevertheless, the language is applied to Christians in the New Testament; for example, see 1 Peter 4:10, "Each of you should use whatever gift you have received to serve others, as faithful stewards of God's grace in its various forms" (see also 1 Cor. 4:1–2; Tit. 1:7; Luke 16:1–8).[10]

A number of environmentalists, including Christians, have criticized the use of the steward concept to describe humans' relationship to the earth. They argue that the concept tilts the balance we have been talking about too far in the direction of humans being separate from the creation. Moreover, the image might suggest the notion of God as an absentee landlord, who has left his creation in the hands of his stewards.[11] These objections have some merit. As we observed in chapter 4, the steward metaphor is not perfect, but we still think it is a useful word for capturing the relationship of humans to their environment. What will be important will be for us to attend carefully to the nature of the two sides of our stewardship. On the one side, the creation we "steward" is not something distant or unrelated to us, but is something in which we ourselves are deeply and irretrievably embedded. On the other side, the God for whom we act as stewards is the active, personal God who rules the earth, not as a distant monarch but as the God who has entered into his world as the incarnate Son.

Human "rule" over creation, then, is seriously conditioned by the theocentric focus of Genesis 1 and of the entire scriptural account. The Old Testament pictures

---

7. See Richard Bauckham, "Stewardship and Relationship," in *The Care of Creation: Focusing Concern and Action*, ed. R. J. Berry (Downers Grove, IL: InterVarsity Press, 2000), 101; Black, *The Dominion of Man*, 56–57.

8. David Larsen notes that a stewardship model, tending toward servanthood, is a key component of the influential "Au Sable theology" (David Kenneth Larsen, "God's Gardeners: American Protestant Evangelicals Confront Environmentalism, 1967–2000" [PhD dissertation, University of Chicago, 2001], 40–45).

9. The declaration states the philosophy of one of the most significant evangelical environmental organizations, the Evangelical Environmental Network. It can be found at http://www.creation-care.org/evangelical_declaration_on_the_care_of_creation.

10. The Greek for "stewards" is *oikonomoi*.

11. See, e.g., Naess, *Ecology, Community and Lifestyle*, 187; Claire Palmer, "Stewardship: A Case Study in Environmental Ethics," in *The Earth Beneath: A Critical Guide to Green Theology*, ed. Ian Ball et al. (London: SPCK, 1992), 67–86. The ambiguity is evident in the insistence of some writers that good stewardship of the earth demands extensive use of technology to turn it into the place God intended it to be (Derr, *Environmental Ethics*, 22; E. Calvin Beisner, *Where Garden Meets Wilderness: Evangelical Entry into the Environmental Debate* [Grand Rapids: Acton Institute, 1997], 17–23). John Black argues that the stewardship metaphor has been molded throughout history by the changing political and social context (*Dominion of Man*, 58–124; see the summary on p. 118). Larsen notes another example: Ronald Reagan's controversial Secretary of the Interior, James Watt, used stewardship language to justify investment in National Park buildings and roads—a program quite the opposite of what most environmentalists using the "stewardship" metaphor would have in mind ("God's Gardeners," 167).

the promised land of Israel as a renewal of Eden, and therefore, many provisions for the care of the land itself are included in the Mosaic law. But even more important in elaborating the nature and extent of the dominion mandate is the accountability side of the stewardship metaphor. As stewards of creation, human beings must please creation's "owner," the Lord God, in the way they carry out their responsibility. The many biblical assertions about the worth of the created world itself thus set implicit parameters for the exercise of dominion. Believers' stewardship must follow the pattern established by Christ himself. "If Christology is our foundational premise both for theological . . . and anthropological . . . doctrine, then 'dominion' as a way of designating the role of *Homo sapiens* within creation can only mean stewardship, and stewardship ultimately interpreted as love: sacrificial, self-giving love (*agape*)."[12] Or, as Philip Hughes puts it, "God, in short, gave man the world to master, but to master to the glory of the Creator, by whom man himself, to be truly human, must first be mastered."[13] And as God's vice-regents, the rule that human beings exercise over creation must imitate the nature of God's own rule of the world, which has been powerfully displayed in the servanthood of the incarnate Son of God.

CARING FOR CREATION AND CARING FOR HUMANS

In the first part of this chapter, we have implicitly claimed that a Christian worldview includes an understanding of humans in creation that is both true to the nature of things—humans as both a part of and distinct within creation—and generative of a robust environmental ethic—humans renewed in God's image through Christ to act as humble stewards in the world. This claim stands in strong and ironic contrast to those who criticize the Christian worldview for undercutting any strong environmental ethic. We now turn from the active side of humans as created beings to the passive side. As stewards of creation, humans act on behalf of it; but as part of creation, humans are also recipients of that stewardship.

We begin with a point that we have made previously: Christian care of creation is rooted in the two "great commandments" that Jesus himself singled out as foundational for his kingdom: love of God and love of the "neighbor" (Matt. 22:34–40). Earlier (see pp. 25–26), we made the point that the "first and greatest" commandment is the most basic reason for Christians to be involved in creation care. Theologian Oliver O'Donovan, in his important book on ethics, *Resurrection and Moral Order*, argues this point particularly clearly. He espouses a "creation ethics," in which, as he puts it, "The way the universe *is*, determines how man *ought*

12. Douglas John Hall, *Imaging God: Dominion as Stewardship* (Grand Rapids: Eerdmans, 1986), 186.

13. Philip Edgecumbe Hughes, *The True Image: The Origin and Destiny of Man in Christ* (Grand Rapids: Eerdmans, 1989), 61.

to behave himself in it."[14] He argues that the resurrection of Christ reaffirms God's original creation decision with respect to Adam, affirming the "order" that God has given to this life. Clearly, it is vital that people learn to live in accordance with that order. Kingdom and creation cannot be set against each other. Humans function in a creation ordered in certain ways by God himself. O'Donovan draws out the consequences for a Christian environmental ethics, founded on the biblical teaching about the intrinsic goodness and ultimate destiny of the created world. Christians ultimately care for creation not because of our own self-interest or even out of love for others, but because the creation is God's.[15]

Much of our book has been concerned with helping us understand the created world against the backdrop of the unfolding biblical narrative of God's plans. Now we want to say a bit more about the second commandment.

Central to new covenant ethics is the command that we love our neighbors (in addition to Matt. 22:34–40 and parallels, see also John 13:34–35; Rom. 13:8–10; Gal. 5:13–15; James 2:8; 1 John 2:7–11). Some contemporary scholars are using the language of "other regard" to capture this central New Testament teaching. Christ's kingdom calls us to shift our gaze from ourselves, our needs, and our wishes, toward others: toward God, first of all, but then also toward all those "others" with whom we have a relationship. The New Testament letters are filled with exhortations about the concern we need to show to the "others": "Therefore, as we have opportunity, let us do good to all people, especially to those who belong to the family of believers" (Gal. 6:10). "Other regard" begins, naturally, with those nearest to us, those in our communities, our brothers and sisters in Christ, but it ultimately extends to all. Jesus famously made this point in the parable of the good Samaritan. Jesus's Jewish interlocutor asks, "Who is my neighbor?", that is, "Whom do I have to love?" Jesus responds, in effect, "Don't ask who is your neighbor; ask rather to whom can I be a neighbor?" (see Luke 10:25–37).

How does this "other regard" fit with creation care? Some are not sure that it does at all. These individuals suggest that Christians might be in danger of spending so much time caring for creation that they end up neglecting pressing human needs. The issue is that some Christians might fall into the sin so memorably parodied by Charles Dickens in the character of "Mrs. Jellyby" in *Bleak House*, who neglects her own family in her passion for foreign missions. However, while neglect of some responsibilities in our passion for others is always a risk, any antithesis between creation care and "other regard" is at bottom quite artificial.

First, of course, God often asks us to do more than one thing. He asks me to love and care for my own family, for my extended family, for my church family, and

---

14. Oliver O'Donovan, *Resurrection and Moral Order: An Outline for Evangelical Ethics*, 2nd ed. (Grand Rapids: Eerdmans, 1994), 17; cf. also Colin Gunton, *The One, the Three, and the Many: God,* *Creation and the Culture of Modernity*, The Bampton Lectures, 1992 (Cambridge: Cambridge University Press, 1993), 124.

15. See also van Dyke, "Beyond Sand County," 44.

for people in my neighborhood, and also to participate in his mission to provide for the poor and spread the gospel to people all over the world. I must prayerfully set priorities, but it is not a matter of caring for my family *or* giving generously to missionaries and aid agencies. Our "other regard" is not a zero-sum game, in which concern for some must inevitably push away concern for others. Likewise, I can care for creation at the same time as I care for other people. The balance of this concern and our particular focus will differ depending on our situation and calling, but there is no reason why meaningful involvement in creation care need interfere with other Christian obligations. Indeed, as we will see in the last chapter, many of the most important things we can do in caring for creation involve simple but difficult lifestyle choices in the way we live—choices we must make whatever our situation or concerns.

Second, creation care and "other regard" in fact go hand-in-hand. We expressed our preference in the first chapter for the language of "creation" over "environment," but the latter term has one distinct advantage: it reminds us that the "creation" we are talking about includes, in fact, the surroundings in which people live. And it is obvious that a person's surroundings will have a huge impact on their well-being. The polluted air that plagues so many of our modern cities has an obvious, negative affect on the people who have to breathe it every day. The harsh realities of the ecological crisis we now face force us to recognize that it is impossible truly to love others without caring for the environment in which they live. At the heart of the modern discipline of ecology is the realization that everything is connected to everything else. We may extend the point with respect to Christian ethics by noting that my own desire to maintain a luxurious Western lifestyle by keeping energy prices low forces power plants to avoid the expense of installing mechanisms to clean effectively their emissions and thus leads to the suffering and even the death of, for instance, asthma sufferers. Moreover, as James Gustave Speth has made very clear, the truly significant environmental issues we now face are global in nature.[16] The "others" whom I am to love are not just my actual neighbors, but the billions all over the planet who might face devastation if global warming becomes as serious as many predict. The warming of our climate, for instance, is causing ocean levels to rise. Countries that have a lot of low-elevation land near the ocean, such as Bangladesh, are at risk of having a significant portion of their land inundated, leading to the forced displacement of millions of people. Other island nations, such as Tuvalu in the South Pacific, are at risk of completely disappearing. Jesus insists that I regard the people of Bangladesh and Tuvalu as my neighbors—people that I need to love.

Even as we recognize the extent of what "neighbor" means across space, we also need to see what it means over time. The "others" I am to put ahead of my own

---

16. James Gustave Speth, *Red Sky at Morning: America and the Crisis of the Global Environment*, 2nd ed. (New Haven, CT: Yale University, 2005).

needs include future generations as well as our own. My (Doug) love for my own grandchildren necessarily includes concern for the kind of "environment" they will live in, and as members of the family of God, we all have a responsibility to consider those who will come after us when making decisions about how we care for creation now.

SUMMARY: LIVING THE WHOLE STORY

The way we live is determined by stories, "narratives" of how the world works and what our role in the world is. We may not always be conscious of these narratives, but they are there, powerfully shaping our lives. The narrative undergirding many of the attitudes of modern people features human beings in the starring role. The story is all about "us": how *our* needs can be met, how *our* lives can be improved, how *our* enjoyment can be maximized. This narrative often claims to be following the script written by God himself in the Bible, according to which humans are created "in God's image" and are charged with "ruling over" the rest of the world. In fact, as we have seen, by stealing a few bits out of the biblical script, this narrative profoundly adulterates God's intent. Human "rule over" creation is guided by care for the creation for which we have been given responsibility and love for the "others" who live with us on this globe. Paul reminds us that ". . . it is required of stewards that they be found faithful" (1 Cor. 4:2 ESV). Christians need to work hard to replace this narrative of our modern Western world with the biblical narrative. Only with deliberate and sustained concentration will we be able to do this. The narrative of modern Western individualism and self-focus is all around us. It is daily reinforced by the media and by most of the people with whom we rub shoulders. Believers need to "indwell"

"The way I look at it, we tend to put the environment last because we think the first thing we have to do is eliminate poverty and send children to school and provide health. But how are you going to do that? In Kenya, one of our biggest exports is coffee. Where do you grow coffee? You grow coffee in the land. To be able to grow coffee you need rain, you need special kinds of soils that are found on hillsides, and that means you have to protect that land from soil erosion so you don't lose the soil. You also want to make sure that when the rains come you're going to be able to hold that water and have it go into the ground so that the streams and the rivers keep flowing and the ground is relatively humid for these plants. For the rains and the rivers you need forests and you need to make sure these your forests are all protected, that there is no logging, that there is no charcoal burning and all the activities that destroy the forest. All this really needs to be done so that you can be able to grow good coffee, so that you can have an income, so that you can send your children to school, so that you can buy medicine, so that you can take them to hospitals, so that you can care for the women, especially mothers. We see that the environment is something to exploit, because we see the environment in terms of minerals for example, or forests, or even raw materials that we produce on our land, or even land itself. We see it in terms of what we can exploit rather than the medium in which all of these activities have to take place. But you can't reduce poverty in a vacuum. You are doing it in an environment."

Wangari Maathai [17]

---

17. Wangari Maathai was a Kenyan scholar, activist, and politician who in 2004 became the first woman from Africa to be awarded the Nobel Peace Prize. This quote is from an interview available at https://kenvironews.wordpress.com/2009/05/22/worldchanging-interview-wangari-maathai.

the biblical narrative by reading Scripture, seeking God in prayer, spending time with the people of God, and worshipping God. It is only when we do this that we will be able to fulfill our role as the stewards of God's creation.

RELEVANT QUESTIONS

1. What are the positive and negative aspects about the idea of Christians as "stewards" of creation?
2. How does the example of Jesus help shape your practice of stewardship of creation?
3. What specific ways could you become a steward of creation in your own town or neighborhood?

CHAPTER 12

WISDOM AND CREATION CARE

The theology of creation that has emerged from our survey of the story of creation in Scripture is, of course, just that: theology. It is by definition rather theoretical. But how are we to move from this theology to the actual practice of creation care? In this chapter, we address that question as a segue into the specifics of creation care outlined in our final two chapters.

DIFFICULT DECISIONS

The theology of creation provides few specific and practical guidelines for responsible Christian decision-making. This leads some, like Thomas Derr, to be pessimistic about the practical usefulness of a theology of creation. He argues that Scripture simply does not reveal enough about God's intentions for nature to enable us to make reasoned ethical decisions. Derr concludes, ". . . I think we must be very, very modest in talking about God's intention for nature. Given the centrality of the divine-human drama in Christian faith, given its proclamation of the redemptive event addressed to humankind, I am certainly willing to say—more than willing, in fact, insistent upon saying—that our focus must be on human life, and that our task with the earth is to sustain the conditions for human life as far into the future as our wits and strength allow. But I am not willing to go much beyond that."[1] From a very different ideological perspective, Arne Naess objects to the "stewardship" metaphor as a way of characterizing the relation of humans and nature for a similar reason: "We know too little about what happens in nature to take up the task."[2]

These reservations are to some extent justified: even if one were to accept all the theological points we have made in this book, disagreement about specific policies would still arise. How we should "steward" creation in specific situations will not always be clear. For instance, we recently saw a very public dispute about a planned extension of the existing Keystone pipeline, known as the Keystone XL, that would channel crude oil derived from the Canadian oil sands more directly to refineries on the Gulf of Mexico. One focus of controversy pitted economics against the environment: building

---

1. *Environmental Ethics*, 26–32 (here, p. 28).   2. *Ecology, Community and Lifestyle*, 187.

the pipeline and refining the oil would produce jobs, but would leaks in the pipeline pollute land and would burning the oil it would carry be "game over for planet earth," as climate scientists and activist James Hansen has claimed? Another focus is political: the Canadian company involved threatened to build a pipeline to western Canadian ports, where the oil could be shipped to the Far East for refining, and at the same time, sued the US government for failing to approve the pipeline. And still another focus lies within the scope of environmental concerns as such: would it be better to build a pipeline or to ship the same oil via rail and truck, a means of transport that has inherently greater risk of spills? We have our own view on this issue—and so do most of you! Our point, however, is simple: people holding the same basic theology about creation might well look at the Keystone pipeline issue and come to different conclusions.

While recognizing the inevitable subjectivity and differences in moving from theology to ethics on any number of issues, we nonetheless think the Christian faith provides resources to help. Once we recognize our role as stewards, one of our first obligations is to seek out the knowledge we need to carry out the task effectively. Paul says that a steward is to be "faithful" (1 Cor. 4:2). We can faithfully "steward" the created world only if we understand that world and what it needs. If I were appointed to steward an estate, I would first of all want to gather all the information I could in order to do my job effectively.[3] Christians who take seriously their responsibility to care for God's creation should likewise seek good information about the world we have been appointed to steward. We begin, of course, with what God tells us in Scripture. However, as we have noted, Scripture does not go into much detail about the nature of our world. It tells us creation is beautiful, fashioned by God for us to inhabit and rejoice in, and designed to stimulate our worship of the Creator. We must, therefore, steward with care, recognizing that we are given responsibility for something of great value. We also learn that God intends creation to last forever, as this world gives way ultimately to the "new heavens and the new earth." We are stewarding something that has lasting value. Beyond these general—though very important!—points, we do not learn much from Scripture about the creation we steward. We need to turn elsewhere for more information.

Humans, it seems, have been created by God with an innate curiosity about this world we live in. Since the beginning of time, people have explored our world, trying to learn about it and to shape it for our own benefit, and (though not often enough!) for its good and God's glory. We continue to do the same today. Farmers, for instance, study their soil and how their crops can best thrive on that soil. Ideally, they will be guided not just by short-term expediency (how can I grow the most crops and make the most money this year?) but by long-term concerns (how can I steward my land for its own good and so that it can be productive for generations to come?). All of us are

3. See also, e.g., Ed Brown, *When Heaven and Nature Sing: Exploring God's Goals for His People and His World* (South Hadley, MA: Doorlight, 2012), ch. 3.

engaged daily, to one degree or another, in the same enterprise of figuring out what our world needs—whether deciding what shrub to plant in a shady part of the lawn or determining where to best locate a housing development being planned.

Some people, however, are more intensely involved in learning about our world. Scientists devote themselves to discovering the nature of the things around us, according to their various specialties. Geologists tell us what kind of rock a mountain is made out of, guiding the road-builder trying to find the best path through a pass or around an outcrop. Chemists discover the nature and operation of various elements, assisting drugmakers in developing the best possible remedies. Meteorologists study the atmosphere, helping us decide whether or not to go to the beach. The Christian who wants to be a "faithful" steward of creation will take advantage of all the information scientists can offer us. Of course, we realize that science itself is always developing. Many of us get somewhat confused about the different recommendations for a healthy diet that are endlessly reported in the media, but we should not be misled into thinking that science in general is always in flux. In fact, there is a large and very stable amount of information about our world on which scientists agree. And, of course, we assume just this in the way we live every day. If I flip a switch and my light does not go on, I don't doubt what scientists tell me about electricity—I change the light bulb.

Let's go ahead here and tackle a controversial example of what we are talking about. Science has determined that the climate of our world is warming, that this warming is significantly linked to human activities, and that the warming is occurring at a rate that will mean serious consequences for the earth and for many who live on it. We all know, of course, that there are very vocal elements among our politicians and a small number of scientists who question one or more of these points. But here is where Christians need to be responsible about their stewardship and seek out the best information available. The consensus about climate change is clear: the vast majority of scientists working in this field agree in significant ways about climate change, its causes, and its consequences

"We have lived by the assumption that what was good for us would be good for the world. . . . We have been wrong. We must change our lives, so that it will be possible to live by the contrary assumption that what is good for the world will be good for us. And that requires that we make the effort to know the world and to learn what is good for it. We must learn to cooperate in its processes, and to yield to its limits. But even more important, we must learn to acknowledge that the creation is full of mystery; we will never entirely understand it. We must abandon arrogance and stand in awe. We must recover the sense of the majesty of creation, and the ability to be worshipful in its presence. For I do not doubt that it is only on the condition of humility and reverence before the world that our species will be able to remain in it."

Wendell Berry[4]

"If the world the Christian message talks about is the same as the world investigated by the sciences, we have to assume that the findings of the sciences have some connection to what Christians believe the world to be."

Christof Schwöbel[5]

---

4. *The Art of the Commonplace*, 20.

5. Christof Schwöbel, "The Church as Cultural Space: Eschatology and Ecclesiology," in *The End of the World and the Ends of*

God: Science and Theology on Eschatology, ed. John Polkinghorne and Michael Welker (Harrisburg, PA: Trinity Press International, 2000), 121.

(for further detail, see the next chapter). We need to factor this information about our world and the way it is changing into a whole host of decisions we need to make as good stewards of God's creation.

THE WAY OF WISDOM

To give the topic of this chapter a biblical anchor, it will be useful to think of these issues in terms of biblical wisdom. Specifically, three aspects of wisdom will help guide Christians who are seeking to steward the creation faithfully: learning about our world, making good decisions, and appreciating our limitations.

Learning about Our World

First, it is useful to think of information about our world as a form of biblical wisdom. Wisdom in the Bible, we will all recall, is rooted in "the fear of the LORD" (e.g., Prov. 1:7). But, while acknowledging God is the necessary beginning of true wisdom, biblical wisdom also involves reflection, from a divine perspective, on the realities of the created world. "The discerning heart seeks knowledge" (Prov. 15:14). Solomon's wisdom included insight into the natural world: "He spoke about plant life, from the cedar of Lebanon to the hyssop that grows out of walls. He also spoke about animals and birds, reptiles and fish" (1 Kings 4:33). A "wise" person is one who governs his or her life in accordance with the reality of the world as God has made it. Therefore, to be wise, a person needs to understand something about how the world works.

"Augustine says simply: 'True wisdom is such that no evil use can ever be made of it.' . . . That is worth our pondering because we, more than any previous generation, are witnessing the evil effects of perverted knowledge, knowledge not essentially connected to goodness. We are seeing those effects manifested, probably for the first time in human history, on a global scale. No other generation has been so successful at using its technological knowledge in order to manipulate the world and satisfy its own appetites. The ecological crisis is essentially a crisis of knowledge run amok."

Ellen F. Davis[6]

Making Good Decisions

Second, wisdom will help Christians to exercise good judgment about some of the competing values involved in decisions about how best to be good stewards of creation. "To humans belong the plans of the heart, but from the LORD comes the proper answer of the tongue" (Prov. 16:1). Should projects like extensions to the Keystone pipeline be supported or fought? What is more important: the immediate need for more energy and jobs or the long-term damage that might be inflicted on the earth? Wisdom is needed to balance these issues and priorities. But not just any wisdom—we need *biblical* wisdom, wisdom that reflects God's own values. Too often, our thinking on such issues is governed by the wisdom of this

6. Ellen F. Davis, *Getting Involved with God: Rediscovering the Old Testament* (Lanham, MD: Rowman and Littlefield Publishers, 2001), 96.

world, the wisdom displayed in political maneuvering and in arguments that tend to make economic good the primary (and, indeed, the only) good. People who think biblically know better. Human flourishing is not a matter simply of wealth or easy lifestyle. Wisdom is a matter not only of thinking well, it is also a matter of having the right standards to guide that thinking.

Appreciating Our Limitations

Third, biblical wisdom reminds us of our limitations. In Job 38:4–7, the Lord reminds Job of his finite and creaturely status:

> Where were you when I laid the earth's foundation?
>   Tell me, if you understand.
> Who marked off its dimensions? Surely you know!
>   Who stretched a measuring line across it?
> On what were its footings set,
>   or who laid its cornerstone—
> while the morning stars sang together
>   and all the angels shouted for joy?

God has given human beings the mandate to use their unique abilities creatively to intervene in the natural world.[7] But these interventions, just because they can have such far-reaching and long-lasting consequences, need to be undertaken with careful and cautious consideration. The hubris that is the result of our sinfulness can often lead us to intervene in creation when a hands-off approach might be wiser. Both conservation and development are integral aspects of human "rule" of the earth.[8] It takes considerable wisdom to determine which is best in any given situation. But the God who gives us this mandate also gives us the resources to carry out that mandate. What is important is that we fully admit our "creatureliness" as we go about caring for the earth, recognizing our own place in the process. As Oliver O'Donovan reminds us,

"What we need is a form of control which is capable of controlling itself."
Eberhard Jüngel[9]

> Man's monarchy over nature can be healthy only if he recognizes it as something itself given in the nature of things, and therefore limited by the nature of things. For if it were true that he imposed his rule upon nature from without, then there would be no limit to it. It would have been from the beginning a crude struggle to stamp an inert and formless nature with the insignia of his will. Such has been the philosophy bred by a scientism liberated from the discipline

---

7. See, e.g., Osborn, *Guardians of Creation*, 129–40.

8. Ron Elsdon, *Green Theology: Biblical Perspectives on Caring for Creation* (Tunbridge Wells: Monarch, 1992), 65.

9. Eberhard Jüngel, *How I Have Changed My Mind: Reflections on Thirty Years of Theology*, ed. J. Moltmann (London: SCM, 1977), 11.

of Christian metaphysics. It is not what the Psalmist meant by the dominion of man, which was a worshipping and respectful sovereignty, a glad responsibility for the natural order which he both discerned and loved.[10]

SUMMARY: STEWARDING WITH RENEWED MINDS

In a passage that resonates with biblical teaching about wisdom, Paul reminds us that we are transformed "by the renewing of your mind" (Rom. 12:2). We rightly value highly the words of Scripture, and we want to be directed by them, but the Bible was not given to us as a book of rules to follow. It simply does not speak directly to many of the most important issues we face in life: Whom should I marry? What profession should I pursue? How should I invest my time and money? It is by thinking about these matters—and everything else—with a renewed mind, a mind governed by biblical values, a mind directed by biblical wisdom, that we will be able to come to decisions that please God. The same goes, of course, for our stewarding of creation. We need, first of all, good data: information about the current state of creation so that we can better appreciate what it needs. But we also need renewed minds so that all our thinking about creation is informed by the values of God and his kingdom.

Biblical wisdom is a very practical thing. It is not only about thinking but also about right doing. The wise person is one who thinks right things and *does* right things. As Jesus reminded us, "wisdom is proved right by her deeds" (Matt. 11:19). Our wisdom about God's creation will likewise be revealed in what we actually do.

RELEVANT QUESTIONS

1. What might you do to find sources of good information about the natural world that would help you live out a commitment to creation care?
2. How do political affiliations influence your commitment to creation care?
3. What kinds of factors should one consider when making decisions that balance development and conservation, economic gain and the health of communities and ecosystems?

---

10. *Resurrection and Moral Order*, 52.

CHAPTER 13

CREATION IN CRISIS?

B iblical wisdom requires attentiveness both to Scripture and to the realities of God's creation if we are to care well for the earth and live out our vocation as God's image bearers. Restoring creation to its proper place in our understanding of the gospel and reconnecting with the living world around us can in fact be a source of great joy, enabling us all the more to enter into the worship of our Creator and Redeemer. Yet, as we discover in this chapter, a growing attentiveness to God's creation will also inevitably bring an awareness of the challenges it is facing. Despite the sorrow that comes with such awareness, we ought not be deterred from our task. In a broken world, to love is to suffer. Our example is Jesus, who did not turn his back on a broken world but entered willingly into its suffering because of God's great love and the glory to come. Moreover, Christians can be powerful witnesses within a culture that often seems to swing between willful ignorance of global environmental degradation, to self-serving propaganda and misrepresentation, to despair and hopelessness. Even as we face squarely and soberly the reality of our situation and come alongside the groaning of all of creation, we ought to cultivate a posture of ongoing gratitude and joy for all the profound goodness that is yet to be discerned in God's world, in the certain hope that God's purposes for his creation will not fail. His will *will* be done on earth, as it is in heaven.

Given the value of non-human creation to God and the impossibility finally of separating the flourishing of human beings from the flourishing of the creation, we are failing in our responsibilities as God's people if we do not take time to pay attention to the health of the earth. Our contemporary culture makes it dangerously easy for most people to remain ignorant about the status and functioning of the very things that sustain life—even as we are kept constantly up-to-date, whether we want to be or not, about the doings of celebrities, the performance of sports teams, the ups and downs of the financial markets, and the shifting fortunes of politicians. It is also the case that our educational system often fails to find space in a crowded and narrowly delineated curriculum for the two things that are most necessary for cultivating the sort of knowledge and wisdom we need: (1) focused attention to the particularities of a place and its life that would be of help for all of us and that would inspire and train amateur naturalists (as well as budding natural scientists); and (2) the sort of wide-ranging, cross-disciplinary attention to complex global challenges that is necessary to leverage the gifts of all sorts of thinkers to help us discover fresh and creative solutions. For most of us, it will take some effort to begin to learn what we need to know about the earth and its life and to follow what is going on. We can't do it all in any case: as with any such global, complex, interconnected issue, we will do best to learn what we can and keep track of the major issues to the extent that we are able, while focusing most of what energy and time we have for it on one or two issues that we actually have some power to address.

In what follows, we provide the most basic and preliminary of sketches of a handful of major planetary-wide challenges facing life on earth. Our focus is mostly global, partly because these are the issues that are of relevance for us all and partly because it is precisely the global scale of our collective impact on creation that is unique to our time. Yet we must not allow the scale of global challenges nor the potentially cataclysmic nature of future prognostications about life on earth to divert our attention from our own local places and the ways we can be better stewards of creation right here, right now. Indeed, focusing our attention wholly on challenges that seem beyond our individual ability to address can too easily excuse an ignorance of the very practical ways we can love and care for the people and the land where we live right now. So even as we necessarily consider global issues, let us not forget that these all have implications for our own homeplaces and that we are called from first to last to love God and to love our neighbor—which includes those around the world but also must include the people next door right now!

In this summary, we have aimed for simplicity, accuracy, and even conservatism in our presentation of the challenges to the health of planet earth. There is a place for stronger, bolder, and more prophetic presentations of the data that may serve better to wake us up to the reality of what many scientists and certainly most environmental activists would describe as an ongoing catastrophe, a catastrophe through which many of us are sleepwalking.[4] Yet there is also a place for sober and restrained assessments, and this is what we have

> "One of the penalties of an ecological education is that one lives alone in a world of wounds. Much of the damage inflicted on land is quite invisible to laymen. An ecologist must either harden his shell and make believe that the consequences of science are none of his business, or he must be the doctor who sees the marks of death in a community that believes itself well and does not want to be told otherwise."
>
> *Aldo Leopold*[1]

> "Only a willful blindness worse than any proverbial ostrich's head in the sand can ignore the facts of environmental destruction and its accelerating pace."
>
> *Christopher J. H. Wright*[2]

> "We are always ready to set aside our present life, even our present happiness, to peruse the menu of future exterminations. If the future is threatened by the present, which it undoubtedly is, then the present is more threatened, and often is annihilated, by the future."
>
> *Wendell Berry*[3]

1. Aldo Leopold, *Round River* (Oxford: Oxford University Press, 1993), 165.

2. Christopher J. H. Wright, *The Mission of God's People*, Biblical Theology for Life (Grand Rapids: Zondervan, 2010), 268.

3. Wendell Berry, *Our Only World* (Berkeley, CA: Counterpoint, 2015), 174.

4. On the use of "apocalyptic" rhetoric among climate and environmental activists, and its connections to the biblical tradition, see Jonathan Moo, "Climate Change and the Apocalyptic Imagination: Science, Faith and Ecological Responsibility," *Zygon: Journal of Religion and Science* 50 (2015): 937–48.

aimed for here. This means that as much as possible we have limited ourselves to presenting information that is well-supported in peer-reviewed scientific literature. Only occasionally, where it seemed necessary due to a lack of data, have we included more tentative sources of evidence—and we make it clear wherever this is the case. Nonetheless, despite our attempt at care and objectivity, all such summaries involve interpretation and are open to future revision. We therefore urge readers to continue reading in these areas and to use discernment in pursuing the sources of information presented in the media or elsewhere. Moreover, as we think becomes clear in any case, we would not want readers to miss the urgency of many of these issues, and though many of our practical ideas for ways we might respond await the next chapter, we have inevitably found it necessary to make occasional suggestions along the way here too. As we come to appreciate this urgency, we will be confronted with our profound responsibility as God's stewards to reconsider our priorities and often to repent and seek to transform our practices.

"THE EARTH IS FULL OF YOUR CREATURES": BIODIVERSITY LOSS

The rule of humankind as described in Genesis 1 is, strictly speaking, not over the earth itself but over other creatures, over "the fish in the sea and the birds in the sky and over every living creature that moves on the ground" (Gen. 1:28).[5] So it makes sense to begin an assessment of the state of creation with a focus on other creatures. Moreover, as we saw in chapter 3, God is portrayed in Scripture as the one who created and delights in the diversity of life on earth, in all the stunning variety of creatures that exist first and foremost for his glory. Ecologists have also discovered—relatively recently—robust quantitative support for what had long been suspected, that biodiversity plays a key role in, among other things, boosting the productivity of ecosystems and making them more stable and resilient to change.[6]

It is sobering in this light to consider the staggering scale of the ongoing loss of creatures in our time. In an earlier book, I (Jonathan) observed that there was a wide range of estimates

> "The most striking feature of Earth is the existence of life, and the most striking feature of life is its diversity."
>
> *David Tilman*[7]

> "Appreciation and enjoyment of the creatures are the hallmark of God's dominion and therefore the standard by which our own attempt to exercise dominion must be judged."
>
> *Ellen F. Davis*[8]

---

5. To be sure, human beings are told to "subdue" the earth, and the Septuagint Greek translator adds the earth to the list of that which is ruled. But the focus of rule in the Hebrew text is solely on other living things.

6. Bradley J. Cardinale et al., "Biodiversity Loss and its Impact on Humanity," *Nature* 486 (2012): 59–67; David Tilman, "Causes, Consequences and Ethics of Biodiversity," *Nature* 405 (2010):

208–11; cf. Yann Hautier et al., "Anthropogenic Environmental Changes Affect Ecosystem Stability Via Biodiversity," *Science* 348 (2015): 336–40; Boris Worm et al., "Impacts of Biodiversity Loss on Ocean Ecosystem Services," *Science* 314 (2006): 787–90.

7. "Causes, Consequences and Ethics of Biodiversity," 208.

8. *Scripture, Culture, and Agriculture,* 64.

for the rate of the recent global decline in biodiversity.[9] There is what scientists call a "natural" or "background" rate of biodiversity loss, as over time some species, due to competition or a changing environment, fail to reproduce at greater rates than they die. There have also been five major prehistoric events when this rate has been exceptionally high—the last of these was largely the result, it seems, of a huge asteroid striking the earth (the impact of which left a 100-mile wide, twelve-mile deep crater that was discovered under the Yucatan Peninsula). Such "natural" die-offs of species, and especially the major extinction events (which profoundly shaped the assemblage of creatures in our world today), may understandably raise questions for us about God's purposes and the nature of his good creation. Such questions are, in the end, more pointed ways of probing the mystery of a God who for his purposes created and even delights in a world that involves predation and death. But the most relevant question that faces us now is this: as God's image bearers, would we consider it an appropriate outcome of our rule over other creatures for us to cause their extinction on a scale not seen since that asteroid hit the Yucatan 65 million years ago?

For such is the situation we are facing today. When I wrote that earlier book, estimates for the present extinction rate ranged from 100 to 1,000 times the background rate. Since then, however, a more definitive estimate has been published by Stuart Pimm and his colleagues in the leading journal *Science*. The results are not encouraging. We are almost certainly in the upper range of previous estimates, probably causing the extinction of other species at a rate at least 1,000 times higher than the natural background rate.[10] Moreover, the rate itself is increasing. We are, according to many scientists, in the midst of a sixth great extinction event.

Pimm and his colleagues more optimistically suggest we still stand on the verge of such an event, and they point to reasons for hope that we may prevent the worst-case scenarios for biodiversity loss in the coming decades. Technology enables us more easily than ever before to discover and track species and their habitats and to learn what is needed to protect them. Moreover, much of the world's biodiversity is concentrated in particular hot spots, mostly around the tropics. Action by wealthier nations to provide financial and other support to the often poorer nations where these regions are found would go a long way toward ensuring that we halt the worst declines in biodiversity that are currently underway. Moreover, the financial costs are actually relatively modest, particularly when compared to the long-term costs of losing forever all the species that otherwise will go extinct.

The question in such cases is what we care about and value. Science can only give us an idea of what the situation is and what the likely outcomes are; it cannot tell us how to act. Do we value other species enough to bear some cost to protect them? Are,

9. Moo and White, *Let Creation Rejoice*, 34.
10. Stuart L. Pimm et al., "The Biodiversity of Species and Their Rates of Extinction, Distribution, and Protection," *Science* 344 (2014). DOI: 10.1126/science.1246752.

for example, the citizens of wealthier nations willing to advocate for and support the costs of conservation both at home and abroad? Are the citizens of those countries where there are high concentrations of biodiversity willing to collaborate in finding other means of economic support than the short-term exploitation of their natural resources?[11] Christians have an obvious potential role to play, both in lobbying their own governments and in working together with our brothers and sisters across the globe, in finding sustainable ways of living and working that protect the diversity of life created by God—not only for the long-term benefits to humanity but also for its own sake as valuable before God.

The urgent need to preserve biodiversity inevitably turns our attention to how we can support our brothers and sisters in the global south, where much of this biodiversity is to be found. But we can also play a role, as we will discuss later in this chapter, by opting to shift our consumption habits such that there is less need, for example, for tropical forests to be cut down in the first place. We might further ask whether our role as rulers over other life on earth might include not only preserving what we can of the wondrous diversity of God's creation but also providing space throughout the earth for other creatures to flourish. We recall, for example, that God blesses both us and other creatures with the command to "be fruitful and multiply." Ought we not have some concern for seeing not just biodiversity hot spots preserved but also setting aside space in all parts of the earth where other creatures can thrive?

One of the most shocking realizations we have had about the sheer scale of our human impact on other life on earth was when we encountered an estimate of the absolute number of animals that now live on our planet compared to the recent past. In what is necessarily a speculative number, the tenth edition of the World Wildlife Fund's Living Planet Report in 2014 estimated that between 1970 and 2010 the total number of wild mammals, birds, reptiles, amphibians, and fish around the globe dropped fifty-two percent.[12] This means that there is less than half the number of God's creatures on earth than there was even at the time many readers of this book were born. The decline of terrestrial animals alone was thirty-nine percent. Such figures are inevitably imprecise and impossible to verify with the level of certainty of other figures presented in this chapter. However, it is the best scientific estimate we have, and there is no doubt about the accuracy of the general picture painted by the report.

What are the causes of such dramatic losses, of such a profound diminishment in the diversity and abundance of life on earth? The answers, as it turns out, are not difficult to discover, even if the root causes are more complicated.[13] The solutions for reversing

---

11. Given that in our globalized age locals often retain only a fraction of the financial benefits of the exploitation of their resources, such support can usually be obtained so long as wealthier countries are willing to share in the cost of foregoing such activities and to provide alternative and more just and equitable economic opportunities.

12. *Living Planet Report 2014: Species and Spaces, People and Places* (Gland, Switzerland: WWF International, 2014); cf. *Living Blue Planet Report: Species, Habitats and Human Well-Being* (Gland, Switzerland: WWF International, 2015).

13. For an analysis that attempts to address the root causes of biodiversity loss, focusing especially on demographic and economic

such trends depend on people who are both aware of the issues and willing to make a concerted effort to choose a different path than the one we are headed down now.

"PEOPLE GO OUT TO THEIR WORK, TO THEIR LABOR UNTIL EVENING": DOMINION OR DOMINATION?

By far the primary driver of the decline in the diversity and abundance of other life on earth is the loss of suitable habitat in which other creatures can live. Some species, and especially many local populations of land animals, are still threatened by overhunting, and overfishing is a major contributor to declines in fish populations. Climate change is also beginning to have an increasing, strongly negative effect on biodiversity. But it remains primarily human modification of the land and oceans that is driving other species to extinction.[14]

Humankind now exerts an influence on our planet that is comparable to a major geological force, leading some to dub our age the "Anthropocene," or "age of humanity."[15] This influence is driven in part by the recent exponential increase in human population. At the time of Jesus, there were perhaps 250 million people on earth; a thousand years later, human population had slowly grown to perhaps 300 million; not long after the start of the industrial revolution, in 1800, we had reached 1 billion for the first time; by 1900, there were just over 1.5 billion people; this had grown to over 6 billion by 2000; then, within just twelve years, we added another billion. The figure now stands at around 7.4 billion (fig. 1). The collective influence of this many people multiplied by increasing individual consumption levels is seen most obviously and dramatically in humankind's conversion of "natural" ecosystems into urbanized or intensively forested, grazed, or farmed land (fig. 2). Over half the entire land surface of the earth has been physically modified by human beings;[16] every year, we collectively move more of the earth than all natural erosion processes combined.[17] Human agriculture alone has replaced seventy percent of the world's grasslands, fifty percent of the savanna, forty-five percent of temperate deciduous forest, and twenty-seven percent of tropical forest.[18] Taken all together, an estimated eighty-three percent of the earth's ice-free land is now directly influenced by human beings in one way or another.[19] As Christians

issues, see Alexander Wood, Pamela Stedman-Edwards, and Johanna Mang, eds., *Root Causes of Biodiversity Loss* (London: Earthscan Publications, 2000).

14. See the *Living Planet Report 2014*, 20; cf. Wood, Stedman-Edwards, and Mang, *Root Causes of Biodiversity Loss*.

15. The now-popular term was first proposed for our era by Paul J. Crutzen and Eugene F. Stoermer, "The 'Anthropocene'," *IGBP Global Change Newsletter* 41 (2000): 17–18.

16. Roger LeB. Hooke and José F. Martín-Duque, "Land Transformation By Humans: A Review," *GSA Today* 22 (2012): 4–10.

17. Roger LeB. Hooke, "On the History of Humans as Geomorphic Agents," *Geology* 28 (2010): 843–46; idem, "On the Efficacy of Humans as Geomorphic Agents," *GSA Today* 4 (1994): 217, 224–25.

18. Jonathan A. Foley et al., "Global Consequences of Land Use," *Science* 309 (2005): 570–74.

19. E. W. Sanderson et al., "The Human Footprint and the Last of the Wild," *BioScience* 52 (2002): 891–904. Interestingly, the authors of this article begin by citing the "dominion" mandate of Gen. 1:28 and claim, "The bad news, and the good news, is that we have almost succeeded [in subduing the earth]."

who value, as Scripture does, the flourishing of human life and the gifts of human work and culture, we ought to recognize that such modification and influence can be good and honoring to God. But when we learn of the negative impact that we are having on the ability of other creatures even to live, we must confront the reality that our influence can too often dishonor our Creator and Lord.

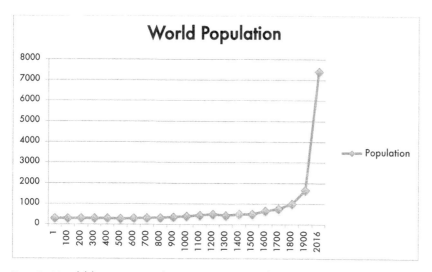

Fig. 1. World human population, in millions, from A.D. 1–2016.

Data based on that provided by the Population Reference Bureau (www.prb.org).

Fig. 2. Estimates of global land cover and use, not including land under ice sheets.

"Infrastructure" includes urban and industrial areas, housing, and roads; "Agriculture and Forestry" includes crops, pasture, and logged areas; "Forest" includes both ancient forests as well as forests that have been dramatically altered by human activity; "Other" is mostly land unsuitable for agriculture, such as high mountains, desert, and tundra.

Figures are based on 2007 estimates provided by Hooke and Martín-Duque, "Land Transformation," 6.

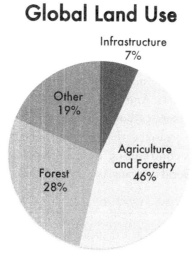

Global Land Use

WHERE "BIRDS MAKE THEIR NESTS" AND "SING AMONG THE BRANCHES": LOSS OF THE WORLD'S FORESTS

Perhaps the most obvious and well-known global example of our collective negative effect on earth is the ongoing destruction of the world's forests, especially in the tropics. In one year alone, 2014, the most recent year for which data are available, 45 million acres (an area greater than North Dakota, or twice the size of Portugal) of tree cover was lost worldwide, over half of which was in the tropics—where the rate of loss is actually accelerating.[20] There are many causes of deforestation. Cutting down trees for fuel and building materials and to make way for small-scale subsistence farming are the oldest causes and are still significant, above all in areas facing demographic and economic pressure. But in recent times, the greatest impact has come from the demands that our consumption habits place on the earth's resources and from the rise of industrial, large-scale forestry and agriculture to support those demands.[21] Demand for beef leads to the burning and chopping down of forests in South America to make way for cattle ranches; demand for biofuels leads to the cutting down of vast swaths of richly diverse and productive forests in southeast Asia and their replacement with barren monocultures of palm oil trees; and the same demand for biofuel and animal feed drives the replacement of tropical forests in the Americas with vast fields of soybeans.

The impact of the dramatic losses of the world's forests is above all felt, as we have already observed, in severe declines in the number and diversity of God's creatures. This is not only a cause for lament in its own right, but the decline in biodiversity leads in turn to a loss of resilience and leaves communities more vulnerable to other environmental changes. Moreover, the removal of trees increases the risks posed by erosion and extreme weather events, even as the local climate may itself be dramatically changed by the loss of moisture-enhancing forests. And the loss of forests that serve as some of the world's great carbon sinks (where carbon dioxide is sequestered in the living biomass of the trees) means increased carbon dioxide concentrations in the atmosphere. This, as we will see, is contributing to changed global weather patterns and to acidification of the world's oceans.

---

20. These data come from a collaborative initiative between the University of Maryland, Google, the U.S. Geological Survey, and NASA that utilizes satellite imaging to determine tree cover. The results are available at www.globalforestwatch.org, where a wide variety of fascinating data and interactive maps enables users to explore the state of forests both globally and locally.

21. For a helpful summary, albeit with a focus only on the tropics, see Doug Boucher et al., *The Root of the Problem: What's Driving Tropical Deforestation Today?* (Cambridge, MA: Union of Concerned Scientists, 2011).

"THE SEA, VAST AND SPACIOUS, TEEMING WITH CREATURES BEYOND NUMBER": THE PLIGHT OF THE WORLD'S OCEANS

The world's forests seemed boundless to early European settlers in the American northwest and, perhaps, to residents of the Amazon basin today. In the same way, people have often gazed at the expanse of the oceans and concluded that their bounty is infinite. This has proven a dangerously mistaken assumption.

In less than four and a half decades, between 1970 and 2012, there has been an estimated forty-nine percent decline in the number of marine vertebrates, including half of those fish species used by human beings.[22] And those that are left are under severe strain: it is estimated that over thirty-one percent of the world's fisheries are being overharvested and so inevitably face further decline, and another fifty-eight percent are being fully exploited, such that even a small increase in harvest would mean sending those populations into decline.[23] This is despite the dramatic increase in farmed fish production and consumption during the same period, which has benefits in taking some pressure off wild fish stocks but poses significant challenges of its own.

A quarter of all marine life depends on coral reefs. Yet half of the world's corals have now been destroyed.[25] The causes range from pollution, physical destruction by fishing techniques (especially trawling), warming seas, and acidification as a result of increased carbon dioxide in the atmosphere (much of which is absorbed by the oceans). At the current rates of ocean acidification and temperature rise, coral reefs could disappear completely by 2050.[26]

The mangrove forests that miraculously grow in the intertidal zone between earth and sea and support a tremendous diversity and abundance of both terrestrial and sea life (and potentially protect coastlines from the impact of storms and tsunamis) are likewise in severe decline. Between 1980 and

> "To stand at the edge of the sea, to sense the ebb and flow of the tides, to feel the breath of a mist moving over a great salt marsh, to watch the flight of shore birds that have swept up and down the surf lines of the continents for untold thousands of years, to see the running of the old eels and the young shad to the sea, is to have knowledge of things that are as nearly eternal as any earthly life can be."
>
> *Rachel Carson* [24]

> "The cod fishery, the herring fishery, the pilchard fishery, the mackerel fishery, and probably all the great sea fisheries, are inexhaustible. That is to say, that nothing we do seriously affects the number of the fish."
>
> *Thomas Henry Huxley, in 1883* [27]

---

22. See again the *Living Blue Planet Report*.

23. FAO, *The State of World Fisheries and Aquaculture 2016: Contributing to Food Security and Nutrition for All* (Rome: Food and Agriculture Organization, 2016), 5–6.

24. Rachel Carson, *Under the Sea-Wind* (London: Penguin Classics, 2003), 3.

25. O. Hoegh-Guldberg et al., *Reviving the Ocean Economy: The Case for Action* (Gland, Switzerland: WWF International, 2015).

26. O. Hoegh-Guldberg et al., "Coral Reefs under Rapid Climate Change and Ocean Acidification," *Science* 318 (2007): 1737–42. The estimate is based on ten years of studies that indicate an atmospheric carbon dioxide concentration of 450 parts per million would lead to the complete disappearance of coral-reef dominated ecosystems, the richest marine ecosystems in the world.

27. The quote appears in *Living Blue Planet Report*, 26.

2005 alone, some twenty percent of mangroves has been lost, mostly due to coastal development (although the rate of loss has thankfully been declining recently).[28] In total, it is estimated that we have only half the mangrove forests that there once were.

Meanwhile, 8 million metric tons of plastic waste are dumped in oceans each year, equivalent to fifteen large garbage bags for every single meter of coastline. Without action to change our practices of waste disposal, that number will increase by an order of magnitude by 2025.[29] Some of the effects of plastic waste are obvious, such as dead seabirds, for example (graphically illustrated in the haunting photos of Chris Jordan[30]), but we are only beginning to understand how the long-term persistence of plastics in the oceans, especially tiny particles, may harm life from microorganisms upward.

What can be done? The complex range of policies that could be addressed is beyond the scope of this book. Our goal is only to provide readers with a glimpse of the scale of the challenges we face and, in the next chapter, to suggest a handful of general practices relevant for us all. But it is worth making two observations at this point. First, if we eat fish, there are two relatively simple ways to ensure that we do not directly contribute to the ongoing decline of the world's fisheries: (1) eat only fish that are recommended by the Monterey Bay Aquarium Seafood Watch program (easily accessed with a downloadable guide or smartphone app)[31] or that we catch ourselves (since most sport-fisheries in rich countries are well-managed), and (2) advocate for more sustainable management of the world's fisheries and fight against perverse government subsidies that contribute to the devastation of local and global fish stocks.

It is important, in this area as in many others related to environmental steward-ship, to be aware of the strength and influence of those lobbies that seek to convince us that stricter regulations will put poor traditional fishermen (or farmers or loggers or ranchers, etc.) out of business. For one thing, it is worth reminding ourselves that there is rarely anything very traditional about the industrial scale and methods used in these activities in our time. But more important, if an activity (e.g., overfishing) is unsustainable, let us remember what that means: it is *unsustainable*. By definition, it cannot go on forever. There will have to be changes. There is going to be disruption in any industry that is destroying the source of its wealth, and the disruption will be more severe and dramatic for all of us the longer we wait. Why not address the challenges now and set things on a more sustainable course that is better for all, now and in the future?

28. FAO, *The World's Mangroves 1980–2005* (Rome: Food and Agriculture Organization, 2007), 12.

29. R. Jambeck et al., "Plastic Waste Inputs from Land into the Ocean," *Science* 347 (2015): 768–71. The figure of 8 million metric tons is the average of the range provided by Jambeck et al. between 4.8 and 12.7 million. The translation into number of garbage bags is courtesy of the *Living Blue Planet Report*, 26.

30. Photographs from Chris Jordan's project "Midway: Message from the Gyre" can be viewed at chrisjordan.com.

31. See www.seafoodwatch.org.

Finally, there are plenty of positive examples of fishermen and loggers and ranchers and farmers who have opted to find better ways to do their work, sometimes at great risk and cost to themselves. Sometimes it has even been the gospel that has led to such transformation. These examples need to be celebrated. And those of us whose primary interaction with those who provide our food and harvest our building materials is as consumers owe it to them and to an entire groaning creation to choose whenever possible to support them, even if it means spending more money—as it usually does.

"BRINGING FORTH FOOD FROM THE EARTH": AGRICULTURE IN CRISIS?

Not addressed in the previous section are the vast dead zones that now form in portions of the world's oceans, as well as in countless lakes and rivers. One of the better known of these, the second largest in the world, forms in the Gulf of Mexico each year after farmers have fertilized their fields. Much of this fertilizer finds its way into the Mississippi River and washes out to sea, where the artificially increased concentrations of nutrients collapse oxygen levels. The result is that any marine life that can't get away suffocates and dies. What is left, in the case of the Gulf of Mexico, is an area the size of Connecticut that is devoid of life, a veritable desert in a sea that ought to be teeming with life.

Such dead zones are but one of the unfortunate consequences of agriculture's reliance on synthetic fertilizers to boost crop productivity and grow our food. Provided there is enough water, nitrogen is usually the limiting nutrient for plants. Although nitrogen molecules make up eighty percent of our air, they are unusable by plants until helpful bacteria living in the soil and in the roots of some plants (legumes) fix the nitrogen and make it available in a form plants can use. In the last century, human beings have worked out how to fix nitrogen from the air and to apply it directly to the soil to boost its productivity. In another sign of how humankind has become a major player in the basic geochemical cycles of the earth, it is estimated that we collectively now are responsible for twice the amount of nitrogen fixation as all natural sources combined. Humankind has had a greater impact on the nitrogen cycle than on any other event over the last 2.5 billion years.[32] Meanwhile, just between 1960 and 2000, the amount of nitrogen fertilizer being applied worldwide has increased by 800 percent.[33]

The ability to fix nitrogen and fertilize the soil has without question been a tremendous gift, enabling far more food to be grown worldwide, even as the human

---

32. Donald E. Canfield et al., "The Evolution and Future of Earth's Nitrogen Cycle," *Science* 330 (2010): 192–96 (here 195).

33. Ibid., 195.

population and demand for food has rapidly accelerated in recent decades. Yet the overuse and misapplication of nitrogen and phosphorous fertilizers also has, as we are seeing, some profoundly negative effects on the functioning of the earth's ecosystems. The solution need not mean entirely giving up the use of fertilizers for growing food (and in fact, in some food-insecure regions with low soil fertility, a case can be made for greater access to fertilizer),[34] but it may involve both a return to time-honored practices like crop rotation as well as the ongoing development of new crop varieties and the recycling of nutrients that otherwise are lost. It also can often be a simple matter of far greater carefulness in the amount, timing, and method of the application of fertilizer.[35] Even better would be a combination of the application of our dramatically increased knowledge along with the wider adoption of the traditional techniques of crop rotation and the use of organic fertilizers.

As always, what is needed is both wider awareness of the problem and then a commitment to changing our practices and our consumption. For those of us who are not farmers ourselves, we might of course consider more carefully the sources of our food and the sort of agricultural policies our politicians support. (And we might also ask whether there can be any justification for the use of synthetic fertilizers merely to keep our lawns artificially green.)[36]

Widespread use of synthetic fertilizer is a key part of our contemporary system of intensive industrial agriculture, which more broadly is contributing to one of the gravest challenges facing humanity: the degradation and loss of our topsoil. As a result of poor farming practices, the living mantle of the earth that sustains our life is being lost at rates that are orders of magnitude greater than it can be replenished.[37] It takes on average a thousand years for just three centimeters of topsoil to form, and we are losing soil at an average rate that is ten to forty times that. Overplowing, overgrazing, poor irrigation techniques, the failure to control for erosion and to leave stubble in fields after harvest, and the widespread overuse of synthetic fertilizers, herbicides, and pesticides means that, according to a major recent report, "[T]he majority of the world's soil resources are in only fair, poor, or very poor condition." Moreover, "The current outlook is for the situation to worsen—unless concerted actions are taken by individuals, the private sector, governments, and international organizations. . . . The current trajectories in soil condition have potentially catastrophic consequences that will affect millions of people in some of the most vulnerable regions over coming decades."[38]

34. Luca Montanarella et al., "World's Soils Are under Threat," *Soil* 2 (2016): 79–82; Jonathan A. Foley et al., "Solutions for a Cultivated Planet," *Nature* 478 (2011): 337–42.

35. Canfield, "The Evolution and Future of Earth's Nitrogen Cycle," 196.

36. Besides nitrogen, phosphorous and potassium are the most important elements used to fertilize the soil, and the supplies of these are limited to what can be mined from the earth's rocks.

Coming shortages and the uneven distribution of these resources (e.g., the United States has only 1–2 percent of the world's potassium reserves and will run out of phosphorous within a few decades) portend other challenges in years to come and add another argument for curbing their overuse. See Ronald Amundson et al., "Soil and Human Security in the 21st Century," *Science* 348 (2015): 647.

37. Montanarella et al., "World's Soils Are under Threat," 79–82.
38. Ibid., 81.

Maria-Helena Semedo, the deputy director of the UN's Food and Agriculture Organization, recently claimed that, at the current rate of topsoil loss and degradation, the world's soils may be able to support only a further sixty years of harvests.[39] Other soil scientists have made similar claims. This may be overblown (we've not found such precise claims in the peer-reviewed literature), and of course soil loss varies greatly from place to place: like most issues, it is ultimately local in its causes and effects. But such dramatic statements by experts in the field ought at least to wake us up to the potential severity of the situation we face. Business as usual is not an option.

Degraded soil also holds less water. At the moment, seventy percent of freshwater use is for agriculture, and severe scarcity in the availability of freshwater is projected for the coming decades.[41] In many places—parts of western North America, northwestern India, northern China, and the Middle East, for example—such scarcity is a present reality. Of the world's largest known aquifers, twenty-one of thirty-seven are being depleted more quickly than they are being replenished.[42] Human water use alone has increased the frequency of droughts globally by twenty-seven percent.[43]

We face all of these interrelated challenges in the context of a world where even now nearly 1 billion people do not have enough to eat . . . and where it is expected we will have over another 2 billion people to feed by 2050. Yet there are thankfully some things that can be done to make agriculture sustainable and to help us go on feeding a growing population. One of the most obvious things is to reduce the wasting of food. It is estimated that anywhere from a third to a half of all food is never eaten, due to problems with transport or storage (a problem especially in poorer countries) or to consumer waste (a problem especially in richer countries).

"I find it quite ironic that while the Mars Curiosity Rover is poking around looking for life in Martian soil, we're in the process of extinguishing life in our own."
John Crawford[40]

"The soil is the great connector of lives, the source and destination of all. It is the healer and restorer and resurrector, by which disease passes into health, age into youth, death into life. Without proper care for it we can have no community, because without proper care for it we can have no life."
Wendell Berry[44]

"When the well's dry, we know the worth of water."
Benjamin Franklin[45]

39. Quoted in Chris Arsenault, "Only 60 Years of Farming Left if Soil Degradation Continues," *Scientific American* (Dec. 5, 2014). Available at http://www.scientificamerican.com/article/only-60-years-of-farming-left-if-soil-degradation-continues.

40. Quoted in an interview by the World Economic Forum in *Time* (Dec. 14, 2012). Available at http://world.time.com/2012/12/14/what-if-the-worlds-soil-runs-out.

41. Yoshihide Wada and Marc F. P. Bierkens, "Sustainability of Global Water Use: Past Reconstruction and Future Projections," *Environmental Research Letters* 9 (2014). DOI: 10.1088/1748–9326/9/10/104003.

42. Alexandra S. Richey, et al., "Quantifying Renewable Groundwater Stress with GRACE," *Water Resources Research* 51 (2015): 5217–38.

43. Yoshihide Wada, et al., "Human Water Consumption Intensifies Hydrological Drought Worldwide," *Environmental Research Letters* 8 (2013). DOI: 10.1088/1748–9326/8/3/034036.

44. *The Art of the Commonplace*, 283–84.

45. The saying appears in Benjamin Franklin's *Poor Richard's Almanack* of 1746, though he may not have coined it himself.

Another obvious step is to shift our diets, especially for those of us in richer countries. Many crops are grown for animal feed, which is a tremendously inefficient use of our planet's limited agricultural resources when compared to growing food for direct human consumption. In fact, if all the crops currently used for purposes other than feeding people (i.e., for animal feed, biofuels, and other non-food uses) were instead consumed directly by human beings, we would have nearly a third more food available globally.[46] Raising animals for food also requires a huge amount of water, and the livestock industry is a major contributor to climate change. Eating much less meat overall and, when we do eat meat, choosing more often poultry, pork, and only pasture-raised beef can make a significant impact.

If we take seriously what we have learned about the value of animal life to God, we should in any case have concerns about our industrial food system, in which animals are typically kept in awful conditions. Reduced to mere machines and treated even worse, they are deprived of any opportunity to be what they were created to be. Of course, it is easy for most of us to ignore this situation since we often buy our meat neatly wrapped in the supermarket, but plenty of information about these food production systems is available. God expects us to gather the information we need to make moral choices. Realizing the conditions in which the animals who supply our meat are kept will lead many thoughtful Christians to elect not to eat such meat. The alternative is to be a vegetarian, or to spend more effort and money in finding alternative sources for meat. Thankfully, a growing market for so-called "ethical" meat means that such supplies are increasingly available. Whatever choice we make about eating such meat, we all should be deeply concerned about the conditions in which so many animals are kept. Domestic animals, including those we eat, are part of the community of creation, valued by God and entrusted to our care as his image bearers.

In addition to wasting less food and shifting our diets, there is of course the need for the practice of agriculture itself to be transformed and made sustainable—even as we continue to produce enough food for the world. This is not the space to suggest all the ways in which this might be accomplished, nor to advocate at length for one particular method over others.[48] We will only observe that there is great potential, still largely untapped, for organic agriculture to be taken up more widely and in ways that not only take into account the

"Climate change, supposedly, is recent. It is apocalyptic, 'big news,' and the certified smart people all are talking about it, thinking about it, getting ready to deal with it in the future. Land abuse, by contrast, is ancient as well as contemporary. There is nothing futurological about it. It has been happening a long time, it is still happening, and it is getting worse. Most people have not heard of it. Most people would not know it if they saw it."

Wendell Berry[47]

---

46. Foley et al., "Solutions for a Cultivated Planet," 340.

47. *Our Only World*, 172.

48. Nor can we enter into the important discussion of the merits or otherwise of genetic engineering as one of the ways to develop new crop varieties. We will only, on this point, acknowledge that though we strongly support the best use of science and technology to address all of the challenges outlined in this chapter, we also recognize the wisdom of caution and the need for limits. And we are aware of the

best practices of the past but also combine them with insights from contemporary science. In the next chapter, we will observe that, for many of us, one immediate way of living out our calling as stewards of God's creation is to be more thoughtful about the sources of our food. Often one of the easiest ways to support agricultural practices that are more sustainable—that are more healthy for people and for the rest of creation—is to buy organic food and/or food grown by local farmers and ranchers we know and trust.

"THE SUN KNOWS WHEN TO GO DOWN": A CHANGING CLIMATE

We have postponed our discussion of climate change until the end, as too often it is pushed to the front of the "environmental" agenda when there are many other issues that equally need to be considered and addressed. But the reality is that climate change affects everything else we have discussed in this chapter. To be sure, one still finds occasional—but sometimes very loud!—voices protesting that there simply is not enough scientific evidence for climate change—or, at least, not enough evidence to support the idea that humans are the main drivers of climate change. However, there is little room for skepticism about climate change or its causes anymore: too many scientists, from too many different countries and different perspectives, are convinced that the earth is warming and that human activity is the primary cause of it. Christians, as we have seen, need to have wisdom about the creation we are stewarding in order to do it well, and it would be irresponsible for us to ignore this very important data about the world we live in and are called to care for. In the discussion that follows, we have space to highlight only a few of the key issues.

As with all the issues discussed above, but especially in this case, readers are urged to continue reading elsewhere to gain a more comprehensive understanding of climate change. One of the leading climate scientists in the United States, Katharine Hayhoe, is also a thoughtful, committed Christian and has written a book with her pastor-husband, Andrew Farley, called *A Climate for Change: Global Warming Facts for Faith-Based Decisions*.[49] Another short, recent book that is generally reliable, up-to-date, and easy to read is Joseph Romm's *Climate Change: What Everyone*

---

fact that the primary use of genetically engineered crops thus far has been to enable the indiscriminate application of herbicide, and it remains associated both with the ongoing planting of monocultures (a much wider problem of today's industrial agriculture) and with injustices in the treatment of the poor and of farmers who refuse to purchase genetically modified products. So though we are not personally opposed in principle to the use of genetic technology in this area, it is understandable why many find it necessary to oppose genetically modified crops due to the uncertain ecological impacts and the ways in which they are currently used. (The concern about their potential impact on human health receives much more media attention, but this seems less substantiated, even if it must be acknowledged that the data one way or another is sparse.)

49. Katharine Hayhoe and Andrew Farley, *A Climate for Change: Global Warming Facts for Faith-Based Decisions* (New York: Faith-Words, 2009). A new edition of this book is due to be published soon. For a Christian perspective, we also recommend Nick Spencer, Robert White, and Virginia Vroblesky, *Christianity, Climate Change and Sustainable Living* (Peabody, MA.: Hendrickson, 2009).

Needs to Know.[50] For a more in-depth textbook-style approach, we recommend John Houghton's *Global Warming: the Complete Briefing.*[51] (We are both acquainted with Sir John Houghton, who is one of the world's leading climate scientists and a deeply committed Christian.) Finally, for keeping up-to-date with the current scientific consensus, the reports of the UN Intergovernmental Panel on Climate Change (IPCC) are indispensable.[52] There are a handful of scientists who will say these reports are too extreme in their assessments and predictions, and others think the IPCC is too conservative in its estimates and too slow to include recent data, but that's the point: the IPCC attempts to present a middle-of-the-road consensus of as many scientists and peer-reviewed studies as possible. For those of us who are nonexperts and looking for understanding or policy guidance, it is a rare gift to have such a complex array of scientific findings distilled in this way by an international team of experts. Such information can never tell us how to act; for that we need to consider what we care about and what our values are, individually and as a society.[53] But it provides an indispensable basis for understanding our situation and making

> "Climate change will have a bigger impact on your family and friends and all of humanity than the Internet has had. . . . Climate change is now an existential issue for humanity. . . . Since everyone's family will be affected by climate change—indeed, they already are—everyone needs to know the basics about it, regardless of their politics."
>
> *Joseph Romm*[55]

informed choices. It must be taken seriously by anyone who considers us to have some responsibility toward the earth and toward our brothers and sisters around the world, now and in the future. It is especially the IPCC report that lies behind the summary below, although in places we provide updated data that were not available at the time of the last IPCC report.[54]

It seems like everywhere I (Jonathan) have lived, people talk about how changeable the weather is—something along the lines of Mark Twain's, "If you don't like the weather in New England now, just wait a few minutes." The vagaries of the weather from day to day and season to season make it difficult for us to appreciate why it might matter that the world's climate is, on average, getting warmer right now. The summer of 2015 here in Spokane, Washington, was extraordinarily hot and very dry, the sky often orange with the smoke from record-breaking wildfires, many of which burned beloved forests where I spend much of my time. It was easy at times to feel that the worst effects of climate change were upon us. And, indeed, it is likely that the summer would not have been *quite* so hot or the fires *quite* so bad in the absence of climate change. But

50. Joseph Romm, *Climate Change: What Everyone Needs to Know* (Oxford: Oxford University Press, 2016).

51. John Houghton, *Global Warming: The Complete Briefing*, 4th ed. (Cambridge: Cambridge University Press, 2009).

52. These reports, including the most recent major fifth assessment (2014), are available for free online at http://www.ipcc.ch. The *Synthesis Report: Summary for Policy Makers* is the best place to begin.

53. On the inevitable ways in which climate change becomes a construct into which we import our values and ideologies, see

Mike Hulme, *Why We Disagree about Climate Change*, 4th ed. (Cambridge: Cambridge University Press, 2009).

54. I (Jonathan) have also been greatly helped and influenced by my conversations and earlier collaboration with geophysicist Robert S. White, with whom I wrote *Let Creation Rejoice*, which has a more extensive discussion of climate change (pp. 54–79), although it was written before the most recent IPCC report.

55. *Climate Change: What Everyone Needs to Know*, xiii.

it still would have been plenty hot, and there still would have been lots of fires. There have always been years of heat and drought, just as there have always been years that are colder and snowier. So for someone like me, living at a temperate latitude where the daily and seasonal weather fluctuations are dramatic (and where the effects of climate change are not yet as pronounced as, for example, in the Arctic), it is easy to be blasé about "climate change." It sounds sensible and wise to observe that the weather has always changed, so why be concerned now?

As with weather, the world's climate—which is just a way of describing the average weather over a period of time—has always fluctuated. Indeed, over the history of the earth, the climate has been both much warmer and much colder than it is now. Most recently, during the last ice age, which was at its most extreme around 24,000 years ago, glaciers covered huge swaths of the globe, sea levels were over a 100 meters lower than they are now, and islands and continents that are now separated by seas were connected by land bridges. Over thousands of years, the globe slowly warmed—by around 9 degrees Fahrenheit (5 degrees Celsius) in over 5,000 years. And in the relatively stable climate of the last 10,000 years, human civilization has thrived and expanded to all corners of the globe.

So what is the difference between the warming that attended our emergence from the most recent ice age, for example, and the warming that we are experiencing today? There are two key differences that are significant for us: (1) the cause of the recent warming, and (2) the rate at which the planet is now warming. What is most critical, however, is the impact that recent and ongoing climate change will have on a vastly expanded human population and on all other life on earth that is already facing the challenges outlined earlier in this chapter.

There is no doubt that the planet is significantly warmer than it was just a century and a half ago and that most of this warming has occurred over the last fifty years or fewer. Not only does every single global temperature record indicate this, but the effects of increased temperatures on declining ice cover and rising sea levels are evident. Between 1880 and 2012, the global temperature has increased by approximately 1.5 degrees Fahrenheit (0.85 degrees Celsius). This is likely warmer than it has been for the last 1,400 years and possibly for much longer than that.[57]

"Warming of the climate system is unequivocal, and since the 1950s, many of the observed changes are unprecedented over decades to millennia."

IPCC[56]

And although it can be misleading to pay much attention to year-to-year fluctuations in the global temperature, since it varies dramatically because of short-term factors like El Niño, it is perhaps worth observing that, since the IPCC report appeared, 2014 turned out to be the hottest year ever recorded. It didn't keep that

---

56. *Synthesis Report 2014*, 2.
57. The unusual warmth of the famous "Medieval Warm Period" now seems to have been confined largely to areas around the North Atlantic. See PAGES 2k Consortium, "Continental-Scale Temperature Variability during the Past Two Millennia," *Nature Geoscience* 6 (2013): 339–46.

title for long, because 2015 ended up "shattering" the record of 2014, with a global temperature 1.62 degrees Fahrenheit (0.90 degrees Celsius) above the twentieth-century average (and a full degree Celsius above the nineteenth-century average).[58] Meanwhile, as the final edits of this book were being made, NOAA released its Global Climate Analysis for 2016 and confirmed that 2016 again broke the previous year's record, with a global temperature 1.69 degrees Fahrenheit (0.94 degrees Celsius) above the twentieth-century average.[59]

Nevertheless, by the time you're reading this, it is almost certain that we will have had months or years substantially cooler than 2015 and 2016, as natural fluctuations (related, for example, to El Niño and La Niña) exert a powerful influence on our weather. What is significant, however, is that the range of fluctuations is higher and higher, such that even "cool" months and years are now much warmer than the long-term average. There has not been, for example, a single year in the last forty years that was below normal, despite lots of La Niña years and even volcanic eruptions, both of which temporarily cool the earth. Many readers of this book have never in their lives experienced a year where the global temperature was not warmer than normal.

"[The] effects [of anthropogenic greenhouse gas emissions], together with those of other anthropogenic drivers, have been detected throughout the climate system and are extremely likely to have been the dominant cause of the observed warming since the mid-20th century."

IPCC[60]

What's the cause of this recent warming? There is now little doubt that human factors are the primary cause. Industrialization has meant the burning of vast amounts of fossil fuels, releasing into the atmosphere carbon that was stored over the course of millennia in ancient forests that have been converted into coal. The combination of the burning of coal and other fossil fuels and the dramatic land-use changes described earlier in this chapter have meant that human beings have significantly altered the composition of the earth's atmosphere. The concentration of carbon dioxide, methane, and nitrous oxide is higher than it has been for at least 800,000 years. In fact, carbon dioxide concentrations, now at 400 parts per million, have not been this high since long before human beings. And the last time they were so high, a few million years ago, the earth was unsurprisingly several degrees warmer than now, and the sea levels were dramatically higher.

It is unsurprising that temperatures would have been warmer when carbon dioxide concentrations were higher, because scientists have known for nearly two centuries that atmospheric gases like carbon dioxide, methane, and water vapor trap

58. NOAA National Centers for Environmental Information, *State of the Climate: Global Analysis for Annual 2015*, published online January 2016, retrieved on July 28, 2016 from http://www.ncdc.noaa.gov/sotc/global/201513.

59. NOAA National Centers for Environmental Information,

State of the Climate: Global Analysis for Annual 2016, published online January 2017, retrieved on February 26, 2017 from https://www.ncdc.noaa.gov/sotc/global/201613.

60. *Synthesis Report 2014*, 4. Note that "extremely likely" is defined by the IPCC as 95–100% probability.

heat. These gases in our atmosphere prevent some of heat near the surface of the earth from escaping into space, similar to how a greenhouse allows the sun's rays to warm the inside of the greenhouse while trapping some of outgoing radiation, so that it's much warmer inside than out. Greenhouse gases keep us as much as 60 degrees Fahrenheit warmer than we would otherwise be: without them, the earth would be a ball of ice floating through space. But increasing the concentration of these gases, as the Swedish scientist Svante Arrhenius worked out already in 1896, increases their ability to trap heat and leads to a warmer and warmer earth.

Since Arrhenius, scientists have learned much more about how the earth's climate works and the complex, interrelated factors that affect it. Yet Arrhenius's basic insight has been borne out by subsequent study, and even his estimate of the effect on global temperature of doubling atmospheric carbon dioxide concentrations—which inevitably left out various factors that are much better understood now—was not terribly far off. Today, when scientists combine all of the factors known to influence climate, they are able to produce models for global temperatures that closely match what has in fact been measured over time. These models emphatically do *not* work if the human-caused increase in greenhouse gases is not included. In fact, if it were not for the effect of increased greenhouse gases, the climate would probably be cooling very slightly. Instead, it is warming at a nearly unprecedented rate. The human fingerprint on recent warming has become increasingly clear and is now almost indisputable; the IPCC suggests that the probability is 95% or higher. A comparison is often drawn with human health: climate scientists are as confident about the effect of human-caused greenhouse gas emissions on increased global temperatures as health experts are about the fact that smoking causes cancer.[61]

For the last 11,000 years, the global temperature has generally varied by not more than 1 degree Fahrenheit. But in the last hundred years alone, it has already risen by up to 1.5 degrees Fahrenheit. Moreover, most of this rise has taken place in just the last few decades. The rate of recent temperature rises is unprecedented in human history and indeed is unusual in the history of the earth. It is partly this rapid rate of temperature increase that makes recent global warming[62] so concerning. It is much more difficult to adapt when things change so quickly—above all on a fragmented globe already under severe pressure.

What is also concerning is that we seem to be near only the beginning of many decades and even centuries of increasing global temperatures. Some of this warming

---

61. One of the reasons for the popularity of this comparison may be the sad fact that some oil companies hired the same people the cigarette companies once used to sow doubt about smoking's effect on lung health to spread disinformation about climate change. See Naomi Oreskes and Erik M. Conway, *Merchants of Doubt: How a Handful of Scientists Obscured the Truth on Issues from Tobacco Smoke to Global Warming* (New York: Bloomsbury, 2011).

62. We have not entirely given up using the term "global warming," because it accurately describes what is in fact at the heart of recent changes in climate: a globe that is on average getting warmer. As we will see, however, this warming is associated with all sorts of other effects that affect us more directly than merely the increase in temperature, and hence the popularity now of the term "climate change."

already is built into the system and is inevitable, but the future trajectory of global temperatures can also be significantly affected by the actions of human beings. Every projection of future temperature rise is thus tentative, dependent in part on the collective choices we make going forward, and there are also plenty of factors and unforeseen events that remain beyond our control. It would be silly to think we can merely turn a thermostat up or down to get the climate "we" want. Yet, as we consider our actions now and going forward, it is necessary to seek the best information we can and to consider what responsible actions we may be called to undertake, both to mitigate future temperature rises and to adapt to the changes that likely are coming.

"Surface temperature is projected to rise over the 21st century under all assessed emission scenarios. It is very likely that heat waves will occur more often and last longer, and that extreme precipitation events will become more intense and frequent in many regions. The ocean will continue to warm and acidify, and global mean sea level to rise."
IPCC[63]

The most recent IPCC report suggests that, if we were not to make efforts to decrease greenhouse gas emissions, the climate would warm by 7 degrees Fahrenheit (4 degrees Celsius) or more by the end of the century. The consequences of such a rise, some of which are summarized below, would be devastating for much of the world. Unfortunately, even this projection fails to take into account recent studies that suggest the situation could be even worse. These studies identify what are called "positive feedback loops," which could accentuate the warming already occurring (such as, for example, the release of methane from the melting of the permafrost). And some previous predictions have already proven to be far too optimistic: for example, arctic sea ice is being lost at a rate that is several times faster than what was projected. Nevertheless, everything we do to mitigate greenhouse gas emissions now and in the future has the real potential to limit future temperature increases, hopefully well below the 7 degrees predicted if we take no action. Based on the highly probable, devastating consequences if we fail to act, it can be argued that we have a moral imperative to do what we can, especially as Christians.

The impacts of increasing global temperatures are complex and vary widely from place to place. There are a growing number of programs and studies devoted to exploring local impacts: for the USA, for example, readers can consult the National Climate Assessment produced by a team of scientists under the auspices of the US Global Change Research Program (available at http://nca2014.globalchange.gov).[64] Here we will summarize just a handful of the more significant impacts that combine to make climate change perhaps the greatest medium-term threat to human (and non-human) life and flourishing.

A warmer planet is also a wetter planet, since warm air can hold more moisture. As a result, one of the effects of global warming that has already become significant is

63. *Synthesis Report 2014*, 10.
64. Jerry M. Melillo, Terese (T.C.) Richmond, and Gary W. Yohe, eds., *Climate Change Impacts in the United States: The Third*

National Climate Assessment (Washington, DC: U.S. Global Change Research Program, 2014). DOI: 10.7930/J0Z31WJ2.

a greater incidence of high-precipitation events of the sort that often result in flooding. Ironically, a related effect of the intensification of the water cycle is the expansion and intensification of drought. For many areas, the frequency and intensity of droughts will increase at the same time that the precipitation they do get comes in the form of intense rainstorms. This is obviously challenging for anyone trying to grow food, for local ecosystems, and also for towns and cities that are already suffering more frequent and devastating floods. This is above all a challenge in poorer parts of the world, where there are fewer resources to adapt to changing conditions—although there are limits even in rich countries when the rain simply doesn't come when it is needed, or comes all at once. One of the awful things about the effects of climate change is that they often hit poorer countries first and hardest. Christians in richer countries will be called all the more to continue to work across borders to help those suffering the effects of climate change and environmental degradation and, in many cases, need to prepare to welcome refugees from places that are likely to become uninhabitable in coming decades.

Extreme weather events in general increase with a warming climate. Storms have the potential to be more powerful, as was likely the case with "Superstorm" Sandy in 2012. Warmer water and higher sea levels likely intensified that storm's damaging effects on the East Coast of the United States. The frequency of such extreme events is inevitably increasing with an intensified water cycle. It is not that any one event can be attributed to climate change, as convenient as that would be for activists and the media; it is rather that the entire climate is in a new mode, one in which the likelihood of such events has indeed gone up and where there is a far greater possibility of genuinely unprecedented heat and storms and droughts.

It is the impact of extreme weather that is likely to be the most obviously damaging effect of climate change, rather than merely the increase in average temperature alone. Today, as I sit writing on the front porch of a friend's house, it is a hot day in Spokane, in the mid-90s. This is 10 degrees above normal, but it's hardly unusual. We have a number of such days every summer. So it's hard to see that it would matter much even if the average temperature were indeed 7 degrees warmer. But here's the thing: if the average temperature here increases by 7 degrees, really hot days in summer will exceed anything experienced in recent centuries. A longer growing season would be nice for my tomatoes, but the increase in pests and drought and extreme heat will be challenging, not only for my garden but especially for farmers and all those wild species that make their homes here and are adapted to quite different conditions. For the forests that stretch to the north and east, already under attack by beetles that are no longer kept in check by cold winters, the effects may eventually be much more severe. At a minimum, species composition will change dramatically, and we have to hope that forests and their associated life are able to shift quickly enough north and to higher ground if we are not to lose some forest communities entirely. Winters will likely have more high-precipitation events, and a warming climate means that those events will far more often come in the form of rain rather than snow. Since we depend on snowmelt from the mountains for our water here—to feed our rivers and replenish our aquifer—replacing snow with rain that runs quickly into the rivers and out to sea in the winter could mean too little water in the summer, when it's already very dry. Just as our winters might get wetter, our summers are projected to be even drier. The combination of drought and excessive heat will mean that last summer's unusual warmth and record-breaking fires could be normal by mid-century. A truly warm and dry summer later in this century could be catastrophic on a scale almost unimaginable today. . . . And I live in a part of the world that is considered a future refuge from the worst effects of climate change.

For some other parts of the world, life will become impossible. Consider low-lying islands or the over seventeen million people in Bangladesh who currently live on land that is 1.5 meters or less above sea level. Even a modest rise in sea level means higher storm surges that cause immediate physical destruction and also leave behind salt that can ruin agriculture and make water unfit to drink. The 2014 IPCC projections for sea level rise (due to thermal expansion and the melting of land-ice) by the end of the century range between 0.26 and 0.98 meters (0.9–3.2 feet), the wide range reflecting in part the uncertain trajectory of future greenhouse-gas emissions.[65] But it should be acknowledged that it is particularly here that the IPCC's estimates have been accused of being far too low. This is, to be fair, mostly because a number of significant studies have been published in the last few years that were not available at the time of the last assessment. In any case, the risk is that if the Greenland ice sheet should melt faster than was previously expected, or if the West Antarctic ice sheet should collapse (both of which some recent studies suggest may be happening), sea level rise could be far higher in the next century.

We have already observed that these rising seas are becoming much more acidic due to their uptake of carbon dioxide. The world's oceans currently absorb just over a quarter of all the carbon dioxide emitted by human activity. And while this has been helpful in lowering the effect on levels in the atmosphere, it has also led to the oceans being more acidic than they have been in 300 million years. As we have seen, this acidification, along with warming seas, is terrible for coral reefs, upon which a quarter of marine life depends. Such an impact on marine life threatens the food supply of many millions of people.

Unfortunately, climate change also poses a tremendous challenge to the world's ability to grow enough food, and this comes in addition to the basic problem of topsoil loss and degradation described above. In a previous book, I was slightly more

65. J. A. Church et al., "Sea Level Change," in *Climate Change 2013: The Physical Science Basis. Contribution of Working Group I to the Fifth Assessment Report of the Intergovernmental Panel on Climate Change*, ed. T. F. Stocker et al. (Cambridge: Cambridge University Press, 2013), 1140.

optimistic about the impact of rising emissions on global food supply. After all, increased carbon dioxide concentrations are actually beneficial for lots of plants. It was hoped that, with the ability and willingness to adapt quickly to a changing climate in terms of where and when we grow crops, the longer growing seasons at higher latitudes would open up vast new areas to agriculture that could make up for those areas lost to the negative effects of climate change. Nonetheless, even then it was recognized that if global temperatures rise above 3 degrees Celsius (5.4 degrees Fahrenheit), the net effect on our ability to grow food would begin to become negative, and so there was all the more reason to act swiftly and strongly to limit future greenhouse gas emissions. Moreover, the negative impacts of climate change will be felt most keenly in those places already on the edge and facing food insecurity. More recent studies have only increased such concerns.[67] It also now seems possible that even with far more modest increases in average temperature, our ability to grow food globally will decline. This is due largely to the sort of extreme weather events (particularly hot days, drought, flooding, etc.) that are exacerbated by climate change. The threat to the world's food supply and security is almost certainly the greatest threat that climate change poses to humanity, and it is perhaps the greatest challenge of our century.

"Climate change is not just an issue that affects the entire planet, it is one that disproportionately affects those who do not have the resources to cope with this change—those whom we are explicitly told as Christians to care for. . . . When I look around, the biggest way in which we are failing to care for those in need is through ignoring climate change and acting like it doesn't exist. As a Christian, I believe that is something the church needs to know."

Katharine Hayhoe[66]

"[Climate change poses the] [r]isk of food insecurity and the breakdown of food systems linked to warming, drought, flooding, and precipitation variability and extremes, particularly for poorer populations in urban and rural settings."

IPCC[68]

ASSESSING OUR CUMULATIVE IMPACT

Before we consider in the next chapter some ways we as Christians might respond to all of this, it is worth examining one of the more interesting recent attempts to step back and assess our cumulative impact on the earth and determine which issues are most critical. This is the work of a group of scientists now known as the "planetary boundaries" group. These scientists have attempted to determine boundaries within which human activity must be constrained if the earth is to be able to go on supporting human life.[69] For example, just how much land can safely be brought

66. Katharine Hayhoe is a prominent climate scientist and evangelical Christian, whose book, *A Climate for Change*, we have recommended above. The quote is from an interview with Ann Neumann, "Katharine Hayhoe: God's Creation Is Running a Fever," *Guernica* (Dec. 15, 2014). Available at https://www.guernicamag.com/gods-creation-is-running-a-fever.

67. See, e.g., Tim Wheeler and Joachim von Braun, "Climate Change Impacts on Global Food Security," *Science* 341 (2013): 508–13.

68. IPCC, "Summary for Policymakers," in *Climate Change 2014: Impacts, Adaption and Vulnerability*, 13.

69. Will Steffen et al., "Planetary Boundaries: Guiding Human Development on a Changing Planet," *Science* 347 (2015). DOI: 10.1126/science.1259855.

under cultivation or intensively used in other ways without jeopardizing the healthy functioning of the planet? How much freshwater can be appropriated for human use? How much can we safely transform the earth's biogeochemical flows through our use of nitrogen and phosphorous fertilizers?

It must be acknowledged that an inevitable problem with this approach is that it can lead us to think we are perfectly "safe" so long as some planetary boundary has not been crossed. On the one hand, we need to be cautious about thinking we know for certain where the boundaries lie, and we need to account for the possibility of tipping points beyond which changes may rapidly accelerate and run away from our ability to stop them. On the other hand, even where global boundaries have been accurately identified, we must always remain attentive to the effects of our activities on individual communities—all the more so given that many of these issues are primarily local in their causes and effects. For example, even if we were within what the team identifies as a safe operating space for our use of nitrogen and phosphorous fertilizers (for which they consider we have unfortunately far exceeded the safe boundaries globally), there would nevertheless remain the need to consider carefully the impact that our *local* use of fertilizer is having on the health of our *local* soil and lakes and rivers.

Nevertheless, the "planetary boundaries" approach is one way of taking seriously the truly global nature of the effect humankind is having on earth, and it can help us identify where some of the greatest problems lie. According to the most recent update of the "planetary boundaries" team, they estimate that humankind is nearing the boundary for "land-system change," and so we are in a zone of increasing risk as we continue to transform the surface of the earth. So too with the boundary for "climate change." We are moreover dramatically overshooting the boundary they label "biosphere integrity," which means that the profound impact we are having on the abundance and diversity of other species and the healthy functioning of the earth's ecosystems has taken us into a zone they label "high risk." According to the lead author of the study, transgressing any one of the nine boundaries identified, but especially this one for biosphere integrity and the one for climate change, "increases the risk that human activities could inadvertently drive the Earth System into a much less hospitable state, damaging efforts to reduce poverty and leading to a deterioration of human wellbeing in many parts of the world, including wealthy countries."[70]

Notice, by the way, that the focus here is entirely on human well-being. Christians have reasons to care about the well-being of other life too, but given the challenges we face, the focus of most such studies is understandably on human life

---

70. See http://www.stockholmresilience.org/research/research-news/2015-01-15-planetary-boundaries---an-update.html.

and flourishing—even when it is realized that this cannot be separated from the health of the local ecosystems and natural communities of which we are a part.

SUMMARY

We happen to live in a time when the scale of our impact on earth is out of all proportion to what it has ever been before. The collective force of our recent actions is comparable to geological forces that usually operate over millennia. Other creatures are disappearing at a rate never experienced in human history. The earth's ancient forests, those great reserves of biodiversity and moderators of our climate, continue to be cut down and burned. Life in the world's oceans, severely diminished already, remains under profound threat from overharvesting, pollution, acidification, and the loss of coral reefs. The topsoil in which we grow our food continues to blow away and run off into the sea at rates impossible to sustain. Meanwhile, all of life, already in the balance, faces the challenge of adapting to a climate that is changing at a rate and in ways never before experienced by humankind.

It is overwhelming to confront these realities. We prefer to avert our eyes from signs of suffering. We'd rather focus on tasks that seem more immediate. We're tempted to suppress what we might learn if we were truly attentive to the earth and its life. We decide that we have too much else to do and can't get involved. It is easier to leave these so-called "environmental" issues to others. Yet the biblical vision of our place before God within the community of creation won't let us off so easily. Our first vocation as human beings, as God's image bearers, is to rule within creation, to work and keep the earth. In Christ, we are being renewed in God's image, and the signs of our reconciliation with our Creator are to be lived out in our reconciliation with other people and with the earth too. Though we indeed all have our own particular tasks and vocations, not one of us is exempt from living faithfully in how we relate to God's creation.

The challenges we face require our fresh and imaginative thinking, creative approaches to problems old and new, novel ways of framing what faithful Christian lives and communities might look like in our time. As we take up this task, we can be grateful that, though the gifts of technology are not all benign, its flourishing has meant the development of previously unimaginable tools that can be of profound help in enabling us to care well for creation. The question, as always, is what do we choose to develop and to what end? Will we use the powers and abilities we have to promote the flourishing of all of life on earth, now and in the future, or to serve narrow interests and short-term wants? At the end of the day, despite whatever might be new and unprecedented in our context, our task remains the most ancient of ones: careful working and keeping of the earth. The traditional virtues that have long been thought to mark the Christian life—prudence, justice, restraint, courage, faith, hope, and love—are no less relevant now than they ever have been. In fact, they have much to teach us today about how to live well and rule within God's creation.[71] The living world around us, though it faces unprecedented challenges, diminishment, and loss, is also resilient. In its beauty and its goodness, God's creation still invites us into joy and praise, even through our tears and in the midst of our sorrow. It is not only in our faithful and responsible work to care for creation but above all perhaps in our love and joy and hope that we will be beacons of the new creation in Christ, overcoming the darkness of despair by our trust in the God who will never abandon us or his groaning creation.

RELEVANT QUESTIONS

1. Which of the issues discussed in this chapter have you experienced or noticed affecting life where you live? Which ones are new or surprising to you? Which ones will you commit to learning more about?

2. What might be the most effective way to communicate some of the realities summarized in this chapter to other people in your church?

3. What difference does our hope in Christ make to how we think about and respond to the challenges outlined here?

4. Before reading the next chapter, make a list of some ideas, small and large, for how our Christian faith might shape the way we care for creation and live in relationship to others and the earth in our time and place.

---

71. Steven Bouma-Prediger explores the relevance of Christian character and virtue ethics in his excellent book, *For the Beauty* *of the Earth: A Christian Vision for Creation Care*, 2nd ed. (Grand Rapids: Baker Academic, 2010), 131–54.

CHAPTER 14

CARING FOR CREATION AND WORSHIPPING THE CREATOR

For the Christian, creation care is part of our worship of God. Caring for creation is to honor God's purposes for it, to accept his own assessment of its goodness, and to acknowledge the value it has before its true owner and Lord. Caring for creation is to live in our true identity as the bearers of God's image, priests and kings whose first vocation is to "work and keep the earth." Caring for creation is to stand against all the powers of destruction unleashed by human sin, to reject the lie that we are gods striding on earth, and instead to find our life in Christ and his kingdom. Caring for creation is to live as children of God and members of the new creation in the certain hope that God has not abandoned his purposes for his people or his whole groaning creation. Caring for creation is to see our keeping of the earth as inextricable from the gospel itself. Caring for creation is to recognize that our stewardship is a necessary expression of both our love for God and our love for neighbor. Finally, caring for creation is to join with the rest of God's creatures in the cosmic chorus of praise that we offer to our Creator and Redeemer by being the people he has created us to be in Christ.

But how do we actually go about doing this? Chapter 12 sketched some of the general considerations that can guide us as we think practically about how we translate the biblical theology of creation care into practice. We are called to cultivate a biblical wisdom that teaches us both to think rightly about the world and to act in accordance with this reality and the purposes of God, while always admitting our own limited knowledge and limited sight. In the previous chapter, we summarized some of the realities of our contemporary

> "Our ecological crisis is attributable not so much to a wrong ethic as to a bad ethos; it is a cultural problem. In our Western culture we did everything to desacralize life, to fill our societies with legislators, moralists, and thinkers, and we undermined the fact that the human being is also, or rather primarily, a liturgical being faced from the moment of birth with a world that he or she must treat either as a sacred gift or as raw material for exploitation and use. We are all born priests, and unless we remain so throughout our lives we are bound to suffer the ecological consequences we are now experiencing. We must allow the idea of priest of creation to reenter our culture and affect our ethos. An ethic that is not rooted in ethos is of little use to ecology."
>
> *Metropolitan John (Zizioulas) of Pergamon* [1]

---

1. Metropolitan John (Zizioulas) of Pergamon, "Proprietors or Priests of Creation?" in *Toward an Ecology of Transfiguration: Orthodox Christian Perspectives on Environment, Nature, and Crea-tion*, ed. Ecumenical Patriarch Bartholomew (Bronx, NY: Fordham University Press, 2013), 171.

situation in terms of the health of the earth and our relationship to it. In this chapter, we aim to carry that discussion forward by suggesting concrete steps that churches and individuals may adopt (and which many have already adopted) in order that our actions might match our theology.

TWO NECESSARY THINGS

Before we begin, however, there are two practices that we consider absolutely indispensable for all of us. These are two things that we hope every reader of this book will embrace, whether or not they have been convinced at every point and whether or not they even adopt any of the practical suggestions given in this chapter for caring for creation—though of course we certainly hope you do!

Putting Creation Back into New Creation

The first necessary practice for us all, and especially those in leadership, is to teach and preach the whole of the gospel. Wherever and whenever possible, we need to highlight how the good news of Jesus Christ embraces all of reality and to proclaim the breathtaking grandeur and cosmic scope of God's purposes. We need, as it were, to put creation back into new creation. Moreover, as we have seen, one of the causes of the contemporary church's often weak and measly theology of creation is a neglect of the Old Testament, a failure to read and teach the whole of Scripture. Much of what the Bible has to say about creation is found in the Old Testament. And for all of the New Testament writers, their Bible *is* the Old Testament. What it teaches about God and creation is a part of the assumed background for what they write, the story of which they see themselves a part. We must then devote ourselves to the reading, studying, and teaching of the Old Testament alongside the New Testament. This is important for many reasons, but among them is that too much of the contemporary Christian church has preached an attenuated gospel, while neglecting what the Old Testament reveals about non-human creation and our responsibility to care for it.

As we observed in chapter 3, there are only two occasions where we actually have a record of how Paul preached the gospel for the first time to those who had no background knowledge of the Old Testament. In both cases, he begins with Creator and creation (Acts 14:15–17; 17:24–30).[2] This suggests something about the necessary content for our own proclamation of the gospel in what is an increasingly post-Christian world. When we take the time to share the grand sweep of the biblical narrative that encompasses all of life and creation, we often find a deep resonance in people who are seeking, whether they know it or not, a story they can become

---

2. This point is developed at greater length in Moo and White, *Let Creation Rejoice*, 87–94.

a part of, a story that is bigger than themselves, a story that is both timeless and of profound relevance to the greatest issues of our time.

For pastors whose primary duties, week in and week out, are to preach and teach the Word and administer the sacraments, and who perhaps are harried by constant calls to address new causes and take up new ministries, it is important to observe that these primary responsibilities always ought to remain at the center. Depending on the structure of a church or para-church ministry, it will often be the case that laypeople are the ones who will need to organize and do much of the on-the-ground work that finally is necessary if our actions are to match our theology in regard to creation care. Yet this will not happen if Christians fail to see the connection between their faith and care for the earth, if their imaginations are not captured by the possibilities of what it is to live wholly as children of God in the midst of a groaning creation. If we are to be mobilized to go about all the work that God calls us to, we need pastors and teachers who are faithfully administering the sacraments and reminding us of their connection to Jesus's incarnation, life, death, resurrection, and coming again, proclaiming the whole Word of God and drawing out its relevance for us now.

There are few things more relevant and needed in our time than God's people taking up their responsibility to care well for his creation. The challenges facing the healthy functioning of the earth's ecosystems that sustain us and all of life is one of the central issues of our day, and it is one that desperately needs a biblical perspective brought to bear on it. It is also one that the worldwide church is uniquely situated to address: we have brothers and sisters around the world who are connected by networks of denominations, missions, and relief and development agencies. Moreover, we all are joined together in the Spirit of God in Christ and are able by his power to accomplish more than we can dream of. Might not God use his Church, the bulwark of the new creation, to display his purposes for the whole of the earth and display his glory in the transformation of his people's relationships with each other and with all of creation? We pray it may be so.

Putting Ourselves Back into Creation

The second practice we consider indispensable for us all is not so much the doing of any one thing as it is a posture towards God's creation of gratefulness, joy, and worship. Reclaiming a biblical theology of creation invites us to see the world afresh as the arena of God's glory, to enter into the praise of the Creator to whom creation all around us testifies by merely being what it is created to be. We are invited to accept with joy our own identity as limited human creatures—part of the vast orchestra of creation, connected to all of life—and to acknowledge again our dependence on the earth itself and on the one who created and sustains it. We can be humbled by our weakness, our finitude, and our apparent insignificance in the face of an immense and terrifyingly awesome creation, while at the same time celebrating the incomprehensible grace of a God who enters into relationship with us and gives us purpose within this vast kingdom.

This posture of gratefulness, joy, and worship will be profoundly aided by time spent in God's creation. Of course, in reality that is the only place we ever spend time. The densely populated central London neighborhood where I (Jonathan) am living this year is no less God's creation than the Cabinet Mountains Wilderness of northwest Montana where my wife and I backpacked last summer. You cannot leave God's creation, but in our day, especially, it has become easy to pretend that we are separate from the rest of creation, to pretend that we are not dependent upon the earth, to pretend that we have transcended nature. As we all know, the very benefits of contemporary technology—the way it opens up new possibilities for thinking about ourselves and our world, makes information and cultural riches accessible to so many, and connects people from around the world—can become liabilities too. We can allow technology to cast a spell over us, to inure us to reality, to make us anxious and confused about our identity and worth, to disconnect us from the immediate world around us, to lead us to forget who we are, where we are, and whose we are.

The antidote to such forgetfulness is not merely to spend time in God's creation but purposefully to contemplate and engage actively with the non-human world around us in all its wonder and diversity. For some of us, this may indeed occasionally take the form of forays into wild places where we encounter most dramatically our own limits and the sometimes-terrifying beauty and awesomeness of God's creation. For many more of us, this can take the form of growing and gathering at least some of our own food. Gardening, gathering wild berries, fishing, and hunting are all ways of participating actively in the life of the earth, which can reconnect us to God's creation in the most basic and ancient of ways—even if our circumstances limit some of us to a window box of herbs! For every single one of us, the challenge above all is fostering a willingness to engage day by day with the beauty and brokenness of the world at our doorstep. We might walk more often (or, if we are infirm, just find ways to spend more time out-of-doors), paying attention to the living world around us and making an effort to get to know something of the ecology and natural history of the place where we live. What is needed is a posture of attentiveness and wonder to the world around us that honors God and his creation, that recalls us to our true identity, and that can, if we let it, open up vistas of joy and possibility in our lives.

If we are to be awakened to the beauty and goodness of non-human creation around us, we must make time in our lives to disengage from the technological, "always-on" culture in which many of us spend much of our time. To disconnect regularly may well have important mental, psychological, and other health benefits, as we are often told—it would be surprising if it didn't—but without question it has become in our time a necessary spiritual discipline. It is an extension of the principle of Sabbath rest. Like all spiritual disciplines, it can be challenging for all sorts of reasons—job, school, social pressures, our need to feel connected—but it is too important to neglect. We simply must take regular time away from all those forms of technology that distract us from the here and now, that distance us from our immediate neighbors and our place, that prevent sustained reflection on Scripture, and that keep us from celebrating and caring intimately for the creation around us.

As we begin to take seriously our call to be responsible members of our communities and citizens of God's kingdom, and as we reconnect with our homeplace, we will be surprised to discover all sorts of things we may have never noticed before. We are likely to have a growing list of questions about the natural and human history of our home, about the rocks and the trees and the grasses and the flowers and the seasons and all the creatures with which we share this place. If our imagination needs some prodding to help us perceive the fascinating and nearly endless possibilities for study and exploration all around us, there are plenty of good, accessible books on local ecology and natural history to help.[4] And as our curiosity and questions grow, we will find that the resources and technology available to us now also make it easier than it ever has been to learn about the world around us and to begin to find some answers to our questions.

> "In our own contemporary context of the rat race of anxiety, the celebration of Sabbath is an act of both resistance and alternative. It is resistance because it is a visible insistence that our lives are not defined by the production and consumption of commodity goods. . . . It is an alternative to the demanding, chattering, pervasive presence of advertising and its great liturgical claim of professional sports that devour all our 'rest time.' The alternative on offer is the awareness and practice of the claim that we are situated on the receiving end of the gifts of God."
>
> *Walter Brueggemann*[3]

PRACTICING WHAT WE PREACH: TRANSFORMED LIVING FOR A TRANSFORMED WORLD

As we observed in the previous chapter, a deeper attentiveness to the world around us will inevitably force us to confront uncomfortable realities about the profound challenges facing the living world in our time. If it sounds as though we are facing a perfect storm, that's because we are. Usually, to claim that your own time is unique betrays an ignorance of history. And there is no doubt that human civilizations have faced environmental challenges and disasters many times before. But today it is only an ignorance of the earth's history that obscures the reality that our time is indeed unique in many respects, the result of an exponentially increasing population many orders of magnitude larger than the world has ever experienced, multiplied by rapidly expanding levels of consumption. This does not mean, however, that we do

3. Walter Brueggemann, *Sabbath as Resistance: Saying No to the Culture of Now* (Louisville, KY: Westminster John Knox Press, 2014), xiii-xiv.

4. For a stirring description of just how much wonder there can

be to discover in even the smallest plot of earth, see David George Haskell, *The Forest Unseen: A Year's Watch in Nature* (New York: Penguin Books, 2013). Haskell visits and describes over the course of one year a single one-meter square patch of Tennessee forest.

not have much to learn from history or that the basic ethos that is demanded of us is any different than it has been in the past. The situation we face is graver and more global in scale than ever before, and so new things may indeed be demanded of us. Yet, even as we consider what some of these might be, let us remember that these do not mean giving up other things to which God also calls us. As in all things, we seek to embody the life of his kingdom and to love God and neighbor.

Inaction is not an option for those who claim to be disciples of Christ. We are called to lives of faithfulness in all we do, no matter how immense the challenges we face and no matter how insignificant our own individual actions might seem. As reconciled children of God in Christ, renewed in the image of our Creator, we are called to live as who we are—in our relationship with others and with all of creation. We serve a God who is able to do more with even our small and feeble efforts than we imagine. Moreover, whether or not we ever see the results we long for, our call to humble discipleship and living lives of integrity still stands. At the height of the slave trade, many Christians decided they could not buy or use sugar that had been produced at the cost of human life and injustice. Did any one person's decision not to purchase "blood sugar" bring about the end of the slave trade? Of course not. Yet might not that have been one of the disciplines required of a follower of Christ in that era, one way to live as a person of integrity and as an example and a challenge to others? For Christians, the personal, societal, spiritual, and political are all interwoven. So, though we seek wisdom to know how best to effect wide and lasting changes for the cause of Christ's kingdom, we also live here and now in the joy of pursuing gentler and more responsible lives that humbly reflect God's purposes for us in all we do, trusting always in his grace and goodness.

In what follows, we provide a mere outline of possibilities and suggestions to get readers started. There are plenty of resources that focus more extensively on practical advice for "sustainable living," "ecologically friendly" practices, "greening" your church, and environmental and climate activism. In this area, it is especially helpful to be open-minded and, as possible, to keep up-to-date, as advice for best practices can change as we learn more. And new opportunities and options are regularly becoming available as (encouragingly) more people seek and develop better ways of living in our world today. But the most basic advice and practices don't change and simply reflect particular ways of living out in our own time what are traditional Christian virtues.

"The right thing to do today, as always, is to stop, or start stopping, our habit of wasting and poisoning the good and beautiful things of the world, which once were called 'divine gifts' and now are called 'natural resources.'"

Wendell Berry[5]

For those who are convinced, as we are, that the gospel demands transformed lives here and now in how we care for creation, it is also important to remember that we are

---

5. *Our Only World*, 171.

sustained only and always by God's grace. Acknowledging God's grace enables us to extend grace to others and ourselves, and it helps us avoid the related traps of legalism, arrogance, and despair. Legalism is attractive because in a messy world it makes our decisions neat and easy and universally applicable, and to the extent that we abide by the rules we lay down, it allows us a certain sense of superiority over others. Now, it is obviously useful and important to decide on principles, regular practices, and indeed even rules for ourselves that enable us to better reflect in our actions what we claim to believe. Such rules also help us avoid the hassle of having to wrestle at length over every decision. If, for example, we have decided not to eat factory-farmed meat, it is easier to decide at the market or grocery store what to buy (or not buy), which restaurants to visit (or not), and what to order once we are there. But we must beware of thinking we have it all figured out, or looking down on others who have not made the same commitments we have, or falling into despair when we fail or it all seems impossible.

> "We shall never achieve harmony with land, any more than we shall achieve absolute justice or liberty for people. In these higher aspirations the important thing is not to achieve, but to strive."
>
> *Aldo Leopold*[6]

Moreover, we are all part of broken systems in a broken world, and often what we might consider to be best or perfect will simply be unavailable to us. And there are times when we will face conflicting values: if we have made a personal commitment to eating differently, for example, how do we accept gratefully food that has been prepared for us by hosts who do not share our commitments? Accepting God's grace must mean extending it to others, and living in it ourselves. Above all, remembering that the source of our life and our hope is Christ, and worshipping God with all we are and do, will keep our focus where it always must be.

> "So then, let us not be like others, who are asleep, but let us be awake and sober."
>
> *1 Thessalonians 5:6*

Henry David Thoreau famously claimed, "To be awake is to be alive." Given that Paul too calls for us metaphorically to "be awake and sober" (1 Thess. 5:6), we will use the acronym "AWAKE" to summarize some of the ways we can live out a biblical theology of creation care, hopefully making the list of suggestions more memorable.

> "Awake, my soul! Awake, harp and lyre! I will awaken the dawn. I will praise you, Lord, among the nations; I will sing of you among the peoples. For great is your love, reaching to the heavens; your faithfulness reaches to the skies. Be exalted, O God, above the heavens; let your glory be over all the earth."
>
> *Psalm 57:8–11*

Attentiveness

We have already discussed the importance of attentiveness, and by it we mean first and foremost attentiveness to the community of creation where we live. Such attentiveness is birthed and sustained in and begets love—love for God, love for

---

6. *Round River*, 155.

"Mankind has gone far into an artificial world of his own creation. He
has sought to insulate himself, with
steel and concrete, from the realities of
earth and water. Perhaps he is intoxi-
cated with his own power, as he goes
farther and farther into experiments for
the destruction of himself and his world.
For this unhappy trend there is no single
remedy—no panacea. But I believe
that the more clearly we can focus our
attention on the wonders and realities
of the universe about us, the less taste
we shall have for destruction."

Rachel Carson[7]

others, and love for God's creation—and it can be a source of great solace and joy. Yet our attentiveness must also include an awareness and attentiveness to the suffering of creation, locally and globally. Such attention to our world—God's world—is demanded of us all today.

Walking

By walking, we intend to invoke the whole range of human-powered forms of transportation and alternative ways of getting around that have a smaller impact on the earth. Perhaps more important, walking and bicycling (and longboarding and snowshoeing and cross-country skiing, etc.) connect us more intimately to the world around us, fostering healthfulness and a spirit of attentiveness. We also intend in this section to encourage thoughtfulness about our use of mechanized transport: if we have a car, what kind we drive; what form of transport we choose for short journeys around town and for longer journeys too; and whether we choose to offset the carbon cost of our journeys and lifestyle.

Walking itself is perhaps the best way to connect or reconnect with our local community, and where we can't walk, we can probably bicycle. There are certainly places where these options are not available to us, but it is too often the case, especially for Americans, that we simply have not considered the possibility. Even when it takes longer (though we sometimes neglect to notice how much time is spent in such things as sitting at traffic lights or looking for parking), the benefits of walking to places that are within a mile or two of our home are hard to beat. There is the fresh air[8] and exercise, the opportunity to be attentive to our surroundings, and the chance to bump into people we might not otherwise see. There are also those days of driving rain and sleet. Even then, there is goodness in experiencing, ever so briefly, the wildness of a world that does not exist solely for our ease and enjoyment—and at the end of our walk, we appreciate anew the warmth of buildings and human companionship! This is all besides, of course, the reduction in emissions and pollution caused by driving and the cost—financially and to the environment—of the extra wear and tear on our vehicle. There are obviously many considerations that go into choosing where we live, but the benefits of walking or bicycling—for ourselves, our communities, and the earth—are such that it is hard to see how living within walking or bicycling distance of work or those places we travel to most would not be one of the most significant factors when choosing a home.

---

7. From a speech, "The Real World Around Us," delivered in 1954; quoted in Linda Lear, ed., *Lost Woods; The Discovered Writing of Rachel Carson* (Boston: Beacon Press, 1998), 163.

8. As I am living in central London this year, I (Jonathan) was pleased to learn that even in polluted cities the health benefits of walking outweigh the costs of breathing polluted air.

Transport has received lots of attention in discussions of climate change, because for many of us, it is the most significant, easily measured way in which our personal actions contribute to greenhouse gas emissions. To reduce our individual "carbon footprint," then, it certainly makes sense to focus some of our efforts on travel. Walking and bicycling for short journeys is an obvious choice, and so is taking a train or, even better, a bus when available.

Flying gets bad press, although for long journeys, it can sometimes actually be better (in terms of its contributions to climate change) than other forms of transport. The problem, of course, is that flying makes it so easy to travel immense distances, and despite the remarkable efficiency of modern transportation, there is still a cost in terms of greenhouse gas emissions. As with much in our life today, the costs of exerting our remarkable power and privilege are hidden and often ultimately borne by others. One small way we can become more cognizant of the cost of our travel is to pay for carbon offsets.

Carbon offsetting has been accused of being akin to purchasing "indulgences," enabling the wealthy (i.e., on global terms, anyone who can afford to fly) to pay a small fee and then carry on guilt-free with a lifestyle that remains unjust and unsustainable. Nevertheless, we should not let the perfect (whatever that might be in this case) be an enemy of the good, and a decision both to reduce our greenhouse-gas-intensive travel and to pay for offsets when we do travel seems an excellent step in the right direction. This is all the more so the case when there is a way to do this that simultaneously offsets our travel and supports Christians caring for people and creation in poorer parts of the world. For example, Climate Stewards (www.climatestewards.org), a part of the A Rocha network, a Christian conservation organization, allows you to calculate the carbon cost of any given trip (and other activities too) and then to donate that amount to support their work in such things as community forestry and cookstove projects in Ghana, Kenya, and Mexico. Here's an example: according to the website, a round-trip flight from Chicago to London is estimated to lead to 1,926 kg of carbon emissions for one traveler, and the cost to offset these emissions is $38.41. The money is used for such things as helping communities plant trees, manage native forests, and purchase fuel-efficient cookstoves, initiatives that not only save carbon emissions but also enhance the healthfulness and resiliency of the local communities.

Activism

There are plenty of organizations and activists who will try to convince you that their agendas, their ideas, and their politics provide the best way of addressing some or all of the challenges outlined above. Some of them might be right. But we will leave it to readers, who we hope are from all sorts of backgrounds and political persuasions, to reflect on how, as a society and a nation and a world, we can best transform laws and policies to care better for creation. All of us need to become activists at some level if we are to take seriously both the demands of the gospel and the realities of our current situation. What is important is to separate the issues from party politics and narrowly defined ideological lines and to work together to face our common challenges. Addressing climate change and problems related to human impact on the environment necessarily will involve us deeply in politics if these issues are finally to be addressed at the scale needed, and we will often disagree about the best approaches. But Christians, of all people, ought to be prepared to work with each other across party lines to move our governments and societies toward greater justice and care for the earth and the poor, and we especially ought to be willing to do the hard work of collaborating with all sorts of people to do the on-the-ground work in our own places to see God's creation protected and sustained.

Activism for some may mean engaging in the traditional forms of protest that we can be grateful are available to many of us in democratic countries. It can mean voting for candidates who support policies that will enable us to multiply our efforts in caring better for the earth and for other people. For all of us, it ought to mean working with others to address local issues, signing petitions, writing to our representatives, supporting organizations that are having a positive influence in the halls of power, and actually getting out and doing things like pulling trash out of rivers, planting trees, or volunteering at community gardens. The degree of our involvement will vary depending on our gifts and callings and opportunities, but the scale of the challenges we face means we all must be involved at both local and national/international levels.

"Joy doesn't betray but sustains activism. And when you face a politics that aspires to make you fearful, alienated and isolated, joy is a fine act of insurrection."

Rebecca Solnit[9]

The best place to start with our activism is in the church. This might mean working to bring others on board, helping them to see the way in which the gospel challenges us to care for creation, inviting them to join us in celebrating the wonder and beauty of the earth and in the worship of its Creator. It will mean finding ways that our churches can be examples in our communities by adopting practices that reflect our respect and love for the world God made. It will mean finding ways that our church can join in local efforts to address environmental problems that are harming our communities. It will mean supporting financially and in prayer churches and Christian mission, relief, and aid agencies that are seeking to proclaim the gospel and care holistically for people and communities around the world, not neglecting the creation of which they are a part. It will mean supporting those who are called specifically to environmental missions. It will mean for preachers and teachers to proclaim the whole Word of God. It will mean for laypeople to take

9. Rebecca Solnit, *Hope in the Dark: Untold Histories, Wild Possibilities* (New York: Nation Books, 2004), 17.

up the work themselves and not always to wait for the clergy or others to set the agenda or lead the way.

Konsumerism

Yes, the purposeful misspelling is silly, but that means you might remember it. The point is to challenge our culture of consumerism and what we mean by it. We are all consumers, but most of us who live in richer countries have lots of choices about what we choose to consume, and, far more important, how much to consume. The danger of some fads in environmentalism is that we often merely replace one form of consumerism with another. I'm eco-friendly, so I buy this car instead of that one. I care about the health of the planet, so I shop at this fashion store instead of that one. I'm an ethically conscious outdoorsperson, so I go to this trendy hiking-backpacking-climbing-bicycling-clothing chain store instead of that hunting-fishing-camping-clothing chain store. I am committed to a sustainable lifestyle, so I stay at this eco-friendly tourist resort in Tahiti instead of that one (where they don't even have composting toilets!). You get the point. And the point is not to criticize thoughtful decision-making about the things we purchase. But we ought first to stop and ask who we are, what defines us, in what does our life consist? If it consists merely in acquiring one list of things and experiences over and against another person's lists of things and experiences, we surely have missed what Scripture would tell us about true fulfillment and who we are created to be in Christ.

The most important and radical thing we can do personally to care better for creation is simply to stop. Stop buying things we don't need, step back from our culture's infatuation with the new and the disposable, and assess how our money and time might be better spent for the purposes of God's kingdom. Our personal carbon footprint, for example, often has more to do with the things we buy and own than it does even with our travel. It's just that it's harder to measure our personal carbon footprint for all our stuff, so in charts of greenhouse gas emissions, it conveniently gets offloaded onto "industry."[10] It's easier to point our fingers at "industry" than to consider the energy and resources that were used and the emissions caused by the building of our houses, the production of our cars, and the making of our smartphones. Certainly, we should advocate for industry to adopt standards that are better for the planet—and should preferentially choose those businesses that do adopt them. But even before that, we must ask what things are worth having in the first place.

When we do decide to buy things, of course we ought to act as informed and ethical consumers. This may be a hassle—so many options, so much conflicting information, so many decisions to be made—but if it seems like too much trouble,

---

10. It also can be misleading to focus on sources of emissions just in the United States, for example, where transportation ranks higher than industry because lots of the things we buy are made elsewhere. Globally, industry usually ranks just after energy generation in its contribution to greenhouse gas emissions (and a significant proportion of that energy generation is actually used by industry).

then perhaps that thing is not worth buying in the first place. It's worth remembering what an immense privilege it is to have access to many of the products that are available to us now and to have choices to make. For the vast majority of people who have ever lived and the vast majority of people alive today, they have not had and do not have options.

Besides food and water, which is the subject of the final section, the other thing we all consume is energy for heating, cooling, and cooking. An obvious way we can reduce our personal use of resources and our impact on climate change is to lower the thermostat in the winter and raise it in the summer. The "average" room temperatures to which Americans especially have been acculturated are far warmer in winter and cooler in summer than is necessary or common in the rest of the world. (To put it bluntly, if we're sitting inside wearing a short-sleeve shirt on a cold winter day, we're wasting energy and needlessly polluting the atmosphere.) As we are able, we can also employ renewable sources of energy, use draft stoppers on our doors, insulate our houses far better, and install more efficient windows, furnaces, hot water heaters, and air conditioners (if we absolutely need them). For new building projects, adopting the highest energy-efficient standards available and considering the source of our materials will cost more upfront but is the right thing to do and is likely to pay dividends in the future.

> "Or maybe we could give up saving the world and start to live savingly in it. . . . Spending less, burning less, traveling less may be a relief. A cooler, slower life may make us happier, more present to ourselves, and to others who need us to be present. Because of such rewards, a large problem may be effectively addressed by the many small solutions that, after all, are necessary, no matter what the government might do. The government might even do the right thing at last by imitating the people."
>
> *Wendell Berry*[11]

Eating

Readers will have noticed that we have had to acknowledge a number of times that the sorts of choices we are suggesting are often more expensive. No matter our relative wealth, everyone is tempted to balk at spending extra money. We certainly do ourselves, and there are plenty of times when we have to compromise in our own decisions about what to buy or how to build something due to our limited resources. But we are also aware that nearly all of us could actually decide to purchase much less and to live more simply so that whatever we do buy is better made, longer lasting, more sustainably sourced and produced, and more just in its impact on workers and communities. This is above all the case for food.

We collectively spend less on food, on average, than people ever have in the history of people spending money on food. It is one of the benefits bequeathed to us by modern oil-fueled industrial agriculture and cheap oil-fueled transportation. But this cheap food comes at a price. As we have seen, modern agriculture has significantly

---

11. *Our Only World*, 175.

harmed the environment, and it is unsustainable as it is currently practiced. An unwillingness to pay more for our food has all but excluded those who want to be smaller-scale farmers, who want to take the time and effort to grow and raise food without overreliance on synthetic fertilizers, herbicides, and pesticides, who want to plant a variety of seeds or crops to maintain diversity and resilience, who want to treat animals well, and who want to protect the topsoil from running off into the sea. All these things take more time and more labor and are less "efficient" in the short term and hence cost more money. So cheap food prices have not been good for the earth, nor, for that matter, for the quality of our food. The reality is, if we care about the long-term sustainability of agriculture, to say nothing of biodiversity and climate change and wider ecosystem integrity, we will have to pay farmers more.

> "'Eating is an agricultural act,' as Wendell Berry famously said. It is also an ecological act, and a political act, too. Though much has been done to obscure this simple fact, how and what we eat determines to a great extent the use we make of the world—and what is to become of it. To eat with a fuller consciousness of all that is at stake might sound like a burden, but in practice few things in life can afford quite as much satisfaction."
>
> *Michael Pollan*[12]

We are also going to need a lot more farmers, if agriculture is to be transformed on the scale needed. Even with all the benefits of modern technology, farming sustainably takes more work and hence more workers. They might be welcomed in our depopulated country towns and emptied-out countryside. A return to the land by educated famers who care about the long-term sustainability of the land (and who can be confident that they will actually be able to make a living) would also be a tremendous boon for an agricultural landscape that has in many places become more denuded of wild creatures and more covered in harmful chemicals than the grittiest neighborhood of the nearest city. Thankfully, there are in fact a growing number of such farmers. We owe it to them to support them and to buy their food—and not complain too much that it is more expensive than what is available in the discount store across the street.

Of course, there are many in our communities and around the world who cannot even afford to eat right now, so efforts to ensure the more just and equitable distribution of food must go alongside our efforts to grow food more sustainably. But these realities should not be put at odds with each other, and in fact, the potential for new fulfilling employment for more people and wider access to healthy food means these efforts can and ought to be pursued together (as they are already in a number of places).

Whatever precise decisions we make about what we eat, our attitude ought to be one of profound gratitude for those who grow and raise our food, for the soil and the water that nourishes it, and above all for the God who creates and sustains and

---

12. Michael Pollan, *The Omnivore's Dilemma* (London: Bloomsbury, 2006), 11.

provides it. Eating is one of the most basic of creaturely activities, binding us to the rest of creation and serving to remind us of who we are. In the Lord's Supper, it is the bread and the wine—drawn from God's creation and produced by good human work—that enable us to partake in Christ's body and blood. Let us indeed, every time we eat and drink, remember Christ's incarnation, his death, his resurrection, and his coming again.

SUMMARY

We end where we began: with celebration, joy, and worship. This chapter and the previous one have forced us to confront some hard realities about the challenges facing life on earth, ranging from the loss of other creatures and forests, to the crisis in our warming and acidifying oceans, to the degradation and loss of topsoil, to the potentially catastrophic effects of climate change. We have considered our responsibilities and a possible range of responses, organizing our discussion around the acronym "AWAKE." We are challenged to be *Attentive* to the community of creation around us, to *Walk* more and consider how and where and how much we travel, to become *Activists* for God's kingdom on earth, speaking up and working on behalf of his creation, to reject our culture's way of *Konsumerism*, and to *Eat* joyfully, thankfully, reverently, and ethically.

> "Creation care . . . is an integral part of our mission and an expression of our worship to God for his wonderful plan of redemption through Jesus Christ. Therefore, our ministry of reconciliation is a matter of great joy and hope and we would care for creation even if it were not in crisis."
>
> *The Lausanne Movement's Jamaica Call to Action* [13]

We have acknowledged that everyone has different gifts and different callings, and so our involvement and ways of caring for creation will naturally vary from person to person. But to care for creation is not an option; the only question is whether we do it well or poorly, for we are all creatures of the earth, all caught up in its life and all given responsibility by God to rule as his image bearers. Consider for a moment the apostle Paul. If anyone ever had a well-defined calling, it was Paul. The apostle to the Gentiles was uniquely called and gifted by God to proclaim the gospel, and to this mission he devoted his entire post-conversion life. Yet Paul was encouraged by his fellow believers to "remember the poor," and far from being unwilling, Paul says that this was "the very thing I had been eager to do all along" (Gal. 2:10). So if Paul sees that his urgent missionary task necessarily includes the care of the poor, we can hardly let our own various gifts and callings and busyness allow us to neglect our own responsibilities toward the poor. Nor, if our conclusions in this book are correct, can we neglect our responsibilities toward God's creation. As we have seen, we cannot in any case

---

13. Jonathan Moo, Dave Bookless, and Lowell Bliss, "Call to Action and Exposition," in Colin Bell and Robert S. White, eds., *Creation Care and the Gospel: Reconsidering the Mission of the Church* (Peabody, MA: Hendrickson, 2016), 7.

truly love our neighbors, especially the poor, if we do not care for the creation of which they and we are a part.

We care for creation first and last because of our love of God. It is as faithful stewards of what he has entrusted to us that we do this work and live as he calls us, whatever the results. It is his love that compels us and sustains us, even in work that may sometimes seem hopeless. What we have presented in the previous chapter leads some to despair, and certainly it should lead all of us to lament. But, as the authors of many of the scientific articles cited there would tell us, there are still ways to change the course we are on, to mitigate the damage that is being done, to avoid the worst scenarios for the future—if we are willing to act. And, what is of far more importance is that we can have certain trust and confidence in the God who transforms us and promises to accomplish more than we could ever ask or imagine. It is in him that we place our hope. As the apostle Paul promises us, our "labor in the Lord is not in vain" (1 Cor. 15:58).

SCRIPTURE INDEX

SUBJECT INDEX

AUTHOR INDEX

The Mission of God's People

A Biblical Theology of the Church's Mission

Christopher J. H. Wright

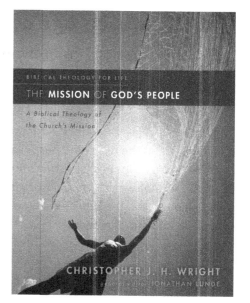

Chris Wright's pioneering 2006 book, *The Mission of God*, revealed that the typical Christian understanding of "missions" encompasses only a small part of God's overarching mission for the world. God is relentlessly reclaiming the entire world for himself. In *The Mission of God's People*, Wright shows how God's big-picture plan directs the purpose of God's people, the church.

Wright emphasizes what the Old Testament teaches Christians about being the people of God. He addresses questions of both ecclesiology and missiology with topics like "called to care for creation," "called to bless the nations," "sending and being sent," and "rejecting false gods."

> *"What do theology and mission have to do with each other? This book powerfully answers the question."*
> — John Goldingay, Professor, Fuller Theological Seminary

As part of the Biblical Theology for Life Series, this book provides pastors, teachers and lay learners with first-rate biblical study while at the same time addressing the practical concerns of contemporary ministry. *The Mission of God's People* promises to enliven and refocus the study, teaching, and ministry of those truly committed to joining God's work in the world.

Available in stores and online!

Biblical Theology for Life

Christians in an Age of Wealth

A Biblical Theology of Stewardship

Craig L. Blomberg

In this book Craig Blomberg addresses the tough questions about the place and purpose of wealth and material possessions in a Christian's life. He points to the goodness of wealth, as God originally designed it, but also surveys the Bible's many warnings against making an idol out of money.

So are material possessions a blessing for which we should long? And what are the dangers that the use or abuse of material possessions can produce?

Blomberg explains how the sharing of goods and possessions is the key safeguard against both greed and covetousness. He expands on the concept of giving generously, even sacrificially, to those who are needier, demonstrating how Christians can participate in God's original good design for abundance and demonstrate the world-altering gospel of Christ.

Available in stores and online!

ZONDERVAN®
.com

Biblical Theology for Life

Following Jesus, the Servant King

A Biblical Theology of Covenantal Discipleship

Jonathan Lunde

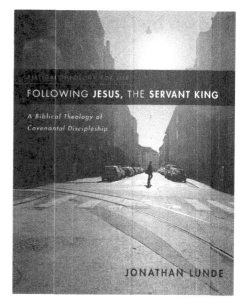

Throughout the Old Testament and into the New, God not only demands righteousness from his people but also showers them in grace that enables them to act. Jesus, of course, provides the ultimate fulfillment of these twin aspects of God's relationship to humanity. In biblical terms, Jesus is the King who demands righteous obedience from his followers, and Jesus is the Servant who provides the grace that enables this obedience.

So what does it mean to follow Jesus? What does God expect from his followers, and how can they be and do what is required?

Jonathan Lunde answers these and other questions in his sweeping biblical study on discipleship. He surveys God's interaction with his people from Eden to Jesus, paying special attention to the biblical covenants that illuminate the character and plans of God. He offers Bible students and teachers—such as pastors, missionaries, and lay leaders—the gift of practical biblical teaching rooted in the Bible's witness on the vital topic of discipleship.

Available in stores and online!

Known by God

A Biblical Theology of Personal
Identity

Brian S. Rosner

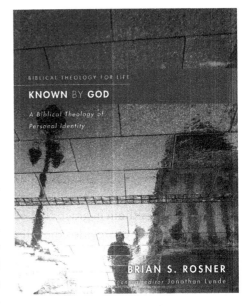

Who are you? What defines you? What makes you, you?

In the past an individual's identity was more
predictable than it is today. Life's big questions were
basically settled before you were born: where you'd
live, what you'd do, the type of person you'd marry,
and your basic beliefs. Today personal identity is a
do-it-yourself project. Constructing a stable and
satisfying sense of self is hard amidst relationship
breakdowns, the pace of modern life, the rise of so-
cial media, multiple careers, and social mobility. Ours is a day of identity angst.

Known by God is built on the observation that humans are inherently social beings; we know
who we are in relation to others and by being known by them. If one of the universal desires
of the self is to be known by others, being known by God as his children meets our deepest
and lifelong need for recognition and gives us a secure identity. Rosner argues that rather than
knowing ourselves, being known by God is the key to personal identity.

He explores three biblical angles on the question of personal identity: being made in the
image of God, being known by God, and being in Christ. The notion of sonship is at the center—
God gives us our identity as a parent who knows his child. Being known by him as his child gives
our fleeting lives significance, provokes in us needed humility, supplies cheering comfort when
things go wrong, and offers clear moral direction for living.

Available in stores and online!